The Great Reset
and the Struggle for Liberty

Unraveling the Global Agenda

Also by Michael Rectenwald from
New English Review Press:

Springtime for Snowflakes:
'Social Justice' and Its Postmodern Parentage (2018)

Google Archipelago:
The Digital Gulag and the Simulation of Freedom
(2019)

Beyond Woke (2020)

Thought Criminal (2020)

The Great Reset and the Struggle for Liberty

Unraveling the Global Agenda

Michael Rectenwald, Ph.D.

Published by New English Review Press
a subsidiary of World Encounter Institute
PO Box 158397
Nashville, Tennessee 37215
&
27 Old Gloucester Street
London, England, WC1N 3AX

Cover Art & Design by Ari Lankin

ISBN: 978-1-943003-74-7

Library of Congress Control Number: 2022948350

First Edition

NEW ENGLISH REVIEW PRESS
newenglishreview.org

Contents

Acknowledgments

THIS BOOK owes a great deal to friends and supporters who have helped to guide its contents, provide vital research, and who encouraged me to bring it to completion.

Perhaps unbeknownst to them, my friends and followers on Facebook and Twitter often provided sparks of insight, which helped to stimulate me as I wrote. You are too many to be named, but I thank you all. You know who you are.

For generous and timely readings of this book's chapters, I owe a great debt of gratitude to Vinay Kolhatkar, the brilliant publisher of the Savvy Street website. Vinay read early and late drafts of most of this book's chapters and offered timely and incisive comments and suggestions, most of which I adopted. Thank you, Vinay!

I owe a great debt of gratitude to John Adam Klyczek, the Taoist Professor, author of *School World Order*, and a veritable encyclopedia regarding the globalist organizations treated in Chapters 8 and 9 of this book (and a lot more). John provided essential research and sketches of the histories of these globalist groups and their Malthusian and neo-Malthusian beliefs. Thank you, John!

Finally, I owe the greatest debt of gratitude to my long-time confidante and sidekick, and editorial and research assistant, Lori R. Price. Lori's tireless and ongoing readings of all parts of this manuscript in every phase of its production have served not only to improve my writing but also to stimulate it. Lori helped me to draft material, provided essential research, and lent editorial assistance at every stage of this book's writing. I cannot say enough about Lori's unflagging support, continual guidance, and steadfast belief that this book would come to fruition. I should also add that Lori's brilliant and important website, *CLG News* (legitgov.org), provided me with up-to-date material that was vital to this book. Thank you so much, Lori!

Without these people, this book would not exist. But any flaws that remain are, of course, my own.

Foreword

WITH ALL THE HORRORS that are unfolding in the world today, it's difficult to avoid the feeling that dark forces are arrayed against those of us who want to live their lives in peace. Michael Rectenwald's excellent and vitally important book, *The Great Reset and the Struggle for Liberty: Unraveling the Global Agenda,* shows better than any other book I know that we are right to feel this way. Rectenwald puts it all together. He shows us who is plotting against us, what they have in mind for us, and—most importantly—what we can do to stop them.

He is superbly qualified to write this book. As his website notes, he is "the author of eleven books, including *Thought Criminal* (Dec. 2020); *Beyond Woke* (May 2020); *Google Archipelago: The Digital Gulag and the Simulation of Freedom* (Sept. 2019); *Springtime for Snowflakes: "Social Justice" and Its Postmodern Parentage* (an academic's memoir, 2018); *Nineteenth-Century British Secularism: Science, Religion and Literature* (2016); *Academic Writing, Real World Topics* (2015, Concise Edition 2016); *Global Secularisms in a Post-Secular Age* (2015); *Breach* (Collected Poems, 2013); *The Thief and Other Stories* (2013); and *The Eros of the Ba-*

by-Boom Eras (1991).

"Michael was a Professor of Liberal Studies and Global Liberal Studies at NYU from 2008 to 2019. He also taught at Duke University, North Carolina Central University, Carnegie Mellon University, and Case Western Reserve University. His scholarly and academic essays have appeared in *The Quarterly Journal of Austrian Economics, Academic Questions, Endeavour, The British Journal for the History of Science, College Composition and Communication, International Philosophical Quarterly,* the De Gruyter anthologies *Organized Secularism* in the United States and *Global Secularisms in a Post-Secular Age,* and the Cambridge University Press anthology *George Eliot in Context,* among others. He holds a Ph.D. in Literary and Cultural Studies from Carnegie Mellon University, a Master's in English Literature from Case Western Reserve University, and a B.A. in English Literature from the University of Pittsburgh. He is a champion of liberty and opposes all forms of totalitarianism and political authoritarianism, including socialism-communism, 'social justice,' fascism, political correctness, and 'woke' ideology."[1]

When you first see the title of this book, one question will spring to your mind: *What is the Great Reset?* Quite simply, it is a plan for the restructuring of society concocted by Klaus Schwab in connection with a vast assemblage of players. It is promoted through his World Economic Forum and its many programs for training the leaders of tomorrow. Rectenwald minces no words in telling us what this mas-

---

1 Michael Rectenwald's website: https://www.michaelrectenwald.com/bio.

ter planners of evil have in store for us:

> The Great Reset means, at the very least, re-
> duced standards of living and carbon use for
> the vast majority. But Schwab and the WEF
> also define the Great Reset in terms of the con-
> vergence of economic, monetary, technological,
> medical, genomic, environmental, military, and
> governance systems. The Great Reset involves
> vast transformations in each of these domains,
> changes which, according to Schwab, will not
> only alter our world but also lead us to "ques-
> tion what it means to be human." In terms of
> economics and monetary policy, the Great Re-
> set amounts to a great consolidation of wealth,
> on the one hand, and the planned issuance of
> universal basic income (UBI) on the other.

> Its goals include a shift to a central bank digi-
> tal currency (CBDC), including a consolidated
> centralization of banking and bank accounts,
> the possibility of immediate real-time taxation,
> negative interest rates, and centralized sur-
> veillance and control over spending, debt, and
> savings. The Great Reset consolidates capital
> flows from central banks and investment firms
> into the hands of preferred producers through
> "stakeholder capitalism." This would amount to
> a virtual oligopoly on top with "actually existing
> socialism" for the majority below. How else are
> we to explain the promise, "you'll own nothing,
> and you'll be happy?"

Now for something that will amaze you. How did
the WEF propose to foist their diabolical scheme on
us? For one thing, they said that a pandemic would
give them a good chance to impose their controls on

people, who would then get used to following orders and living at a reduced level. (See Chapter 1.)

It seems Schwab and his cohorts divide people into three categories: an elite group at the top, the masses who will exist at a low standard of living, made necessary by the efforts to "green" and control the economy, and an intermediate group with some limited social mobility. Those who don't go along with the plan will be destroyed:

> Whether we understand the stakeholder capitalism of the Great Reset as capitalism with Chinese characteristics, as neo-feudalism, as corporate socialism or as economic fascism—the results are the same. The Great Reset amounts to a state-corporate-woke-cartel hybrid administering the economy through the recommendations and decisions of technocrats like those at the WEF, the UN, the World Bank, and, by extension, the World Health Organization—as well as by top corporate decision-makers like BlackRock's Larry Fink . . . The elite will appeal to the downtrodden and weaponize them with egalitarian rhetoric and the distribution of social welfare, while castigating and vilifying non-compliant professionals, entrepreneurs, and business owners. Whatever rhetoric or ideology is propagated by the adherents of the Great Reset, power and control is vested in a consortium of elites, who effectively run the economy as its primary beneficiaries. This is just the kind of tiered social structure that characterized Communist nations. The elite class was the party faithful, and the masses, at times, starved without UBI. We should be very wary, indeed.

Rectenwald points out that this plan for the economy conforms exactly to fascism, as Ludwig von Mises analyzed it. The owners of businesses will not really be owners at all, but will have to do as the government and "the woke cartel" command:

> Corporatism—otherwise known as "economic fascism"—involves the politicization of the economy and the coordination of production and the running of society by a consortium of dominant interest groups, just like the one that the WEF establishes. Woke corporatism, or economic fascism, allows nominal private ownership but effectively puts corporations under the pressures of the woke cartel and the eventual control of legislation promulgated by the state. Aided by the Fourth Estate, the Fifth Estate of the WEF and its corporate partners apply extra-governmental pressure on corporate and individual behavior.
>
> ...Contrary to Larry Fink's assertion, the corporatism he promotes involves the exercise of corporate power, in advance of state sanctions, to achieve a particular ideological and political agenda. That agenda is wokeness.

The last word in this passage, "wokeness," is one of the keys to understanding Rectenwald's book. How does the elite propose to get those in our society who are doing well to accept the lower standard of living their plans envision? The answer is "wokeness." They make people feel guilty for their "privileges," allegedly at the expense of the disadvantaged:

> Wokeness is a selection mechanism for divid-

ing the compliant from the non-compliant—for
businesses in addition to individuals. Just as
non-woke individuals are cancelled from civic
life, so too are non-woke companies cancelled
from the economy, leaving the spoils to the
woke. Corporate cancellations are not merely the result of political fallout. They are being institutionalized and carried out through
the stock market, the banking industry, and
the insurance industry, from which they insinuate themselves into every other industry.
Woke planners wield the Environmental, Social, and Governance (ESG) Index to reward
the in-group and to squeeze non-woke players out of business. The ESG Index serves as a
"Chinese-style" social credit scoring system for
rating corporations...

As Rectenwald writes in *Beyond Woke*:

According to the social justice creed, being
'woke' is the political awakening that stems
from the emergence of consciousness and con-
scientiousness regarding social and political
injustice. Wokeness is the indelible inscription
of the awareness of social injustice on the con-
scious mind, eliciting the sting of conscience,
which compels the newly woke to change their
beliefs and behaviors.[2]

He says furthermore:

And what are the effects of being repeatedly
reprimanded as such, of being told that one has

---

2 Michael Rectenwald, *Beyond Woke*, Nashville, TN: New English
Review Press, 2020, pages 173-174.

been the beneficiary of unmerited 'privilege,' that one's relative wealth and well-being have come at the expense of oppressed, marginalized, and misused Others? Shame, guilt, remorse, unworthiness. And what are the expected attitudinal and behavioral adjustments to be taken by the majority? They are to expect less. Under woke ideology, one will be expected to forfeit one's property rights, because even these rights, nay, especially these rights, have come at the expense of others. Thus, wokeness works by habituating the majority to the reduced expectations of the Great Reset...

Rectenwald argues that the Great Reset did not materialize out of thin air. The WEF is the successor to a long line of globalist organizations:

The WEF is heir to a long line of globalist ideas and policies that extend back to the early twentieth century. In fact, the WEF is modeled after the Rhodes Society, founded in 1903. It derives from successors to Lord Alfred Milner's Round Tables. These successors include the Royal Institute of International Affairs (RIIA, otherwise known as Chatham House, founded in 1920), the Council on Foreign Relations (CFR, founded in 1921), the Bilderberg Group (founded in 1954), and the Club of Rome (founded in 1968). The WEF is essentially a fraternal twin of the Trilateral Commission (founded in 1973)...

As an organization, the WEF outstrips its ancestors in terms of reach, penetration, and "success"... To analogize, we might say that the WEF is to these earlier organizations what Lenin was to Marx. Like Marx, Lenin was a theorist. But unlike Marx, Lenin was also a "practical" revolutionary. Likewise, the WEF theorizes but also administers and coordinates practical applications with immense global consequences. Nevertheless, Lenin would not have been Lenin without Marx and the WEF would not have been the WEF without these earlier Round Table groups.

One thing you may wonder about is this: Don't the planners of the Great Reset realize that what they have in mind will destroy much of humanity? The answer is that this is exactly what they want. Rectenwald's discussion of this topic struck home with me because he shows how the Great Reset ties in with the anti-human ideology of environmentalism. I have often written about this anti-human project. We desperately need to understand that environmentalism views mankind as a cancer that must be eradicated:

> A particularly egregious example of neo-Malthusianism, written in 1971, the year that the World Economic Forum was founded, can be found in the Proceedings of the Eighth Annual Symposium of the Eugenics Society, which included a series of articles entitled Population and Pollution. In the introductory essay, entitled "Ethics and the Population Increase," Eliot Slater stated blankly: "Because there are too many of us, a man does his neighbour more harm than good, just by staying alive." Slater blamed Christianity for the plague of over-population, because the Christian religion "banned the human checks of abortion and infanticide." He argues further: "As human birth takes on a

negative value for society, human death takes on a positive one. In time we shall probably have to allow easy ways out [euthanasia] for those who badly need them."...The Great Reset agenda is rooted in such enviro-neo-Malthusian population "ethics."

The anti-human plotters have another tool to scare us into submission. This is what Rectenwald calls "climate catastrophism." They argue that we have to destroy the world's economy in order to prevent the globe from heating up:

As I write, Democrats on Capitol Hill are pressuring the Biden administration to declare a climate emergency, urging the Biden administration to declare a climate emergency, voicing their doomsday predictions that without immediate action to curb and ultimately end our dependence on fossil fuels, "the planet" and, by implication, every living creature that inhabits it, will die. "If we don't really begin to lower emissions, this planet has no chance," said Representative Alan Lowenthal, a California Democrat. "We have a few years left and that's it. The planet is dying."

I've read a lot about "global warming," but Rectenwald's book is most thorough in its debunking of the claims of the "climate catastrophists." (See Chapter 11.) One detail that Rectenwald adds is new to me and is devastating in its implications:

James T. Moodey, a real-world gas physicist, has tested the claim that CO_2 retains heat long enough for the atmosphere to warm over time.

Moodey and his team first isolated a mixture of vaporous (70 percent humidity) atmospheric air that included carbon dioxide. He then applied heat to the air-carbon dioxide mixture, which closely resembled atmospheric conditions. Once the heat source was discontinued, Moodey measured the rate of heat loss. He had already recorded temperature drops in the atmosphere over a period of a year at varying altitudes and in numerous climates. He noted that the atmosphere warms, on average, about 22 degrees every sunny or partly sunny day, regardless of the daytime high temperature. The vaporous air-carbon dioxide mixture that he tested cooled by 22 degrees in about 11 hours, 45 minutes. This, by no coincidence, closely matched the cooling rate of our atmosphere. In the next series of tests, Moodey heated pure CO_2. The results varied by the type of container used, but he found that at the low end, the CO_2 lost all 22 degrees of heat in three minutes and 45 seconds.

From these tests and his recordings of atmospheric temperatures, he concluded that carbon dioxide in the atmosphere cools as rapidly as vaporous air and the sun allow. "Even the vaporous mixture cools faster than [in] 24 hours...In other words, carbon dioxide is not a greenhouse gas."

. . .Carbon dioxide is a heavy gas with a specific gravity of 1.62. It is 62 percent heavier than air. The CO_2 produced by emissions tends to fall to the Earth and its oceans and is absorbed, where it serves plants in the process of photosynthesis. I asked Moodey how it is that climate scientists do not know these simple facts about carbon dioxide, or indeed about all so-called greenhouse gases (GHGs). He answered that when the money began to pour in for climate science research, it was directed entirely at academia, where the scientists learn theoretical gas physics to the exclusion of real-world gas physics.

We learn that the WEF plans are so bad that they parallel Mao's "Great Leap Forward," which caused the death of tens of millions of people:

Suffice it to say that the Great Leap Forward precipitated the worst famine in recorded history. Deaths attributable to the famine of 1958-1961 numbered between 20 and 43 million, including those children who were murdered, boiled, and turned into fertilizer.

...The putative object of the Great Leap Forward was to increase gross domestic product to equal or surpass that of developed nations, particularly Great Britain, and to raise the standard of living of the peasants and the population at large. The Great Reset, on the other hand, represents deliberate de-growth and reduced standards of living of the lower and middle classes in the developed world and the squelching of growth in the developing world. While the Great Leap Forward was implemented to hasten the arrival of full communism, the Great Reset establishes corporate socialism, economic fascism, and neo-feudalism. Despite the technological innovations of the Fourth Industrial Revolution, the Great Reset is a de-civilizational project.

Yet, the Great Leap Forward and the Great Reset share one essential feature: the arbitrary imposition of a collectivist unscientific ideology on all human activity and nature. During the Great Leap Forward, Lysenkoism was adopted from the Soviet Union for ideological reasons, despite its disastrous effects there. During the Great Reset, climate catastrophism has been adopted on equally ideological, unscientific grounds...We are told that industrial production must be carried on using non-fossil-fuel inputs. These demands are as delusional as anything advocated by Chairman Mao.

The outlook is dire, but like the great Murray Rothbard, Rectenwald is an optimist. We can defeat the plot of the anti-humans to destroy us, and he has a concrete nine-point program to do this. (See the Conclusion.)

Rectenwald is a hero of liberty, so it is an honor to be asked to write the Foreword to *The Great Reset and the Struggle For Liberty*. After you read it, you will never see the world in the same way again.

— Llewellyn H. Rockwell, Jr., former editorial assistant to Ludwig von Mises and congressional chief of staff to Ron Paul, is founder and chairman of the Mises Institute, and editor of LewRockwell.com. He is the author of *Against the State* and *Against the Left*.

Introduction:

The Elite's Greatest Hits

S o far, elites have orchestrated the Great Purge, the Great Terror, the Great Leap Forward, and the Great Society—to mention only the most conspicuous "great" modern projects. Despite the disastrous consequences of such hubristic undertakings, "the Great Reset" and "the Great Narrative" roll unironically from their lips.

The Great Reset is on everyone's mind, whether everyone knows it or not. It was presaged by the measures undertaken by states, intergovernmental organizations, health agencies, and corporations in response to the covid-19 crisis. I mean by "crisis" not the so-called pandemic itself, but the responses to a novel virus called SARS-CoV-2 and the impact of the responses on social and economic life.

In their book, *COVID-19: The Great Reset*, World Economic Forum (WEF) founder and executive chairman Klaus Schwab and co-author Thierry Malleret write that the covid-19 crisis must be regarded as an "opportunity [that] can be seized to make the kind of institutional changes and policy choices that will put economies on the path toward a fairer, greener future."[1] Although Schwab has been promoting the Great Reset for years, the covid crisis has provided an initial pretext for finally enacting it. According to Schwab, we should not expect the post-covid world system to return to its previous modes of operation. Rather, Schwab and company suggest that changes will be, or should be, enacted across interlocking, interdependent domains to produce a "new normal."

The covid crisis has been used by the WEF and its partners to accelerate the adoption of a pre-ordained set of policies and beliefs, the "sustainability" goals of Agenda 2030, to which the WEF is a partner. On its webpage announcing the Great Reset, the WEF claims that the covid crisis has made it necessary to adopt three goals: 1) "fairer outcomes," 2) "investments [to] advance shared goals, such as equality and sustainability," and 3) "to harness the innovations of the Fourth Industrial Revolution to support the public good."[2]

Under the first head, the WEF claims that the covid crisis means that the "'stakeholder economy" should be established. It then suggests that the stakeholder economy "may include changes to wealth taxes, the withdrawal of fossil-fuel subsidies, and new rules governing intellectual property, trade, and competition." Under the second head, we learn that investments to advance "shared goals" means "large-

---

1   Klaus Schwab and Thierry Malleret, *COVID-19: The Great Reset* (n.p.: Forum Publishing, 2020), page 57.

2   "Now Is the Time for a 'Great Reset,'" World Economic Forum, 2020, https://www.weforum.org/agenda/2020/06/now-is-the-time-for-a-great-reset.

scale" government spending to advance "equal outcomes." The WEF praises the $826 billion recovery fund then planned by the European Commission and plans by nation states, including Japan, China, and the U.S. to unveil similar packages. The investments should not merely shore up "the old system," but must be used to establish "a new one." This new system we learn must involve "building 'green' urban infrastructure and creating incentives for industries to improve their track record on environmental, social, and governance (ESG) metrics." Under the third head, we learn that harnessing the Fourth Industrial Revolution to support the public good means "companies, universities, and others" working "to develop diagnostics, therapeutics, and possible vaccines; establish testing centers; create mechanisms for tracing infections; and deliver telemedicine."

What could the covid crisis have to do with the world economic system, the environmentalist objectives of the WEF and its partners, or the Fourth Industrial Revolution? None of these policy recommendations makes sense without understanding the economic system that the WEF and its partners have promoted for decades, the beliefs and history of the "green" movement, and the technologies being developed under the rubric called the Fourth Industrial Revolution. I address each of these elements throughout the pages of *The Great Reset and the Struggle for Liberty*. These topics overlap considerably, but I have endeavored to issue as tidy a discussion of them as possible. Here, I present a summary of what follows.

The Great Reset means, at the very least, reduced standards of living and carbon use for the vast majority. But Schwab and the WEF also define the Great Reset in terms of the convergence of economic, monetary, technological, medical, genomic, environmental, military, and governance systems. The Great Reset involves vast transformations in each of these domains, changes which, according to Schwab, will not only alter our world but also lead us to "question what it means to be human."[3]

In terms of economics and monetary policy, the Great Reset amounts to a great consolidation of wealth, on the one hand, and the planned issuance of universal basic income (UBI) on the other.[4] Its goals include a shift to a central bank digital currency (CBDC),[5] including a consolidated centralization of banking and bank accounts, the possibility of immediate real-time taxation, negative interest rates, and centralized surveillance and control over spending, debt, and savings.

The Great Reset consolidates capital flows from central banks and investment firms into the hands of preferred producers through "stakeholder capitalism." This would amount to a virtual oligopoly on top with "actually existing socialism" for the majority below. How else are we to explain the promise, "you'll own nothing, and you'll be happy?" I address stakeholder capitalism and the primary mechanism

---

3 Klaus Schwab, *The Fourth Industrial Revolution*, New York: Crown Business, 2017, page vii.

4 Kanni Wignaraja and Balazs Horvath, "Universal Basic Income Is the Answer to the Inequalities Exposed by COVID-19," World Economic Forum, Apr. 17, 2020, https://www.weforum.org/agenda/2020/04/covid-19-universal-basic-income-social-inequality/.

5 "The Fed Explores Possibility of Issuing Digital Currency," BitIRA, Jan. 9, 2020, https://www.bitira.com/fed-explores-digital-currency/.

it involves—the Environmental, Social, and Governance Index (ESG) in Part I. The ESG Index represents a means by which the corporate economy is being transformed into a pre- or extra-governmental regulation system—to be codified by legislation or executive fiat soon after. For many corporate players, who are otherwise mere bystanders to the Great Reset, the appeal is to get in front of governmental regulations, which are slated to follow. In a business strategy sense, businesses secure the "first-mover advantage"[6] sought after by business executives and shareholders. I call the favored companies "the woke cartel." The elite money managers have promised that companies that do not abide by the ESG Index eventually will be eliminated from the market. Thus, the Great Reset reveals the extent and scope of what has been called "woke capitalism."

I explain the economic model of the Great Reset in terms of "corporate socialism," "capitalism with Chinese characteristics," "neo-feudalism," and "economic fascism" (Part I). It is enough to say for now that the WEF claims that the economy must be "transformed" for "a fairer, greener future" and that this future must be dramatically different from the past. The transformation amounts to a vast consolidation of wealth and economic control in the hands of the corporate partners and others abiding by the dictates of the WEF. The pretext of this consolidation is, of course, the supposed looming climate catastrophe posed by global warming (discussed in Part III), while the more proximate pretext has been the covid

---

6 "First Mover Advantage," Corporate Finance Institute, February 7, 2022, https://corporatefinanceinstitute.com/resources/knowledge/strategy/first-mover-advantage/.

crisis.

The upshot of the covid crisis has led some commentators to conclude that covid was the creation of the "Davos crowd," since it has worked to their distinct advantage.[7] According to this line of thinking, covid allowed the globalists to remove Donald Trump from office. His presidency posed what was perhaps the final obstacle to their plans. It also provided justification for beginning the reset of the economy with the destruction of small businesses and the reduction of the consumption and prospects for the vast majority. Since the Great Reset lends itself to such "conspiracy theories," I treat the question of conspiracy in connection with the Great Reset in the first chapter and devote Part V to the question of conspiracy theory itself. Do concerns about the Great Reset necessarily implicate one in conspiracist thinking? If so, does that invalidate such concerns and thinking?

While every aspect of the Great Reset involves technology, the Great Reset specifically entails "the Fourth Industrial Revolution,"[8] or 4-IR, including transhumanism: the expansion of genomics, nanotechnology, and robotics and their penetration into human bodies and brains (Part IV). The 4-IR involves the redundancy of human labor, to be re-

---

7 Mark Wauck, "Tom Luongo's Theory of Everything," *Meaning In History*, August 6, 2022, https://meaninginhistory.substack.com/p/tom-luongos-theory-of-everything.

8 Klaus Schwab, "The Fourth Industrial Revolution: What It Means, How to Respond," World Economic Forum, Jan. 14, 2016, https://www.weforum.org/agenda/2016/01/the-fourth-industrial-revolution-what-it-means-and-how-to-respond/; Klaus Schwab, *The Fourth Industrial Revolution*, New York, NY: Crown Business, 2017; Klaus Schwab and Nicholas Davis, *Shaping the Fourth Industrial Revolution*, Geneva: World Economic Forum, 2018.

placed by AI and robotic automation in increasing sectors. But the 4-IR extends well beyond the outmoding of labor. Among key 4-IR technologies are the digital identity, the Internet of Things (IoT), the Internet of Bodies (IoB), central bank digital currencies (CBDCs), the metaverse, and transhumanism. The Great Reset means the issuance of digital identities, replete with vaccine passports and the transparency of medical records, inclusive of medical history, genetic makeup, and disease status. It entails wearable devices that report on organs and organ systems to central databases. But, according to the architects of the Great Reset, it could also include the implanting of microchips or nanobots that would read and report on genetic makeup and brain states, and more immediately, brain scans such that "[e]ven crossing a national border might one day involve a detailed brain scan to assess an individual's security risk."[9]

In military terms, the Great Reset entails the creation of new battle spaces, including cyberspace and the human brain as a battle space.[10]

In terms of governance, the Great Reset means increasingly centralized, coordinated, and expanded government and "governmentalities,"[11] the conver-

---

9 Klaus Schwab and Nicholas Davis, *Shaping the Future of the Fourth Industrial Revolution: A Guide to Building a Better World*, New York: Currency, 2018.

10 Tim Requarth, "This Is Your Brain. This Is Your Brain as a Weapon.," *Foreign Policy*, Sept. 9, 2015, https://foreignpolicy.com/2015/09/14/this-is-your-brain-this-is-your-brain-as-a-weapon-darpa-dual-use-neuroscience/. I do not treat the military implications of the Great Reset.

11 Michael Rectenwald, "The Google Election," Mises Institute, November 10, 2020, https://mises.org/wire/google-election. I have adopted the term "governmentality" from Michel Foucault and

gence of corporations and states in governance systems, and the digitalization of governmental functions, including, with the use of 5G and predictive algorithms, real-time tracking and surveillance of bodies in space and the "anticipatory governance" of human and systems behavior.[12]

The Great Reset initiative has apparently ushered in the controlled demolition of the economy and the social order that we've experienced of late. The unrestrained pumping of currency into the market, the subsequent spiking inflation, the impetuous efforts to "green" the economy, the resultant soaring energy costs, the rising interest rates, the supply chain disruptions, the looming food shortages, the increasing consumer debt, and the possible tanking of the stock market are arguably consequences of the Great Reset.

On the social front, the effects of the Great Reset may be gleaned in the elevated rates of suicide, homicide, violent crime, and excess mortality. Great Reset-connected policies are responsible for the quasi-open southern American border and the flood of illegal immigrants, Critical Race Theory in the schools, plummeting educational standards and outcomes, and even the escalating abortion debate and the burgeoning transgender movement.

---

amended it to include the distribution of state power to extra-governmental agents—in particular to the extension and transfer of state power to supposedly private enterprises.

12　Leon S. Fuerth and Evan M.H. Faber, "Anticipatory Governance Practical Upgrades: Equipping the Executive Branch to Cope with Increasing Speed and Complexity of Major Challenges," NDU Press, October 2012, https://ndupress.ndu.edu/Portals/68/Documents/Books/CTBSP-Exports/Anticipatory-Governance.pdf?ver=2017-06-16-105921-030.

On the geopolitical front, the onslaught of non-stop propaganda, the censorship of dissident views and persons, the crisis in election integrity, the elite's war on populism, and the declining trust in establishment authorities are arguably Great Reset effects.

All that having been said, the Great Reset is but a coordinated propaganda campaign, shrouded under a cloak of inevitability. It is the wrapping on a giant package of plans and policies delivered to the world at large by various governments, international governance bodies, non-governmental organizations, and corporations. This package is not sold wholesale as "the Great Reset" but rather is distributed under various retail names, depending on the destination. It can only "succeed" if these parties adopt and administer the package and only if it is accepted by those it means to administer. Unfortunately, to a significant extent, the bills of sale have been signed by many world leaders, including corporate heads, and the Great Reset project is already well underway. Rather than the imaginary construction of conspiracy theorists, as the *New York Times* has suggested,[13] the Great Reset is an open, avowed plan in progress—not merely the "wishful thinking"[14] of socioeconomic planners to have corporate "stake-

---

13 Davey Alba, "The Baseless 'Great Reset' Conspiracy Theory Rises Again," *New York Times*, Nov. 17, 2020, https://www.nytimes.com/live/2020/11/17/world/covid-19-coronavirus#the-baseless-great-reset-conspiracy-theory-rises-again.

14 Alberto Mingardi, "The Great Reset: Between Conspiracy and Wishful Thinking," *Library of Economics and Liberty* (Econlib), Dec. 1, 2020, https://www.econlib.org/the-great-reset-between-conspiracy-and-wishful-thinking/.

holders"[15] and governments adopt the desiderata of the WEF but the coordinated means for resetting the global economy and reconfiguring the social order worldwide.

To sell this package, the WEF mobilizes the warmed-over rhetoric of "economic equality," "equity," "fairness," "inclusion," and "a shared destiny," among other euphemisms and doublespeak.[16] Together, such phrases represent the collectivist, socialist, or "woke" political and ideological component of the envisioned corporate-and-state-run socialism.[17]

The Great Reset entails a neo-techno-feudalist-corporate-socialist global order, with socioeconomic planners and corporate "stakeholders" at the helm and the greater part of humanity in their thrall. The mass of humanity, the planners would have it, will live under an economic stasis of vastly reduced expectations, with individual autonomy greatly curtailed by regulations if not obliterated by pandemics, cyber intrusions, and the planned remote control of human beings. As Ludwig von Mises suggested, central planners are always authoritarians who mean

---

15 "Stakeholder Capitalism: A Manifesto for a Cohesive and Sustainable World," *World Economic Forum Blog*, Jan. 14, 2020, https://www.weforum.org/press/2020/01/stakeholder-capitalism-a-manifesto-for-a-cohesive-and-sustainable-world/.

16 Nicholas Davis, "What Is the Fourth Industrial Revolution?," World Economic Forum, Jan. 19, 2016, https://www.weforum.org/agenda/2016/01/what-is-the-fourth-industrial-revolution/.

17 Michael Rectenwald, "Who Funds the Riotous American Left and Why? The Globalist Billionaire Class, Which Uses It to Build Corporate Socialism," Michael Rectenwald (website), Oct. 12, 2020, https://www.michaelrectenwald.com/essays/why-capitalists-fund-socialism.

to supplant the plans of individual actors with their own centralized plans and schemes. In the past, such socialist/communist/fascist plans and schemes, at national levels, have inevitably imploded, but their adoption nevertheless exacted an enormous toll over several generations. But now, for the first time in history, this is a global order equipped with superior technology and with sovereigns, including Western liberal nation-states and multinational mega-corporations, eager to buy in.

A Back Story of the Great Reset

As should be clear by now, Francis Fukuyama's declaration in *The End of History: The Last Man* (1992) that we had arrived at "the end of history" did not mean that classical liberalism, or laissez-faire economics, had emerged victorious over communism and fascism, or that the final ideological hegemony signaled the end of socialism.[18] In fact, for Fukuyama, the terminus of history was always democratic socialism or social democracy. As Hans-Hermann Hoppe noted in *Democracy: The God That Failed*, "the Last Man" standing was not a capitalist *homo economicus* but rather "*homo socio-democraticus.*"[19] The end of history, with all its Hegelian pretenses, did not entail the defeat of socialism-communism but rather of classical liberalism. Evidently, the Big State and Big Capital were supposed to have reached an inevitable and final détente. The Great

---

18   Francis Fukuyama, *The End of History and the Last Man*, London: Penguin Books, 2020.

19   Hans-Hermann Hoppe, *Democracy, The God That Failed: The Economics and Politics of Monarchy, Democracy, and Natural Order*, New Brunswick: Transaction Publishers, 2007, page 222.

Reset is the elite's desired consummation of this final détente.

The elite subversion of the free-market system and republican democracy had already been underway for many decades before "the end of history." According to W. Cleon Skousen in *The Naked Capitalist*, elites positioned within major banks, large corporations, leading think tanks, influential publishing companies, the media, tax-exempt foundations, the educational system, and the U.S. government sought to remake the U.S. in the image of its (former) collectivist arch rival since at least the early 1930s.[20] According to Carrol Quigley's *Tragedy and Hope: A History of the World in Our Time* (1966), elites propagated socialist, communist, and other collectivist ideologies at home. They promoted international policies that led to the deliberate abandonment of Eastern Europe and Southeast Asia to the communist scourge.[21] According to Anthony C. Sutton, they funded and armed the Bolsheviks in Russia and the Communists in Vietnam.[22]

---

20 Cleon W. Skousen, *The Naked Capitalist* (The Naked Series Book 2), Verity Publishing, 2011, pages 57-68. See also René A Wormser, *Foundations: Their Power and Influence*, Dauphin Publications, 2014; freebroadcasting, "G. Edward Griffin Interviews Norman Dodd on Subversive Activities of Wall Street Foundations- Youtube.com," March 8, 2020, https://www.youtube.com/watch?v=gyBrd74EJ-g; "Norman Dodd, Interviewed by G. Edward Griffin," Hidden agenda transcript, accessed May 10, 2022, https://web.archive.org/web/20080209100842/http://realityzone.stores.yahoo.net/hiddenagenda2.html.

21 Carrol Quigley, *Tragedy and Hope: A History of the World in Our Time*, San Diego, CA: Dauphin Publications, 2014.

22 Antony C. Sutton, *Wall Street and the Bolshevik Revolution*, Forest Row: Clairview, 2016; Antony C. Sutton, *National Suicide: Military Aid to the Soviet Union*, Dauphin Publications Inc., 2021.

For many in the U.S., at least, the goal of advancing collectivism has been most evident in the alacrity with which the institutions of higher education have absorbed and circulated Marxist, neo-Marxist, and post-Marxist collectivist ideologies in their various guises at least since the early 1930s—including Soviet propaganda, critical theory, postmodern theory, and the most recent variants, critical race theory, critical whiteness studies, and LGBTQIA+ ideology. The dreaded "long march through the institutions"[23] was never a bottom-up, grassroots project. Rather, it was an inside job undertaken by elites in positions of power and influence. When the philosophers, sociologists, and psychologists of the Frankfurt school of critical theory emigrated to the U.S. in 1933—armed with the Marxist theory of revolution and Antonio Gramsci's model for socialist cultural hegemony— they hardly inaugurated this march. Rather, they were welcomed by elites and funded by tax-exempt foundations, whose work was already well underway.[24] The so-called long march through the institutions was a stampede within them.

At the same time, as discussed in Part II, international NGOs (culminating in the WEF) have planned and sought to implement a global socialist economic and social order, using population "ethics"

---

23 "Long March through the Institutions," Wikipedia, January 27, 2022, https://en.wikipedia.org/wiki/Long_march_through_the_institutions.

24 The Frankfurt School theorist, Herbert Marcuse, for example, was funded by The American Council of Learned Societies, the Louis M. Rabinowitz Foundation, the Rockefeller Foundation, and the Social Science Research Council. See Herbert Marcuse, *One-Dimensional Man*, London: Routledge, 2002 (1964), page iv, where Marcuse acknowledges such funding.

and environmentalism as the pretexts for elite control. The World Economic Forum draws on the anti-capitalist, anti-human, neo-Malthusian environmental movement that began in the late 1960s. This movement sees humanity, especially the masses, as a scourge on the planet, a scourge whose consumption, and even whose population, must be curbed if not dramatically reduced.

To understand the Great Reset, then, we must recognize that the project represents the completion of a least a century-long and ongoing attempt to destroy classical liberalism (the free market and liberal democracy), constitutionalism (especially American constitutionalism), and national sovereignty vis-à-vis an elite-administered socialism and the "watermelon" green movement. The idea of resetting capitalism suggests that capitalism had previously been pure. But the Great Reset is the culmination of a much longer collectivization process and socialist project, with the corresponding growth of the state and intergovernmental, international governance bodies, especially the United Nations. Despite being pitched as the antidote to the supposed weaknesses of the free market, which WEF founder and chairman Klaus Schwab and company equate with "neoliberalism," the Great Reset is meant to intensify and complete an already prevalent economic and social interventionism.

New means are being deployed to bring about this economic and social interventionism. But we should not imagine that the Great Reset project was born *ab nihilo*. It is the culmination of decades of elite thinking, activism, and social engineering.

In this book, I explore just what the Great Reset

entails, according to its architects and subscribers. I have relied on the claims of Klaus Schwab and his WEF contributors, the WEF's partnerships, developments that stem from the project, and the implications that can be reasonably drawn from proposals and their implementation. I have also explored the anatomy and deep history of the WEF (Part II). Understanding this global reset requires a theoretical and historical treatment, material that is vital for countering the program.

In the conclusion, I consider the chances for "success" of the Great Reset project, and just what success might mean. I end by discussing how the momentum of this juggernaut might be impeded. One consolation is knowing that the structure of this "New World Order" is, ironically, unsustainable.[25] But left unopposed, the damage that the Great Reset would leave in its wake would be enormous. Likewise, we must work to thwart the plans of the Davos crowd. Although there is no silver bullet that would mortally wound the giant that we face, we are not entirely helpless in countering the Davos Agenda. But we should not hope to replace the "utopian" plans of the Great Reset with plans of an alternate utopia. Much damage has already been done, and much of what we undertake will amount to damage control. Still, we must have ideals in mind, and therefore I assert that free-market, pro-liberty ideals must underly our analysis and guide our responses.

---

25 Jakub Bożydar Wiśniewski, "Why the 'New World Order' Is Impossible to Implement without Creating Mass Chaos," Mises Institute, July 25, 2022, https://mises.org/wire/why-new-world-order-impossible-implement-without-creating-mass-chaos.

CHAPTER ONE

The Great Reset:
History and Conspiracy

B EFORE GRAPPLING with the main components
of the Great Reset, a history of the idea and its
development is in order. The history intersects with
"conspiracy theory," which the Great Reset project
seems to generate, as if spontaneously. It is as though
the architects of the Great Reset intentionally sprin-
kle breadcrumbs that lead potential detractors into
conspiratorial thinking, thereby discrediting and de-
flecting legitimate criticism and concerns. To avoid
such pitfalls, here I merely present a timeline of this
history and leave conjecture to the reader. It's not as
if I am concerned about being labeled a "conspiracy theorist." As I will discuss in a chapter devoted to
the question of conspiracy theory per se, the blithe
dismissal and/or routine denigration of conspiracy
theories is epistemologically unsound. My aim is to
show just why the Great Reset has generated such
speculation.

Although, as we will see, its philosophical roots

go much deeper, the Great Reset can be traced to the inception of the World Economic Forum, founded as the European Management Forum in 1971. In the same year, Klaus Schwab, an engineer and "economist" by training, published his first book, *Modern Enterprise Management in Mechanical Engineering*, written in his native German.[1] Here, Schwab first introduced what he would call "stakeholder capitalism," arguing, as the WEF website notes, "that the management of a modern enterprise must serve not only shareholders but all stakeholders to achieve long-term growth and prosperity."[2] Schwab and the WEF have promoted the multistakeholder concept ever since. The WEF is the proximate source for the stakeholder and "public-private partnership" rhetoric and policies embraced by governments, corporations, non-governmental organizations (NGOs), civil society organizations, and international governance bodies worldwide. Public-private partnerships have played a key role in the response to the covid crisis and are instrumental in the response to the "climate change" crisis.

The exact phrase, "the Great Reset," came into general circulation in 2010 with the publication of the book, *The Great Reset*, by the American Urban Studies theorist Richard Florida[3]—although others claim that they used the phrase before he did. Florida's Great Reset was a response to the 2008 finan-

---

1 "Klaus Schwab," World Economic Forum, accessed October 27, 2021, https://www.weforum.org/about/klaus-schwab.

2 Ibid.

3 Richard L. Florida, *The Great Reset: How New Ways of Living and Working Drive Post-Crash Prosperity*, New York, NY: HarperCollins, 2010.

cial crisis and he argues that the 2008 crash was the latest in a series of Great Resets, including the Long Depression of the 1870s and the Great Depression of the 1930s. Far from being the fallow years typically depicted, according to Florida, Great Resets are periods of paradigm-shifting innovation and geographical reconfiguration. Schwab apparently appropriated the phrase and adapted it to represent his stakeholder vision for a new kind of capitalism and world economic system.

At the WEF annual meeting in 2014, Schwab declared: "What we want to do in Davos this year...is to push the reset button."[4] By this, he referred to an imaginary reset button on the world economic system of "neoliberal" capitalism. A graphic depiction of a reset button would later appear on the WEF's website. In 2017, the WEF published a paper entitled, "We Need to Reset the Global Operating System to achieve the SDGs [Sustainable Development Goals]" of the United Nations (UN).[5]

Next, the WEF organized two events that eerily anticipated the covid-19 crisis. Covid-19 became the proximate inspiration for launching the Great Reset project. In May 2018, the WEF collaborated with the Johns Hopkins Center for Health Security to conduct the CLADE X Exercise, a "tabletop" simulation of a

---

4   "WEF Chairman Hopes Forum Will Help Push 'Reset' Button on World Economy," YouTube, July 31, 2015, https://www.youtube.com/watch?v=RAjYAXYGPuI.

5   Homi Kharas, "We Need to Reset the Global Operating System to Achieve the SDGs. Here's How," World Economic Forum, January 13, 2017, https://www.weforum.org/agenda/2017/01/we-need-to-up-grade-the-sustainable-development-goals-here-s-how/.

national response to a pandemic.[6] The exercise simulated the outbreak of CLADE X, a novel strain of a human parainfluenza virus with genetic elements of the Nipah virus. According to *Homeland Preparedness News*, the CLADE X simulation demonstrated that "[t]he lack of both a protective vaccine and a proactive worldwide plan for tackling the spread of a catastrophic global pandemic resulted in the death of 150 million people across the Earth."[7] Clearly, preparation for a global pandemic was in order.

A little over a year later, in October 2019, the WEF's uncanny prescience was again on display, only this time with greater precision. Along with the Bill and Melinda Gates Foundation, the WEF teamed up with Johns Hopkins University to stage another pandemic exercise, called Event 201. Event 201 simulated the international response to the outbreak of a novel coronavirus—just two months before the covid-19 outbreak became international news and a mere five months before the World Health Organization (WHO) declared it a pandemic. The Johns Hopkins Center for Health Security's summary of the exercise closely resembles the actual covid-19 scenario, including apparent foreknowledge of so-called asymptomatic spread:

---

6   Julia Cizek, "Clade X, a Tabletop Exercise Hosted by the Center for Health Security," Johns Hopkins Center for Health Security, January 7, 2019, https://www.centerforhealthsecurity.org/our-work/events/2018_clade_x_exercise/.

7   Kim Riley, "Mock Clade X Pandemic Decimates Human Population; Denotes Global Pre-Planning Needs," Homeland Preparedness News, May 21, 2018, https://homelandprepnews.com/countermeasures/28548-mock-clade-x-pandemic-decimates-human-population-denotes-global-pre-planning-needs/.

Event 201 simulates an outbreak of a novel zoonotic coronavirus transmitted from bats to pigs to people that eventually becomes efficiently transmissible from person to person, leading to a severe pandemic. The pathogen and the disease it causes are modeled largely on SARS, but it is more transmissible in the community setting by people with mild symptoms.[8]

The CLADE X and Event 201 simulations anticipated practically every eventuality of the covid crisis, notably the responses by governments, health agencies, conventional media, social media, and elements of the public. The responses and their effects included worldwide lockdowns, the collapse of businesses and industries, the adoption of biometric surveillance technologies, an emphasis on social media censorship to combat "misinformation" and "disinformation," the flooding of social and legacy media with "authoritative sources," widespread riots, and mass unemployment.[9]

These premonitory exercises and other covid curiosities have contributed to the "plandemic" narrative—speculation that the covid-19 crisis may have been staged by global elites centered around the WEF as an alibi for initiating the Great Reset. In addition to the pandemic exercises just referenced,

8   JHCHS website, "The Event 201 Scenario: A Pandemic Tabletop Exercise," Johns Hopkins Center for Health Security, October 18, 2019, https://www.centerforhealthsecurity.org/event201/scenario.html.

9   Tim Hinchliffe, "A Timeline of the Great Reset Agenda: From Foundation to Event 201 & the Pandemic of 2020," *The Sociable*, July 20, 2021, https://sociable.co/government-and-policy/timeline-great-reset-agenda-event-201-pandemic-2020/.

Swiss Policy Research points to the WEF's role in promoting digital biometric identity systems, thrusting its Young Global Leaders into major roles in the governmental management of the covid crisis and advocating the vaccination of children as "an entry point for digital identification."[10]

In June 2020, the WEF held its Great Reset summit as the fifty-first annual meeting of the World Economic Forum—delayed and refocused due to the covid crisis—and announced the Great Reset's official launch.

Just months into the covid crisis, on July 19, 2020, and a mere month after the annual meeting, Klaus Schwab and Thierry Malleret published *Covid 19: The Great Reset*. Steve Umbrello, the Managing Director at the Institute for Ethics and Emerging Technologies at the University of Turin, wrote in his academic review of the manifesto:

> Although not impossible, the speed at which a book on this particular topic, proposing these theses...was produced does play into the conspiratorial aesthetic that the book has since induced. Even though the authors are transparent about writing and publishing the book within a month's time, this neither confirms the veracity of such claims nor dispels suspicion from those who question its expediency.[11]

---

10 "The WEF and the Pandemic," Swiss Policy Research, October 27, 2021, https://swprs.org/the-wef-and-the-pandemic/.

11 Steven Umbrello, "Should We Reset? A Review of Klaus Schwab and Thierry Malleret's 'Covid-19: The Great Reset,'" *The Journal of Value Inquiry*, February 17, 2021, 1–8, https://doi.org/10.1007/s10790-021-09794-1, page 7.

The short interval between the Great Reset summit and the book's publication is not the only factor that has fed "the conspiratorial aesthetic" surrounding the Great Reset. Schwab's writing with Malleret and other WEF statements have stoked the speculations. In *Covid-19*, the co-authors declare, without noting the irony, that covid-19 represents an "opportunity [that] can be seized,"[12] and "we should take advantage of this unprecedented opportunity to reimagine our world,"[13] and "the moment must be seized to take advantage of this unique window of opportunity,"[14] and "[f]or these companies the pandemic is a unique opportunity to rethink their organization and enact positive, sustainable and lasting change,"[15] and "[f]or those fortunate enough to find themselves in industries 'naturally' resilient to the pandemic [like Big Digital Tech], the crisis was not only more bearable, but even a source of profitable opportunities at a time of distress for the majority."[16] This last statement is suggestive of the Great Reset's overall effects: profitable opportunity for the global elites and distress for the majority.

In his welcoming remarks at the 2022 annual meeting of the WEF, Schwab suggested that current global conditions, including the war in Ukraine and the post-pandemic "new normal," made this year's forum the most important in its 50-year history. Schwab then stated that covid-19 represented the

---

12　Klaus Schwab and Thierry Malleret, *COVID-19: The Great Reset*. n.p.: Forum Publishing, 2020, page 57.

13　Ibid., pages 18-19.

14　Ibid., page 143.

15　Ibid., page 173.

16　Ibid., page 204.

most severe health crisis of the last hundred years yet warned that something worse may be on the horizon: "We have to reinforce our resilience against a new virus, possibly, or other risks which *we have on the global agenda*" (8:30 mark, emphasis mine). "The future is not just happening," Schwab later declared, *"the future is built by us, by a powerful community, as you here in this room"* (11:20 mark, emphasis mine).[17]

Recognizing that the Great Reset project has sparked an enormous public backlash, Schwab and Thierry Malleret penned a second Great Reset book—*The Great Narrative*—to recast the Great Reset as both necessary and benign and to reinforce the official narrative.[18] One would think, then, that Schwab might have refrained from suggesting that a "new virus" or "other risks" are part of "the global agenda"—as if the WEF and its corporate and state partners were planning such events. And Schwab might have weighed his words more carefully than to state blatantly: "the future is built by us, by a powerful community, as you here in this room."

Schwab apparently let the cat out of the bag. Or did he intentionally make such statements to generate "conspiracist" thinking and thereby discredit critics? In other words, is it possible that Schwab and others intentionally sow the seeds of conspiracy theories about the Great Reset? The WEF and the

---

17   "Welcoming Remarks and Special Address, World Economic Forum Annual Meeting 2022, Davos," World Economic Forum, May 23, 2022, https://www.weforum.org/events/world-economic-forum-annual-meeting-2022.

18   Klaus Schwab and Thierry Malleret. *The Great Narrative (The Great Reset)*, Cologny/Geneva, Switzerland: Forum Publishing, 2022.

UN can then dismiss all objections to the Great Reset by labeling them "conspiracy theories" while working to ban such content and its promulgators from the Internet.

The WEF and the United Nations (UN) have become proactive in thwarting "conspiracy theories" about a global agenda. In a podcast, the WEF announced its recruitment of "hundreds of thousands of 'information warriors'" to patrol the Internet and police social media and other forums for "misinformation" and conspiracy content, which will then be systematically shut down.[19] In the WEF podcast entitled "The World Vs Virus," the "virus" is not the coronavirus but rather the virus of "misinformation." The interviewee, the UN's Under-Secretary-General for Global Communications, Melissa Fleming, calls misinformation an "info-demic" and "pollution."[20] Fleming's voice quavers as she dismisses counter-claims about the virus and vaccines and argues that such "misinformation" should not be allowed expression.

The UN Secretary-General similarly announced a "communications response initiative" aimed at "conspiracy theories" regarding covid. The campaign promises "to flood the Internet with facts and science while countering the growing scourge of mis-

19 Baxter Dmitry, "Un Declares War on 'Dangerous' Conspiracy Theories: 'the World Is Not Secretly Manipulated by Global Elite,'" *News Punch*, August 4, 2022, https://newspunch.com/un-de-clares-war-on-dangerous-conspiracy-theories-the-world-is-not-se-cretly-manipulated-by-global-elite/.

20 "Where's the Cure for the Infodemic? Our World vs Virus Podcast," World Economic Forum, accessed August 19, 2022, https://www.weforum.org/agenda/2020/11/misinformation-infodem-ic-world-vs-virus-podcast/.

information, a poison that is putting even more lives at risk."[21]

The United Nations Educational, Scientific and Cultural Organization (UNESCO) also announced a joint campaign with the European Commission, Twitter, and the World Jewish Congress called #ThinkBeforeSharing. The campaign hopes to teach Internet users how to "pre-bunk and debunk" "dangerous" conspiracy theories, especially those purportedly linked to "antisemitism."[22]

Such efforts on the part of the WEF and the UN to shut down expression that deviates from official narratives only serve to augment distrust and further fuel speculation about the role of the WEF and its partners in connection with the covid crisis and their relationship to the Great Reset. But perhaps this is the objective.

---

21 "New United Nations Strategy Aims at Countering Viral Hatred, Covid-19 Conspiracy Theories, Secretary-General Says, Urging World to Unite against Virus | UN Press," United Nations, accessed August 19, 2022, https://press.un.org/en/2020/sgsm20044.doc.htm.

22 Director-General, UNESCO, "#Thinkbeforesharing - Stop the Spread of Conspiracy Theories," UNESCO, April 14, 2021, https://en.unesco.org/themes/gced/thinkbeforesharing.

Part I

The Economics of the Great Reset

It is not merely a question of changing the institutions but rather, and this is more important, of totally changing human beings in their attitudes, their instincts, their goals, and their values.
— Herbert Marcuse

Affluence is the biggest threat to our world...
— Sam Fleming, WEF

CHAPTER TWO

Who Is Dr. EV-il?

GENERAL MOTORS' (GM) 2022 Super Bowl advertisement, "Dr. EV-il," summoned viewers to ponder the issue of climate change.[1] The ad introduced the company's electric vehicles, stylized as "EVs," before apparently committing the corporation to a "net-zero" future. In the same breath, GM subtly suggested that it would use what is purported to be a looming catastrophe to its advantage.

The ad reprised the theme of the Austin Powers series. Mike Myers, Seth Green, Rob Lowe, and Mindy Sterling play Dr. Evil, Dr. Evil's son Scott, Number Two, and Frau Farbissina, respectively. As his cohorts inform him, despite having taken over GM, Dr. Evil has been displaced by climate change from his position as the world's number-one threat. Not to be outdone, nor to have his plans for world domination thwarted, Dr. Evil co-opts Frau Farbissina's words, vowing to regain his Number One status by

---

1 GMblogs, "Dr. EV-Il | #Everybodyin | 90 Second Spot," YouTube, February 10, 2022., https://www.youtube.com/watch?v=uEuEBT0T-WQE.

becoming part of the climate solution: "I will help save the world first, then take over the world!"

Dr. Evil: I will help save the world first, then take over the world!

The irony of GM's Dr. Evil appropriation was not lost on *Gizmodo* columnist Molly Taft, for whom GM is a real-life supervillain openly pretending to be a superhero and making its pretensions blatant: "GM's long history of climate denial makes this ad painfully literal—and is a warning about how polluting companies are now trying to greenwash their own reputations."[2] For Taft, GM is Dr. Evil himself; marshaling this iconic character is too clever by half and cuts matters too close to the bone.

The ad should strike us as ironic too, but GM's playful Dr. EV-il ad was a joke on such observers as

---

2 Molly Taft, "GM's Dr. Evil Super Bowl Commercial Is a Little Too Literal," *Gizmodo*, February 14, 2022, https://gizmodo.com/gms-dr-evil-super-bowl-commercial-is-a-little-too-lite-1848533642.

Taft. The company ironically suggested that it is not the criminal force that Taft and others make it out to be. Dr. Evil is, after all, a fictional villain, and not the real CEO of GM.

But even more ironic was GM's (perhaps unintentional) representation of the World Economic Forum (WEF). Just as GM appropriated Dr. Evil and Dr. Evil appropriated Frau Farbissina, the ad seemed to reference the mien and ethos of Herr Klaus Schwab, the chairman and founder of the WEF, who has been popularly likened to Myers's villain.[3]

Klaus Schwab: Every country, from the United States to China, must participate, and every industry, from oil and gas to tech, must be transformed!

Schwab is the world's leading corporate mouthpiece of climate change catastrophism. He, and the

3 "Klaus Schwab (Dr Evil)," YouTube, July 21, 2021, https://www.youtube.com/watch?v=HsxlOlKXyx8.

corporate "stakeholders" signed onto the WEF's agenda, also stand to gain outsized economic and political power as the Great Reset is enacted via Schwab's brainchild, "stakeholder capitalism."[4] Its Environmental, Social, and Governance (ESG) Index already measures corporate compliance with the agenda. Stakeholder capitalism makes partners[5] of corporations in the world's governance system while advancing their monopolistic economic ambitions.

Does GM mean to suggest that Klaus Schwab is Dr. Evil? After all, Dr. Evil's appropriation—"I will help save the world first, then take over the world"—echoes Schwab and the WEF's Great Reset agenda. Given the prevalence of the comparison on the Internet, and the expenditures for the ad, it's highly unlikely that the creative team was unaware of it. But whether the invocation of Klaus Schwab was intentional or not, the ad nevertheless issued a biting tongue-in-cheek criticism of the agenda that GM and consumers are being compelled to accept.

Furthermore, the Dr. EV-il ad tacitly acknowledges that something evil is afoot with the Great Reset agenda. No matter how much the WEF and its partners gloss the project in terms of "equity" and "sustainability," the sense that an evil agenda is being conducted under the imperatives of stakeholder capitalism is irresistible.

4 Michael Rectenwald, "The Great Reset, Part IV: 'Stakeholder Capitalism' vs. 'Neoliberalism,'" Mises Institute, January 26, 2021, https://mises.org/wire/great-reset-part-iv-stakeholder-capitalism-vs-neoliberalism.

5 Javvad Malik, Paddy Padmanathan, and Geoffrey See, "Partners," World Economic Forum, accessed June 30, 2022, https://www.weforum.org/partners/.

CHAPTER THREE

Stakeholder Capitalism

Welcome to my city - or should I say, "our city."
I don't own anything. I don't own a car. I don't
own a house. I don't own any appliances or any
clothes.

It might seem odd to you, but it makes perfect
sense for us in this city. Everything you considered a product, has now become a service. We
have access to transportation, accommodation,
food and all the things we need in our daily
lives. One by one all these things became free,
so it ended up not making sense for us to own
much.[1]

THE PASSAGE ABOVE is the vision of one Ida
Auken, "the first Danish politician chosen to
be a Young Global Leader for the World Economic

---

1 Ida Auken, "Welcome to 2030: I Own Nothing, Have No Privacy
and Life Has Never Been Better," *Forbes Magazine*, April 14, 2022,
https://www.forbes.com/sites/worldeconomicforum/2016/11/10/
shopping-i-cant-really-remember-what-that-is-or-how-differently-
well-live-in-2030/. (This article was previously located on the WEF
website but was taken down.)

Forum and [who] has also been elected to be one out of the 40 most promising young leaders under 40 in Europe."[2] It is an excerpt from her report from the future to the past, our present. The glorified blogger does not project "a utopia or dream of the future," we are told. Yet the future she describes just so happens to meet all the criteria of the Great Reset—low to no carbon emissions, nearly 100% reusable products, "sustainability," and a "happy," compliant, and propertyless population.

The Great Reset is a phrase used by Schwab and the World Economic Forum (WEF) primarily to describe a supposedly new kind of capitalism. It is important to note that the "E" in the WEF stands for "economic," and not "environmental," although the economics of the WEF are determined by its environmentalism.

In their book, *COVID-19: The Great Reset*, WEF founder and executive chairman Klaus Schwab and Thierry Malleret write that the COVID-19 crisis should be regarded as an "opportunity [that can be] seized to make the kind of institutional changes and policy choices that will put economies on the path toward a fairer, greener future."[3] What is this "fairer, greener future," and how would the Great Reset bring it about?

The Great Reset ushers in a bewildering economic amalgam. I've variously called it "corporate

---

2 "Ida Auken - Agenda Contributor," World Economic Forum, accessed June 28, 2022, https://www.weforum.org/agenda/authors/ida-auken.

3 Klaus Schwab and Thierry Malleret, *COVID-19: The Great Reset*, n.p.: Forum Publishing, 2020, page 57.

socialism,"[4] "capitalism with Chinese characteristics,"[5] and "neo-feudalism,"[6] while the Italian philosopher Giorgio Agamben has called this economic fusion "communist capitalism."[7] Schwab and company euphemistically call it "stakeholder capitalism."

The Great Reset would eliminate so-called shareholder capitalism, or "neoliberalism," and universalize "stakeholder capitalism." Stakeholder capitalism, we are told, is a form of capitalism that benefits "customers, suppliers, employees, and local communities"[8] in addition to shareholders in the business operations of the world's major corporations and governments. A stakeholder is anyone or any group that stands to benefit or lose from corporate behavior—other than competitors, we may suppose. Stakeholder capitalism involves changes to the behavior of corporations with respect to carbon-based energy use

---

4   Michael Rectenwald, *Google Archipelago: The Digital Gulag and the Simulation of Freedom,* Nashville, TN: New English Review Press, 2019, pages 54-65 and 123-24; Michael Rectenwald, "The Great Reset, Part II: Corporate Socialism," *Mises Wire,* December 31, 2020, https://mises.org/library/great-reset-part-ii-corporate-socialism.

5   Michael Rectenwald, "The Great Reset, Part III: Capitalism with Chinese Characteristics," *Mises Wire,* December 28, 2020, https://mises.org/wire/great-reset-part-iii-capitalism-chinese-characteristics.

6   Michael Rectenwald, "What Is the Great Reset? Part I: Reduced Expectations and Bio-Techno-Feudalism," *Mises Wire,* December 11, 2020, https://mises.org/wire/what-great-reset-part-i-reduced-expectations-and-bio-techno-feudalism.

7   Giorgio Agamben, "Communist Capitalism," *Ill Will,* December 15, 2020, https://illwill.com/communist-capitalism.

8   Neil Kokemuller, "Does a Corporation Have Other Stakeholders Other Than Its Shareholders?" *Chron.com,* October 26, 2016, https://smallbusiness.chron.com/corporation-other-stakeholders-other-its-shareholders-63538.html.

but also in terms of the distribution of benefits and "externalities" that corporations produce. It means not only corporate cooperation but also major government intervention in the economy. Schwab and Malleret promote "the return of 'big' government," as if it had not been growing all the while. If "the past five centuries in Europe and America" have taught us anything, they assert, it is that "acute crises contribute to boosting the power of the state. It's always been the case and there is no reason why it should be different with the COVID-19 pandemic."[9]

Stakeholder capitalism includes not only corporate-state responses to ecological issues such as climate change, "but also rethinking their commitments to already-vulnerable communities within their ecosystems."[10] This is the "social justice" aspect of stakeholder capitalism and the Great Reset. These special stakeholders include women, and black, brown, indigenous, transgender, and other special identity groups, who supposedly stand to gain from stakeholderism.

Schwab and Malleret typically pit "stakeholder capitalism" against "neoliberalism." Although "neoliberalism" is a weasel word that changes meanings depending on the user, Schwab and Malleret deploy the term to refer to what is otherwise known as the free market. Neoliberalism is, according to Schwab and Malleret, "a corpus of ideas and policies that can

---

9 Schwab and Malleret, *COVID-19*, pages 88-89.

10 World Economic Forum, "The Bold Steps Business Leaders Must Take on Social Justice," *Forbes Magazine*, January 26, 2021, https://www.forbes.com/sites/worldeconomicforum/2021/01/25/the-bold-steps-business-leaders-must-take-on-social-justice/?sh=113639621e61.

loosely be defined as favoring competition over solidarity, creative destruction over government intervention and economic growth over social welfare."[11] Stakeholder capitalism is thus opposed to the free enterprise system—to the competition of the free and open market—to capitalism. If stakeholder capitalism means centralized economic planning so that production and consumption tend toward a greener, fairer economy, we may assume that the obverse of this is also true. That is, corporate-state endeavors that do not tend to benefit stakeholders, according to WEF principles, like the Keystone Pipeline project in the U.S., for example, must be abandoned.

The collectivist planners of the Great Reset intend to drive ownership and control of production to those enrolled in "stakeholder capitalism" and away from other, non-compliant companies. The goal of the WEF and its partners is to vest as much control over production and distribution in these corporate stakeholders as possible, while eliminating producers whose products or processes are deemed either unnecessary or inimical. "Every country, from the United States to China, must participate, and every industry, from oil and gas to tech, must be transformed,"[12] writes Schwab.

Since the overriding pretext for the Great Reset is global climate change, anyone in the world can be considered a stakeholder in the governance of any major corporation. Racial "equity," the promotion of transgender agendas, and other such identity

11 Schwab and Malleret, *COVID-19*, page 78.

12 Klaus Schwab, "Now Is the Time for a 'Great Reset,'" World Economic Forum, June 3, 2020, https://www.weforum.org/agenda/2020/06/now-is-the-time-for-a-great-reset/.

policies and politics are also injected into corporate schemes.

Debates about the efficacy, politics, and ethics of *shareholder* capitalism versus what is now called stakeholder capitalism date at least to the 1970s, if not much earlier. They were stirred up by Milton Friedman's famous essay, "The Social Responsibility of Business is to Increase its Profits," published by *The New York Times Magazine* in 1970.[13] In this seminal piece, Friedman voiced his rejection of the "soulful corporation," which came into focus with Carl Kaysen's essay, "The Social Significance of the Modern Corporation," in 1957.[14] Kaysen had figured the corporation as a social institution that must weigh profitability against a broad and growing array of social responsibilities. For the modern corporation, Kaysen argued, "there is no display of greed or graspingness; there is no attempt to push off onto the workers or the community at large part of the social costs of the enterprise. The modern corporation is a soulful corporation."[15] In Kaysen's "corporate social responsibility" claims, we can descry the roots of stakeholder capitalism.

Friedman noted that the notion of corporate so-

---

13 Milton Friedman, "A Friedman Doctrine— the Social Responsibility of Business Is to Increase Its Profits," *The New York Times*, September 13, 1970, https://www.nytimes.com/1970/09/13/archives/a-friedman-doctrine-the-social-responsibility-of-business-is-to.html.

14 Carl Kaysen, "The Social Significance of the Modern Corporation," in "Papers and Proceedings of the Sixty-Eighth Annual Meeting of the American Economic Association," eds. James Washington Bell and Gertrude Tait, special issue, *American Economic Review* 47, no. 2 (May 1957): 311–19, page 314.

15 Ibid.

cial responsibility imports "the political mechanism" into every form of economic activity, allowing the majority, or a dictator, to force conformity to social (and essentially socialist) dictates through non-democratic means. The imperatives of "social responsibility"—or the running of a corporation for other than profit-making—amount to the undemocratic imposition of taxes on shareholders, customers, and even employees. Further, such rhetoric undermines the foundations of a free society and encourages the "iron fist of government bureaucrats" to impose "socially responsible" behavior on otherwise free market players. Running corporations in terms of "social responsibility," Friedman concluded, "does not differ in philosophy from the most explicitly collectivist doctrine," although it professes to achieve "collectivist ends" without explicitly avowing "collectivist means." Friedman's words sum up the agenda of stakeholder capitalism and its measuring rod, the Environmental, Social, and Governance (ESG) Index, nicely.

If anything, stakeholder capitalism *theoretically* represents a consumptive worm set to burrow into and hollow out corporations from within—a means of socialist wealth liquidation from within capitalist organizations themselves, using any number of criteria for the redistribution of benefits and "externalities."

But don't take my word for it. Take one David Campbell, a British socialist (although non-Marxist) and author of *The Failure of Marxism* (1996). After pronouncing Marxism kaput, Campbell began advocating stakeholder capitalism as a means for achieving the same socialist ends. His argument with the

British orthodox Marxist Paddy Ireland represents an internecine squabble over the best means of achieving socialism, while also providing a looking glass into the minds of socialists determined to try other, presumably nonviolent tacks, like stakeholder capitalism.[16]

Campbell castigated Ireland for his rejection of stakeholder capitalism. Ireland held—wrongly, Campbell asserted—that stakeholder capitalism is ultimately impossible. Ireland argued that nothing can interfere, for very long, with the inexorable market demand for profit. Market forces will inevitably overwhelm any such ethical considerations as stakeholders' interests.

Ireland's more-radical-than-thou Marxism left Campbell flummoxed. Didn't Ireland realize that his market determinism was exactly what the defenders of "neoliberalism" asserted as the inevitable and only sure means for the distribution of social welfare? "Marxism," Campbell rightly noted, "can be identified with the deriding of 'social reform' as not representing, or even as obstructing, 'the revolution.'" A typical anti-reformist Marxist, Ireland failed to recognize that "the social reforms that [he] derided *are* the revolution."[17] Socialism is nothing if not a movement whereby "the purported natural necessity represented by 'economic' imperatives is replaced by conscious *political* decisions about the allocation of

---

16 David Campbell, "Towards a Less Irrelevant Socialism: Stakeholding as a 'Reform' of the Capitalist Economy," *Journal of Law and Society* 24, no. 1 (1997): 65–84.

17 Campbell, "Towards a Less Irrelevant Socialism," pages 75-76, emphasis in original.

resources" (emphasis mine).[18] This political socialism, as against Marx's orthodox epigones, is what
Marx really meant by socialism, Campbell suggested. Stakeholder capitalism is socialism.

Ireland and Campbell agreed that the very idea
of stakeholder capitalism derived from companies
having become relatively autonomous from their
shareholders. The idea of managerial independence
and thus company or corporate autonomy was first
treated by Adolf A. Berle and Gardiner C. Means
in *The Modern Corporation and Private Property* (1932) and after them in James Burnham's *The
Managerial Revolution* (1962). In "Corporate Governance, Stakeholding, and the Company: Towards a
Less Degenerate Capitalism?," Ireland wrote of this
putative autonomy:

> [T]he idea of the stake-holding company is root-
> ed in the autonomy of 'the company' from its
> shareholders; its claim being that this autono-
> my...can be exploited to ensure that companies
> do not operate exclusively with the interests of
> their shareholders in mind.[19]

This apparent autonomy of the company, Ireland argued, came about not with incorporation or
legal changes to the structure of the corporation, but
with the growth of large-scale industrial capitalism.
The growth in the sheer number of shares and with
it the advent of the stock market made for the ready

---

18   Campbell, "Towards a Less Irrelevant Socialism," page 76.

19   Paddy Ireland, "Corporate Governance, Stakeholding, and the
Company: Towards a Less Degenerate Capitalism?," *Journal of Law
and Society* 23, no. 3 (September 1996): 287–320, esp. page 288.

salability of the share. Shares became "money cap-ital," readily exchangeable titles to a percentage of profit, and not claims on the company's assets. It was at this point those shares gained apparent autonomy from the company and the company from its share-holders. Ireland wrote:

> Moreover, with the emergence of this mar-ket, shares developed an autonomous value of their own quite independent of, and often dif-ferent from, the value of the company's assets. Emerging as what Marx called fictitious capital, they were redefined in law as an autonomous form of property independent of the assets of the company. They were no longer conceptual-ized as equitable interests in the property of the company but as rights to profit with a value of their own, rights which could be freely and eas-ily bought and sold in the marketplace...

> On gaining their independence from the as-sets of companies, shares emerged as legal objects in their own right, seemingly doubling the capital of joint stock companies. The as-sets were now owned by the company and by the company alone, either through a corpora-tion or, in the case of unincorporated compa-nies, through trustees. The intangible share capital of the company, on the other hand, had become the sole property of the shareholder. They were now two quite separate forms of property. Moreover, with the legal constitution of the share as an entirely autonomous form of property, the externalization of the shareholder from the company had been completed in a way

not previously possible.[20]

Thus, according to Ireland, a difference in interests emerged between the holders of the industrial capital and the holders of the money capital, or between the company and the shareholder.

Nevertheless, Ireland maintained, the autonomy of the company is limited by the necessity for industrial capital to produce profit. The value of shares is ultimately determined by the profitability of the company's assets in use:

> The company is, and will always be, the personification of industrial capital and, as such, subject to the imperatives of profitability and accumulation. These are not imposed from the outside on an otherwise neutral and directionless entity, but are, rather, intrinsic to it, lying at the very heart of its existence.[21]

This necessity, Ireland argued, defines the limits of stakeholder capitalism and its inability to sustain itself.

> The nature of the company is such, therefore, as to suggest that [there] are strict limits to the extent to which its autonomy from shareholders can be exploited for the benefit of workers or, indeed, other stakeholders.[22]

Here is a point on which the "neoliberal" Mil-

---

20 Ireland, "Corporate Governance, Stakeholding, and the Company," page 303.

21 Ibid, page 304.

22 Ibid.

ton Friedman and the Marxist Paddy Ireland would
have agreed, despite Ireland's insistence that the extraction of "surplus value" at the point of production
is the source of profit. And this agreement between
Friedman and Ireland is exactly why Campbell rejected Ireland's argument. Such market determinism is only necessary under capitalism, Campbell
asserted. Predictions about how companies will behave in the context of markets are only valid under
market conditions. Changing company rules such
that profitability is endangered, albeit, or even especially, from the inside out, is the very definition of socialism. Changing the way companies behave in the
direction of stakeholder capitalism is revolutionary
en se.

Curiously, Campbell ended his argument rather
undogmatically by stating that if Friedman was right
and "if these comparisons [between shareholder and
stakeholder capitalism] tend to show exclusive maximization of shareholder value to be the optimal way
of maximizing welfare," then "one should give up
being a socialist."[23] If, after all, the maximization of
human welfare is really the object, and "shareholder
capitalism" (or "neoliberalism") proves to be the best
way to achieve it, then socialism, including stakeholder capitalism, must necessarily be abandoned.

Stakeholder capitalism can be traced, although
not in an unbroken line of succession, to the "commercial idealism"[24] of the late nineteenth and early
twentieth centuries, when Edward Bellamy and King
Camp Gillette, among others, envisioned corporate

23 Campbell, "Towards a Less Irrelevant Socialism," page 81.
24 Gib Prettyman, "Advertising, Utopia, and Commercial Idealism:
The Case of King Gillette," *Prospects 24* (January 1999): 231–48.

socialist utopias via incorporation. For such corporate socialists, the means for establishing socialism was through the continuous incorporation of all the factors of production. With incorporation, a series of mergers and acquisitions would occur until the formation of a singular global monopoly, in which all "the People" had equal shares, was complete. In his *"World Corporation,"* Gillette declared:

> The trained mind of business and finance sees no stopping-place to corporate absorption and growth, except final absorption of all the World's material assets into one corporate body, under the directing control of one corporate mind.[25]

Such a singular world monopoly would become socialist upon the equal distribution of shares among the population:

> CORPORATIONS WILL CONTINUE TO FORM, ABSORB, EXPAND, AND GROW, AND NO POWER OF MAN CAN PREVENT IT. Promoters [of World Corporation] are the *true socialists* of this generation, the actual builders of a co-operative system which is eliminating competition, and in a practical business way reaching results which socialists have vainly tried to attain through legislation and agitation for centuries (italics mine).[26]

This is not altogether different than stakehold-

---

25 King Camp Gillette, *"World Corporation,"* Boston: New England News, 1910, page 4.

26 Ibid., page 9, capitalization in original.

er capitalism. Although the latter does not promise equal ownership in a one-world corporation, it nevertheless promotes monopolies for the benefit of "the People."

Gillette's earlier book, *The Human Drift* (1894), promoted monopoly and railed against competition. Competition, he believed, was "the prolific source of ignorance and every form of crime, and that [which] increases the wealth of the few at the expense of the many...the present system of competition between individuals results in fraud, deception, and adulteration of almost every article we eat, drink, or wear." Competition resulted in "a waste of material and labor beyond calculation." Competition was the source of "selfishness, war between nations and individuals, murder, robbery, lying, prostitution, forgery, divorce, deception, brutality, ignorance, injustice, drunkenness, insanity, suicide, and every other crime, [which] have their base in competition and ignorance."[27] For Gillette, competition was the root of all evil.

Competition is also the bane of existence for the WEF. In a passage that echoes Gillette, Schwab and Malleret figure neoliberalism as "a corpus of ideas and policies that can loosely be defined as favouring competition over solidarity, creative destruction over government intervention and economic growth over social welfare."[28] I must note here that without economic growth, social welfare is impossible for a growing population. Thus, stakeholder capitalism is

---

27 King Camp Gillette, *The Human Drift*, Boston: New Era, 1894, pages 34-35.

28 Klaus Schwab and Thierry Malleret, *COVID-19: The Great Reset*, Forum Publishing, page 78.

neo-Malthusian at base. (See Part II.)

It is essential to state that stakeholder capitalism is not a new form of capitalism at all. Capitalism is the economic system under which governments have nothing to do with the economy, other than protecting property rights—if such rights can be protected rather than infringed by governments.[29] There is no hyphenated form of capitalism as such. But since stakeholder capitalism, as Paddy Ireland notes, cannot result in pure socialism, we must determine what so-called stakeholder capitalism amounts to. If it is not capitalism or socialism, then just what is it? One way to understand stakeholder capitalism is by comparing it to the contemporary Chinese economy.

---

29 For the question of whether governments protect or infringe property rights, see Hans-Hermann Hoppe, *Democracy, The God That Failed: The Economics and Politics of Monarchy, Democracy, and Natural Order*, New Brunswick: Transaction Publishers, 2007, pages 221-238.

CHAPTER FOUR

Capitalism with Chinese Characteristics

T HE TITLE OF THIS chapter represents a play on
the description of the Chinese economy by the
Chinese Communist Party (CCP). Several decades
ago, when China's growing reliance on the for-profit
sectors of its economy could no longer be credibly
denied by the CCP, its leadership approved the slogan "socialism with Chinese characteristics" to describe the Chinese economic system.[1] Formulated by
Deng Xiaoping, the phrase became an essential component of the CCP's attempt to rationalize Chinese
for-profit development under a socialist-communist
political system. "Capitalism" would support socialism until communism was reached.

According to the party, the growing privatization of the Chinese economy was to be a temporary
phase—lasting as long as one hundred years, accord-

---

1 Ian Wilson, "Socialism with Chinese Characteristics: China and
the Theory of the Initial Stage of Socialism," *Politics* 24, no. 1 (September 2007): 77–84.

ing to some party leaders!—on the way to a class-
less society of full socialism-communism. The party
leaders claimed, and still maintain, that socialism
with Chinese characteristics was necessary in China's case because China was a "backward" agrarian
country when socialism-communism[2] was introduced—too early, it was suggested. China needed a
capitalist booster shot.

With the slogan, the party was able to suggest
that China had been an exception to the orthodox
Marxist position that socialism arrives only after the
development of capitalism—although Marx himself
deviated from his own formula late in life. At the
same time, the slogan allowed the CCP to confirm the
orthodox Marxist position. China's communist revolution had come before developed industrial capitalism—an exception to orthodox Marxism. "Capitalism" was thus introduced into China's economic
system later—a confirmation of orthodox Marxism.

Stripped of its socialist ideological pretensions,
socialism with Chinese characteristics, or the Chinese system itself, amounts to a socialist-communist
state increasingly funded by for-profit economic development. The difference between the former Soviet Union and contemporary China is that when it
became obvious that a socialist-communist economy
had failed, the former gave up its socialist-communist economic pretenses, while the latter has not.

Whether the CCP leaders believe their own rhetoric or not, the ideological gymnastics on display

---

2 I use "socialism-communism" rather than either "socialism" or
"communism." The usage acknowledges the fact that Marx did not
distinguish between the two, while it also recognizes that Lenin conceived of socialism as a stage before communism.

are nevertheless spectacular. On its face, the slogan embeds and glosses over a seemingly obvious contradiction to sanctify or "re-communize" Chinese for-profit development as a precondition of full socialism-communism.

However, the Chinese slogan does capture an essential truth about socialism-communism, one that is either unrecognized or unacknowledged by the CCP and denied by Western Marxists. Contrary to the assertions of communist leaders and followers, and even contrary to the claims of many who oppose it, socialism-communism is not primarily an economic system. It is first and foremost a political system. That's because socialism-communism is impossible.

Once in power, socialist-communist leaders recognize that given their control over resources, they have effectively become the new owners of the means of production. (Whereas, as Ludwig von Mises suggested, consumers effectively hold the power of economic disposal in free markets.)[3] In attempting to implement a socialist-communist economy, they recognize that, in the absence of prices, large-scale industrial production requires supervisory decision-making. Likewise, the economy is not democratic in the sense promised by socialist-communist ideologues. Decision-making must be centralized, or at least bureaucratized. Democratic decision-making is precluded by state-owned and state-controlled production and distribution.

Contrary to the claims of its advocates, it is so-

---

3 Ludwig von Mises, *Socialism: An Economic and Sociological Analysis*, 3d ed., New Haven, CT: Yale University Press, 1951, pages 37–42.

cialist-communist production and not capitalist production that is "irrational." Its irrationality is due to
the elimination of the essential indices for determining rational production and distribution—namely,
prices. In what has been dubbed "the calculation
problem," Ludwig von Mises showed that prices
represent the incredibly thick and vital data sets required for allocating resources to production and
calibrating these to demand.[4] Socialism is irrational
because by beginning without prices for the factors
of production, no rational criteria can ever emerge
for allocating resources to specific production processes. Eliminating prices for the factors of production and setting prices for consumer goods based on
labor inputs (derived from the labor theory of value)
rather than demand, the socialist economy cannot
provide the feedback loops required for determining
what to produce, how much of it to produce, or how
to produce it. Cancerous, oversized productive capacities in one sector of the economy are paralleled
by relatively anemic productive capacities in another, and so on. Therefore, socialism-communism cannot exist for long.

This means that socialism fails, not only at resource allocation, but also at the economic representation of the people it claims to champion. Absent
price mechanisms, economic "voters," or consumers,
would have no way to voice their needs and wants.
Production and distribution must be based on the
nondemocratic decision-making of centralized authorities. Without any way of having their needs and
wants reflected in production, socialism represents
anything but "economic democracy." Those who re-

4 Ibid., pages 113-122.

ally care about the working masses must reject socialism for its incapacity to establish economic democracy, its most fundamental reason for being.

This failure was demonstrated by the Soviet Union's attempt at using a centralized planning system called Gosplan, by which central planners attempted to allocate factors of production and consumer goods based on estimates of demand rather than actual demand, and under which the prices for consumer goods, as well as wages, were set according to labor time rather than actual demand.[5]

Theoretically, socialism-communism is a system under which resource allocation is commanded by the state and thus effectively controlled by the state leaders, the real ruling class. The latter retain control through ideology and force. However, a fully socialist-communist economy is impossible. As opposed to a fully implemented economic system, socialism-communism is primarily a political system, under which the political class issues dictates to economic producers. Likewise, socialism-communism can be combined with "capitalism" under such forms as "state capitalism"[6] or "corporate socialism." (The latter is discussed later.) Its economic pretensions will be jettisoned as "capitalist" development is introduced and cleverly rationalized, as in China.

---

5 Michael Rieger, "A World Without Prices: Economic Calculation in the Soviet Union," *Libertarianism.org*, August 1, 2017, https://www.libertarianism.org/columns/world-without-prices-economic-calculation-soviet-union.

6 Western Marxists employ the term state capitalism to exclude the Soviet Union and China from the category of socialism-communism. They thereby reserve, in their own propaganda, at least, the hallowed terms socialism and communism for the never present, always receding, and just-over-the-horizon ideal.

If such pretentions are maintained for long, they will wreck society, as in the former Soviet Union. In either case, the socialist-communist leadership will learn that wealth production requires the accumulation of privately held capital—whether they understand why or not. As I wrote in *Beyond Woke*:

> Without prices, the value of the factors of production are indeterminable; irrationality and systemic chaos must ensue. But prices depend on exchange. And exchange presupposes markets. And markets presuppose property relations. And property relations presuppose private property. And private property presupposes that persons possess property. Therefore, wealth production depends on persons possessing private property.[7]

I'm not the first to make a play on the CCP's rationalization of China's capitalist development with the phrase "capitalism with Chinese characteristics." Yasheng Huang, et al., have written a book by the same title.[8] But for my purposes, in "What is capitalism with Chinese characteristics?," the Chinese scholar Wei Zhao ably characterizes the Chinese system:

> [The] Chinese social structure is a kind of relational market, which has a tributary State on the top and [the] remaining part is composed

---

7 Michael Rectenwald, *Beyond Woke*, Nashville, TN: New English Review Press, 2020, pages 173-174.

8 Yasheng Huang, Sally Stein, and Allan Sekula, *Capitalism with Chinese Characteristics: Entrepreneurship and the State*, Cambridge: Cambridge University Press, 2010.

by small merchant capitalists, without any middle class in between. Therefore[,] there is no separate sphere of "economy" or "market" [apart] from [the] political State or communitarian society.[9]

The Great Reset, I am suggesting, effectively represents the development of the Chinese system in the West, only in reverse. Whereas the Chinese political class began with a socialist political system and introduced "capitalism" (or privately held for-profit production) later, the West began with capitalism and is now aiming to implement a socialist political system directing the economy. It's as if the Western oligarchy looked to the "socialism" on display in China and said, "yes, we want it."

This is attested to by Maurice Strong, the late environmentalist, United Nations Under-Secretary General, first executive director of the United Nations Environment Programme (UNEP), early WEF board member, and avowed socialist, about whom I will have more to say in Parts II and III. In an interview with *The Guardian*, Strong averred:

> *We know that pure capitalism hasn't worked. In China, they have used their system – which they call a socialist market economy – quite well to achieve their objectives.* It's also in a continuous process of evolution. I've had a working relationship with China nearly all my adult life. I've seen the remarkable progress they've made and are still making. They're

9 Wei Zhao, "What Is Capitalism with Chinese Characteristics? Perspective on State, Market, and Society," Research and Regulation: Colloque International, 2015, page 4.

quick learners. They tend to be among the best in terms of business and industry. *They have learned how to use the methods of capitalism to meet their own goals of socialism. China is among the best managed countries today* (emphasis mine).[10]

This is precisely the object of the Great Reset—a Chinese-style system that includes vastly increased state control of the economy on the one hand, and, necessarily, the kind of authoritarian measures that the Chinese government uses to control the population on the other. Eliminating the free market requires a great deal of socioeconomic and political control.

The WEF has attempted to distinguish stakeholder capitalism and China's "state capitalism." In their article, "What is the difference between stakeholder capitalism, shareholder capitalism and state capitalism?,"[11] as part of the Davos Agenda,[12] Klaus Schwab and Peter Vanham argue that stakeholder capitalism is nether the "state capitalism" of China nor the "shareholder capitalism" of most of the Western world. Leaving aside their obvious criti-

10 Leo Hickman, "Maurice Strong on Climate 'Conspiracy', Bilderberg and Population Control," *The Guardian*, June 23, 2010, https://www.theguardian.com/environment/blog/2010/jun/22/maurice-strong-interview-global-government.

11   Klaus Schwab and Peter Vanham, "Stakeholder Capitalism, Shareholder Capitalism and State Capitalism," World Economic Forum, January 26, 2021, https://www.weforum.org/agenda/2021/01/what-is-the-difference-between-stakeholder-capitalism-shareholder-capitalism-and-state-capitalism-davos-agenda-2021.

12   "The Davos Agenda," World Economic Forum, January 25, 2021, https://www.weforum.org/events/the-davos-agenda-2021.

cism of shareholder capitalism—that it supposedly fails to meet the needs of all so-called stakeholders in society—I'll address their treatment of what they call state capitalism. State capitalism, they assert, "solves a major shortcoming of shareholder capitalism because there are mechanisms in place to ensure that private and short-term interests do not overtake broader societal interests." The state does this in three ways:

> First, it keeps a strong hand in the distribution of both resources and opportunities. Second, it can intervene in virtually any industry. And third, it can direct the economy by means of large-scale infrastructure, research and development, and education, health care, or housing projects.[13]

Yet, under state capitalism, they admit, "the government wields too much power." They recommend stakeholder capitalism as the alternative to both state and shareholder capitalism. Under stakeholder capitalism, they suggest, "all those who have a stake in the economy can influence decision-making, and the metrics optimized for in economic activities bake in broader societal interests." They represent their comparison of the three systems in a table:

---

13 Ibid.

Types of Capitalism	State Capitalism	Shareholder Calipatlism	Stakeholder Capitlaims
Key Stakeholder	Government	Company Shreholders	All Stakeholders matter equally
Key Characteristics	Goverment steers the economy, can intervene when necessary	The social responsibility of business is to increase its profits	Society's goal is to increase the well-being of people and the planet
Implication for companies	Business interests are subsidiary to state interests	Short-term profit maximization is highest good	Focus on long-term value creation and ESG measures
Advanced by		Milton Friedman ('70) "Shareholder theory"	Klaus Schwab ('71) "Davos Manifesto" ('73)

Figure 1.1: Stakeholder vs. shareholder and state capitalism

As we have already seen from several citations, the state is one of the major stakeholders under stakeholder capitalism. To refresh the reader's memory, Schwab and Malleret wrote the following in *Covid-19: The Great Reset*:

One of the great lessons of the past five centuries in Europe and America is this: acute crises contribute to boosting the power of the state.

It's always been the case and there is no reason why it should be different with the COVID-19 pandemic.[14]

Schwab and company repeatedly call for "big government."[15] And one of the reasons for stakeholder capitalism, Schwab and Vanham suggest, is to avert environmental catastrophe, which they deem an "acute crisis." What they say about state capitalism is no less true of stakeholder capitalism: the government "keeps a strong hand in the distribution of both resources and opportunities...it can intervene in virtually any industry," and "it can direct the economy by means of large-scale infrastructure, research and development, and education, health care, or housing projects." The WEF has recommended such heavy-handed interventions in countless pages posted to its website. There is no doubt that stakeholder capitalism is closer to state capitalism than it is to shareholder capitalism. Yet, the state is conspicuously absent from their table. Could that be because stakeholder capitalism and state capitalism are barely, if at all, distinguishable?

The WEF has lauded the wonders of China's state capitalism, including in "Geo-economics with Chinese Characteristics," and "8 things you need to know about China's economy," among many others.[16]

---

14 Klaus Schwab and Thierry Malleret, *COVID-19: The Great Reset*, n.p.: Forum Publishing, 2020, page 89.

15 For example, see ibid., pages 88-94, in a section called "The return of big government."

16 Mark Leonard, et al., "Geo-Economics with Chinese Characteristics: How China's Economic Might Is Reshaping World Politics," World Economic Forum, January 2016, https://www3.weforum.org/

Despite the WEF's attempts to distinguish stakeholder capitalism from state capitalism, China's "state capitalism" is the model for the economic and political system being promoted in the West, and the Great Reset is the most forthright articulation of that system—although its articulation is anything but perfectly forthright. The "Chinese characteristics" that the Great Reset aims to reproduce in connection with Western capitalism involve a vastly increased state interventionism in the economy and a great abridgment of property rights.

In effect, socialism with Chinese characteristics and capitalism with Chinese characteristics amount to the same thing. The losers under capitalism with Chinese characteristics are small property owners, not the elite, who will retain control over resources. This makes the economic structure a form of neo-feudalism.

docs/WEF_Geoeconomics_with_Chinese_Characteristics.pdf; Jonathan Eckart, "8 Things You Need to Know about China's Economy," World Economic Forum, June 23, 2016, https://www.weforum.org/agenda/2016/06/8-facts-about-chinas-economy/.

CHAPTER FIVE

Neo-Feudalism, Corporate Socialism

F. A. HAYEK SUGGESTED in his introductory essay to *Collectivist Economic Planning* that socialism can be divided into two aspects: the ends and the means.[1] The socialist means is collectivist planning, while the ends, at least under proletarian socialism, are the supposed collective ownership of the means of production and the "equal" or "equitable" distribution of the end products. Distinguishing between these two aspects in order to set aside the question of the ends and to focus on the means, Hayek suggested that collectivist planning could be marshaled in the service of ends other than those associated with proletarian socialism: "An aristocratic dictatorship, for example, may use the same methods to further the interest of some racial *or other elite* in the service of some other decidedly anti-equalitarian

---

1   F.A. Hayek, "The Nature and History of the Problem," in N.G. Pierson and F.A. Hayek, *Collectivist Economic Planning*, London: Routledge and Kegan Paul, 1963, page 14.

purpose"(emphasis mine)[2] The Great Reset aims at just such an aristocratic dictatorship in the service of an elite, while mobilizing the rhetoric of egalitarianism to bring it about.

Nevertheless, the aims of the Great Reset are not exactly to plan every aspect of production and thus to direct all individual activity. Rather, the goal is to eliminate possibilities for individual activity, including the activity of consumers—by dint of squeezing industries and producers within industries from the economy and thus controlling individual consumption.

As Hayek noted, "when the medieval guild system was at its height, and when restrictions to commerce were most extensive, they were not used as a means actually to direct individual activity."[3] Likewise, the Great Reset aims not at a strict *planning* of the economy so much as it recommends and enacts neo-feudalistic *restrictions* that would go further than anything since the medieval period and arguably further than that. In 1935, Hayek noted the extent to which economic restrictions had already led to distortions of the market:

> With our attempts to use the old apparatus of restrictionism as an instrument of almost day-to-day adjustment to change we have probably already gone much further in the direction of central planning of current activity than has ever been attempted before...It is important to realize in any investigation of the possibilities of planning that it is a fallacy to suppose capi-

2 Ibid., page 15.
3 Ibid., page 23.

talism as it exists to-day is the alternative. We are certainly as far from capitalism in its pure form as we are from any system of central planning. The world of to-day is just interventionist chaos.[4]

The Great Reset takes us toward the kinds of restrictions imposed under feudalism, including the economic stasis that feudalism entailed. I call this neo-feudalism "corporate socialism"—not only because the rhetoric to gain adherents derives from socialist ideology ("fairness," "economic equality," "collective good," "shared destiny," etc.), but also because the reality sought after is de facto shared monopolistic control of production via the elimination of noncompliant producers—i.e., a tendency toward monopoly over production characteristic of socialism. Socialism is nothing if not a monopoly. Only, with the Great Reset, it is a monopoly of a woke corporate cartel. Its economic interventionism not only adds to the "interventionist chaos" already in existence but further distorts markets to an unprecedented degree—excepting perhaps the centralized state-socialist planning of the former Soviet Union.

Corporate Socialism
A socialist-communist sequel is coming to a theater near you. Some of the same old characters are reappearing, while new ones have joined the cast. While the ideology and rhetoric sound nearly the same, they are being put to slightly different ends. This time around, the old bromides and promises are in play, and a similar bait-and-switch is being dan-

---

4   Ibid.

gled. Socialism promises the protection of the beleaguered from the economically and politically "evil," the promotion of the economic interests of the underclass, a benign banning of "dangerous" persons from public forums and civic life, and a primary or exclusive concern for the so-called "common good." China's "One Belt, One Road" initiative may hang the takers in Africa and other underdeveloped regions as if from an infrastructural noose.[5] A different variety is on the docket in the developed world, including in the U.S.

The contemporary variant is corporate socialism. The difference between state socialism and corporate socialism is merely that a different constituency effectively controls the means of production. But both depend on monopoly—one by the state and the other by a corporate-state hybrid. And both depend on socialist-communist ideology, or, in a recent variant, "social justice" or "woke" ideology, to bring it about. (More on woke ideology later.) Corporate socialism is the desired end, while "democratic socialism" or "woke capitalism" are among the means.

By corporate socialism, I don't mean what Democratic socialists and other leftists mean by that term— "corporate welfare"—tax cuts and bailouts for corporations at the expense of workers, etc. My usage follows that of the late historian and Hoover Institute scholar, Anthony C. Sutton:

---

5 Alexandra Ma, "The US Is Scrambling to Invest More in Asia to Counter China's 'Belt and Road' Mega-Project. Here's What China's Plan to Connect the World through Infrastructure Is like.," *Business Insider*, Nov. 11, 2019, https://www.businessinsider.com/what-is-belt-and-road-china-infrastructure-project-2018-1.

Old John D. Rockefeller and his 19th century fellow capitalists were convinced of one absolute truth: that no great monetary wealth could be accumulated under the impartial rules of a competitive laissez faire society. The only sure road to the acquisition of massive wealth was monopoly: drive out your competitors, reduce competition, eliminate laissez-faire, and above all get state protection for your industry through compliant politicians and government regulation. This last avenue yields a legal monopoly, and a legal monopoly always leads to wealth.

This robber baron schema is also, under different labels, the socialist plan. The difference between a corporate state monopoly and a socialist state monopoly is essentially only the identity of the group controlling the power structure...We call this phenomenon of corporate legal monopoly—market control acquired by using political influence—by the name of corporate socialism.[6]

I recognize that monopolies are rare and that corporate socialism is never fully realized. The Great Reset involves a tendency toward corporate-socialist monopolization, via a relational networking of the state, with preferred corporate partners leading to an oligopoly.

The corporate-socialist tendency is thus toward a two-tiered economy, with an oligopoly or woke cartel and the state on top, and "actually existing social-

---

6 Antony C. Sutton, *Wall Street and FDR: the True Story of How Franklin D. Roosevelt Colluded with Corporate America*, Forest Row: Clairview Books, 2013, Chapter 5.

ism" for the majority, below. As Roger Scruton noted, "[a]ctually-existing socialism" is a "[t]erm used in the former communist countries to describe them as they really were, rather than as the official theory required them to be."[7] The corporate socialism of the Great Reset creates a new "actually existing socialism" for the majority.

Whether we understand the stakeholder capitalism of the Great Reset as capitalism with Chinese characteristics, as neo-feudalism, as corporate socialism—or, as I'll discuss in the next chapter, as economic fascism—the results are the same. The Great Reset amounts to a state-corporate-woke-cartel hybrid administering the economy through the recommendations and decisions of technocrats like those at the WEF, the UN, the World Bank, and, by extension, the World Health Organization—as well as by top corporate decision-makers like BlackRock's Larry Fink (also discussed later). This elite colludes with the state to control and regulate production, while private owners retain nominative legal ownership. However, private property is subjected to breaches in property rights—to intrusive oversight and control, and further, to demands of compliance. The compliant class rises in power and prestige, while non-compliant dissidents are eventually cancelled and relegated to the underclass.

Thus, the Great Reset effectively creates three classes: the elite; the downtrodden majority, or those without special abilities surviving on Universal Basic Income; and those with special entrepreneurial, pro-

---

7 *Palgrave Macmillan Dictionary of Political Thought*, by Roger Scruton, 3d ed., New York: Macmillan Publishers, 2007, s.v. "Actually existing socialism."

fessional, or scientific ability, who may choose to join the elite by being compliant so as not to suffer cancellation and relegation to the status of the downtrodden. The elite will appeal to the downtrodden and weaponize them with egalitarian rhetoric and the distribution of social welfare, while castigating and vilifying non-compliant professionals, entrepreneurs, and business owners. Whatever rhetoric or ideology is propagated by the adherents of the Great Reset, power and control is vested in a consortium of elites, who effectively run the economy as its primary beneficiaries.

This is just the kind of tiered social structure that characterized Communist nations. The elite class was the party faithful, and the masses, at times, starved without UBI. We should be very wary, indeed.

CHAPTER SIX

Woke Capitalism

WOKE CAPITALISM involves far more than the public relations and advertising campaigns of companies like Accenture, American Airlines, Amazon, Apple, Coca-Cola, Disney, Gillette, General Motors, Nike, Starbucks, and countless others who virtue-signal to their customers and employees.[1] The popular phrase, "Go woke and go broke" should be immediately discarded and replaced with "Go woke *or* go broke." While "Go woke and go broke" may prove true in the long run, "Go woke or go broke" is the rule of the day. If the managers of woke capitalism continue to have their way, woke capitalism will encompass the entire economic system and include every sector of the economy in a scheme to institute stakeholder capitalism across the board.

The phrase "woke capitalism" was coined by

---

1 Dave Seminara, "Complete List of Woke Companies Including Those Condemning Roe vs. Wade Overturn, Voting Laws & Florida's Incorrectly Labeled 'Don't Say Gay' Law (Updated)," Dave Seminara, September 8, 2022, https://daveseminara.com/complete-list-of-woke-companies-condemning-so-called-racist-voting-laws/.

New York Times editorialist Ross Douthat to describe corporate activism in line with the woke agenda: the promotion by for-profit corporations of identity politics, gender pluralism, transgender rights, lax immigration standards, voting "reform," climate change mitigation, and so on.[2] Upon coining the term, Douthat ventured to explain the phenomenon, arguing that woke capitalism works by substituting symbolic value for economic value. Under woke capitalism, corporations offer workers rhetorical placebos in lieu of costlier economic concessions, such as higher wages and better benefits. The same gestures of wokeness also appease the liberal political elite, whom the woke corporations hope will spare them higher taxes, increased regulations, and antitrust legislation aimed at monopolies.

Business Insider columnist Josh Barro offered another, closely related explanation to Douthat's, essentially claiming that woke capitalism provides a form of *parapolitical* representation for workers and corporate consumers.[3] Given their perceived political disenfranchisement, woke capitalism offers consumers representation in the public sphere, as they see their values reflected in corporate pronouncements.

Still others have suggested that corporations have gone woke only to be spared cancellation by Twitter mobs and other activists, that wokeness is a

---

2 Ross Douthat, "The Rise of Woke Capital," *The New York Times*, February 28, 2018, https://www.nytimes.com/2018/02/28/opinion/corporate-america-activism.html.

3 Josh Barro, "There's a Simple Reason Companies Are Becoming More Publicly Left-Wing on Social Issues," *Business Insider*, March 1, 2018, https://www.businessinsider.com/why-companies-ditching-nra-delta-selling-guns-2018-2.

good "branding tool,"[4] that corporations are merely virtue-signaling,[5] or that progressive shareholders demand corporate activism.[6]

These explanations are woefully inadequate for explaining woke capitalism, mostly because they fail to acknowledge its enormous scope and penetration.

Woke capitalism consists of much more than merely placating coastal leftists,[7] ingratiating left-liberal legislators, or avoiding the wrath of activists. Rather, woke capitalism involves what BlackRock's CEO Larry Fink described as a "tectonic shift" in corporate behavior across all sectors of the economy. As wokeness has escalated and taken hold of corporations and states, and vice versa, it has revealed its true character as a demarcation device, a shibboleth for cartel members to identify and distinguish themselves from their non-woke competitors, who are to be starved of capital investments.

Wokeness is a selection mechanism for dividing the compliant from the non-compliant—for businesses in addition to individuals. Just as non-woke individuals are cancelled from civic life, so too are

---

4   Helen Lewis, "How Capitalism Drives Cancel Culture," *The Atlantic,* July 15, 2020, https://www.theatlantic.com/international/archive/2020/07/cancel-culture-and-problem-woke-capitalism/614086/.

5   SkyNewsAustralia, "There Is a 'Deafening Media Silence' on Global Protests," YouTube, July 16, 2022, https://www.youtube.com/watch?v=lG660H1JjWU.

6   Charles Gasparino, "How Corporations Surrendered to Hard-Left Wokeness," *New York Post*, February 14, 2021, https://nypost.com/2021/02/13/how-corporations-surrendered-to-hard-left-wokeness/.

7   Lythos Studios, "Woke Capitalism," *Praxis Circle*, August 22, 2021, https://praxiscircle.com/blog/woke-capitalism/.

non-woke companies cancelled from the economy, leaving the spoils to the woke. Corporate cancellations are not merely the result of political fallout.[8] They are being institutionalized and carried out through the stock market, the banking industry, and the insurance industry, from which they insinuate themselves into every other industry. Woke planners wield the Environmental, Social, and Governance (ESG) Index to reward the in-group and to squeeze non-woke players out of business. The ESG Index serves as a "Chinese-style" social credit scoring system for rating corporations. In fact, some have questioned whether China actually *has* a social credit scoring system.[9] Given its totalitarian predilections, "China" serves as a handy foil against which the West can favorably compare itself, at least for now. "At least we're not in China," or "we're becoming more like China every day" constitutes a smokescreen to deflect attention from the fact that a social credit system is being implemented in the West, beginning with corporations. Woke investment drives capital away from the noncompliant, while the ESG Index serves as an admission ticket for entry into the woke cartel.

Research suggests that ESG investing favors

---

8 Robert Hart, "'They're Trying to Cancel Me': My Pillow CEO Says Retailers Have Dropped the Brand amid His Baseless Voter Fraud Claims," *Forbes Magazine*, April 14, 2022, https://www.forbes.com/sites/roberthart/2021/01/19/theyre-trying-to-cancel-me-retailers-drop-mypillow-amid-ceos-baseless-voter-fraud-claims/?sh=518f21d46863.

9 Austrian China, "The 'China Dystopia' PSYOP – Social Credit System in China or in the West?," Austrian China, December 25, 2021, https://austrianchina.substack.com/p/china-dystopia-psyop.

large over small companies.[10] Woke capitalism transfers as much control over production and distribution to these large, favored corporations as possible, but such transfers may be reversed when the favored fall out of compliance. Woke capitalism has become a monopoly game—and not only the Hasbro board game of woke *Monopoly*.[11]

ESGs and the Woke Cartel

The ESG Index is a feature and development of stakeholder capitalism, the idea that businesses should not be run strictly for profit but also for the benefit of all so-called "stakeholders," which, by including potential consumers, includes just about anyone. As I have suggested, stakeholder capitalism addresses the supposed "equitable" distribution of benefits and externalities produced by the corporation. The ESG Index is a rubric for analyzing corporate performance along these lines. Companies are graded in terms of their environmental, social, and governance practices and plans. Environmental performance is graded in terms of "sustainability" and with reference to practices affecting climate change. Social performance is graded in terms of whether and how well companies promote "social justice"— the representation of certain favored minorities and women on boards and in management roles, or af-

---

10 "ESG Investing: Practices, Progress and Challenges – OECD," accessed June 30, 2022, https://www.oecd.org/finance/ESG-Investing-Practices-Progress-Challenges.pdf.

11 Joan Verdon, "Time for Mr. Monopoly's Get Woke Moment," *Forbes Magazine*, March 18, 2021, https://www.forbes.com/sites/joanverdon/2021/03/18/time-for-mr-monopolys-get-woke-moment/?sh=f33be62aa2f8.

firmative action.[12] Governance is graded in terms of corporate social responsibility, human rights, transparency, and how well companies cooperate with each other and the government.

Promoters of stakeholder capitalism claim that business practices that take stakeholders into consideration lead to better financial returns in the long run. Yet others suggest that ESGs are generally outperformed by non-ESG funds. Whatever the case, better ESG performance, when it materializes, is a short-term function of the preference for ESG-abiding companies by major asset managers. Asset managers like BlackRock Inc.'s Larry Fink have smuggled ESGs into their most successful portfolios, often without the knowledge of their own investors, to whom they owe a fiduciary duty.[13] Funds are thereby funneled into ESG-abiding companies, boosting ESG stock prices. Retail investors pay premiums on ESG funds in the form of fees that are 43% higher than those for standard exchange-traded funds (ETFs).[14]

As Mark Ray Reavis and David W. Orr note, "stakeholder proponents are seemingly everywhere in American society in 2021. They are seeking a

---

12   Some minorities are nevertheless actively discriminated against. See Vinay Kolhatkar, "Is the Anglosphere Still Prejudiced against Outsiders?" *Savvy Street*, January 9, 2019, https://www.thesavvystreet.com/is-the-anglosphere-still-prejudiced-against-outsiders/.

13   Cam Simpson and Saijel Kishan, "How BlackRock Made ESG the Hottest Ticket on Wall Street," *Bloomberg*, December 31, 2021, https://www.bloomberg.com/news/articles/2021-12-31/how-blackrock-s-invisible-hand-helped-make-esg-a-hot-ticket.

14   Michael Wursthorn, "Tidal Wave of ESG Funds Brings Profit to Wall Street," *The Wall Street Journal*, March 16, 2021, https://www.wsj.com/articles/tidal-wave-of-esg-funds-brings-profit-to-wall-street-11615887004.

higher minimum wage, diversity in the boardroom, increased corporate social responsibility, and higher corporate income taxes."[15] And just who are these proponents? According to Ashley E. Jaramillo, they are small shareholders: "Retail investor demand for socially-conscious exchange-traded funds (ETFs) has skyrocketed—2020 saw a record $27.4 billion invested in US ETFs that indicate a focus on ESG-related practices."[16]

Many other such commentators have figured the woke imperative as a local, bottom-up phenomenon stemming from workers, consumers, activists, and retail investors. But the woke cartel is noteworthy for being the coordinated, top-down construction of international bodies and the global elite. As Nathan Worcester of *The Epoch Times* notes:

> The internationalist, or globalist, nature of ESG is nothing new. In fact, the term "ESG" originated through a collaboration between the United Nations, the Swiss government, and a group of major banks that included Morgan Stanley, Deutsche Bank, Credit Suisse Group, and Goldman Sachs.[17]

---

15 Mark Ray Reavis and David W. Orr, "The Journey of American Capitalism: From Stockholders to Stakeholders," *American Journal of Management* 21, no. 4 (2021): 1–15, page 2, https://doi.org/10.33423/ajm.v21i4.4553.

16 Ashley E. Jaramillo, "Hippies in the Boardroom: A Historical Critique of Addressing Stakeholder Interests Through Private Ordering," *New York University Law Review* 99 (December 2021): 2213–59, page 2224, https://www.nyulawreview.org/wp-content/uploads/2021/12/Jaramillo-ONLINE.pdf.

17 Nathan Worcester, "'Environmental, Social, and Corporate Governance' Scores Are Changing the Oil Industry," *The Epoch Times*, February 8, 2022, https://www.theepochtimes.com/environmen-

Stakeholder capitalism and the ESG Index are not orchestrated by activists and retail investors. Rather, well-heeled, well-placed bureaucratic planners are driving the "demand" for ESG indexing.

BlackRock, Inc., the world's largest asset manager, holds upwards of 10 trillion dollars in assets under management (AUM), including the pension funds of many U.S. states. In 2019, BlackRock's CEO Larry Fink led a US Business Roundtable on stakeholder capitalism.[18] CEOs from 181 major corporations redefined the common purpose of the corporation in terms of stakeholder capitalism, signaling the supposed end to shareholder-driven capitalism. Corporate America has officially gone woke. But what does this mean?

In his "2021 Letter to CEOs," Fink made Black-Rock's own position on investment decisions clear. "Climate risk is investment risk," Fink declared.[19] "The creation of sustainable index investments has enabled a massive acceleration of capital towards companies better prepared to address climate risk."

---

tal-social-and-corporate-governance-scores-are-changing-the-oil-industry_4238488.html. See also: Elliot Wilson, "The United Nations Free-Thinkers Who Coined the Term 'ESG' and Changed the World," *Euromoney,* March 24, 2022, https://www.euromoney.com/article/294dqz2h1pqywgbyh3zls/esg/the-united-nations-free-thinkers-who-coined-the-term-esg-and-changed-the-world.

18   "Business Roundtable Redefines the Purpose of a Corporation to Promote 'an Economy That Serves All Americans,'" *Business Roundtable,* August 19, 2019, https://www.businessroundtable.org/business-roundtable-redefines-the-purpose-of-a-corporation-to-promote-an-economy-that-serves-all-americans.

19   Larry Fink, "Larry Fink CEO Letter," Blackrock, Inc., accessed March 9, 2021, https://www.blackrock.com/corporate/investor-relations/larry-fink-ceo-letter#.

Fink promised a "tectonic shift" in investment behavior, an increased acceleration of investments going to "sustainability-focused" companies. Fink warned CEOs: "And because this will have such a dramatic impact on how capital is allocated, every management team and board will need to consider how this will impact their company's stock." Fink's letter urged every company to provide a net-zero plan.

In thus throwing down the stakeholder gauntlet, Fink echoed the menacing words of Klaus Schwab: "Every country, from the United States to China, must participate," wrote Schwab in June 2020. "Every industry, from oil and gas to tech, must be transformed. In short, we need a 'Great Reset' of capitalism."[20]

But unlike Schwab's admonitions, Fink's dictum of "go woke or go broke" should not be dismissed as the conspiratorial rantings of Dr. Evil. Fink has at least 10 trillion dollars in capital behind him. Fink and company carry out what Schwab and the WEF have mostly promoted with propaganda and urgent recommendations—although, as evidenced by Fink's advocacy, that propaganda and those urgent recommendations have proven quite successful.

Fink's "2022 Letter to CEOs: The Power of Capitalism" continues the strong-armed advancement of stakeholder capitalism, suggesting that stakeholder capitalism has always been the modus operandi of successful capitalist corporations:

---

20 Klaus Schwab, "Now Is the Time for a 'Great Reset,'" World Economic Forum, June 3, 2020, https://www.weforum.org/agenda/2020/06/now-is-the-time-for-a-great-reset/.

Over the past three decades, I've had the opportunity to talk with countless CEOs and to learn
what distinguishes truly great companies. Time
and again, what they all share is that they have
a clear sense of purpose; consistent values; and,
crucially, they recognize the importance of engaging with and delivering for their key stakeholders. This is the foundation of stakeholder
capitalism.[21]

According to Fink, stakeholder capitalism is not
an aberration. Fink provides evidence of the woke
imperative in his denial of the same: "It is not a social
or ideological agenda. It is not 'woke.' *It is capitalism...*" This definition of capitalism would certainly
have come as news to the likes of Milton Friedman
or Ludwig von Mises.

Fink's letter makes clear what's at stake with
stakeholder capitalism: "At the foundation of capitalism is the process of constant reinvention—how
companies must continually evolve as the world
around them changes *or risk being replaced by new
competitors*" (emphasis mine). The corporations
that deserve capital and that will not be "replaced,"
Fink makes clear, are those committed to the net-ze-
ro-emissions economy. All others will face the prospect of extinction.

A letter from the Attorneys General of 19 states
to Larry Fink on August 4, 2022, excoriated Black-
Rock for its ESG-dominated approach to investing
the pension funds of those states. It pointed to Black-
Rock's circumvention of the will of the U.S. elector-

21 Larry Fink, "Larry Fink's Annual 2022 Letter to CEOS," Black-
Rock, Inc., January 2022, https://www.blackrock.com/corporate/
investor-relations/larry-fink-ceo-letter.

ate, as well as its flouting of the U.S. Constitution, which grants to the Senate the exclusive right to ratify treaties, such as the Paris Agreement:

> Based on the facts currently available to us, BlackRock appears to use the hard-earned money of our states' citizens to circumvent the best possible return on investment, as well as their vote. BlackRock's past public commitments indicate that it has used citizens' assets to pressure companies to comply with international agreements such as the Paris Agreement that force the phase-out of fossil fuels, increase energy prices, drive inflation, and weaken the national security of the United States. These agreements have never been ratified by the United States Senate. The Senators elected by the citizens of this country determine which international agreements have the force of law, not BlackRock. We have several additional concerns that fall under our jurisdictional authority as attorneys general.[22]

The AGs further contended that BlackRock's membership in the Net Zero Managers Alliance (NZMA), the Glasgow Financial Allowance for Net Zero (GFANZ), and Climate Action 100+ belies the claims by its Chief Client Officer, Mark McCombe (in his letter to many of these states), that BlackRock maintains "neutrality" with reference to ESG investing:

---

22 "To: Laurence D. Fink, CEO BlackRock Inc., from 19 U.S. Attorneys General," Texas Attorney General, August 4, 2022, https://www.texasattorneygeneral.gov/sites/default/files/images/executive-management/BlackRock%20Letter.pdf.

Mr. McCombe's letter posits that BlackRock is agnostic on the question of energy, and merely offers investing clients a range of investment options in the energy sector. But this claimed neutrality differs considerably from Black-Rock's public commitments which indicate that BlackRock has already committed to accelerate net zero emissions across all of its assets, regardless of client wishes.[23]

The AGs pointed to BlackRock's own statements regarding climate change and its commitment to a net-zero policy by 2050.[24] They also noted statements by NZMA and GFANZ, of which BlackRock is a member, that clearly indicate a desideratum to "'alter the planet's climate trajectory.'" Notably, GFANZ was launched by Mark Carney, who is the UN Special Envoy on Climate Action and Finance, Governor of the Bank of England, Chairman of the Financial Stability Board (FSB), Member and Chairman of the Board of the Bank for International Settlements, and Chairman of the Group of Thirty. Carney also sits on the Board of Trustees of the WEF.[25]

Finally, the AGs suggested that BlackRock may be breaking the law with its ESG-oriented invest-

---

23 Ibid.

24 "Pursuing Long-Term Value for Our Clients – BlackRock," BlackRock, Inc., accessed September 13, 2022, https://www.blackrock.com/corporate/literature/publication/2021-voting-spot-light-full-report.pdf; "Our Approach to Sustainability – BlackRock," BlackRock, Inc., accessed September 13, 2022, https://www.black-rock.com/corporate/literature/publication/our-commitment-to-sustainability-full-report.pdf.

25 "Mark Carney - Agenda Contributor," World Economic Forum, accessed September 13, 2022, https://www.weforum.org/agenda/authors/mark-carney.

ment strategy and demanded that BlackRock honor its fiduciary duties:

> BlackRock's actions on a variety of governance objectives may violate multiple state laws. Mr. McCombe's letter asserts compliance with our fiduciary laws because BlackRock has a private motivation that differs from its public commitments and statements. This is likely insufficient to satisfy state laws requiring a sole focus on financial return. Our states will not idly stand for our pensioners' retirements to be sacrificed for BlackRock's climate agenda. The time has come for BlackRock to come clean on whether it actually values our states' most valuable stakeholders, our current and future retirees, or risk losses even more significant than those caused by BlackRock's quixotic climate agenda.[26]

BlackRock's supposed "neutrality" was shown to be a mere subterfuge when Dalia Blass, BlackRock's head of external affairs, responded in a letter to the group of Attorneys General. She stated that climate change is becoming a major risk and that investors and clients want to be apprised of the risks to achieve better returns:

> Governments representing over 90% of global GDP have committed to move to net-zero in the coming decades...We believe investors and companies that take a forward-looking position with respect to climate risk and its implications for the energy transition will generate better long-term financial outcomes. These opportu-

---

26 "To: Laurence D. Fink, CEO BlackRock Inc., from 19 U.S. Attorneys General," op. cit., page 7.

nities cut across the political spectrum.[27]

Rather than extending McCombe's "neutrality" ploy, BlackRock now simply doubled down on its investment policies by pointing to other believers in climate change catastrophism (treated in Part III). This pattern of assert, deflect, and reassert has been typical of BlackRock's attempts to counter opposition to its dictatorial climate change-directed investment strategies.

Larry Fink sits on the Board of Trustees of the WEF, along with Mark Carney, Al Gore, Chrystia Freeland, and others.[28] Although BlackRock's influence over corporate behavior should not be underestimated, BlackRock is only one of hundreds corporate partners aligned ideologically and politically with the WEF, Schwab's stakeholder capitalism, and the ESG metric.

The WEF's own stakeholder metrics provide ESG reporting over and above that imposed through the stock market. The metrics break down the environmental, social, and governance guidelines into a granularized guide for corporate behavior. On January 26, 2021, the WEF reported that a growing list of over eighty companies "announced their commitment to report on the Stakeholder Capitalism Metrics," those specifically proposed by the WEF. The list

---

27 Qtd. in Zachary Halaschak, "BlackRock Hits Back at Republican Attorneys General Critical of Its ESG Policies," *Washington Examiner*, September 8, 2022, https://www.washingtonexaminer.com/policy/economy/blackrock-esg-republican-attorneys-general.

28 "Leadership and Governance," World Economic Forum, accessed September 13, 2022, https://www.weforum.org/about/leadership-and-governance.

included Accenture, Bank of America, Credit Suisse, Dell Technologies, Deloitte, Dow, HP, IBM, Mastercard, McKinsey & Company (discussed in Chapter 10), Mitsubishi, Nestlé, PayPal, Royal Dutch Shell, Sony, and others.[29] By the 2022 annual meeting of the WEF, 160 major companies included the metric in their reporting materials.

Bank of America (BoA) is among the leaders promoting stakeholder capitalism and ESG indexing. At the 2022 annual meeting of the WEF, in a forum on globalizing ESGs and stakeholder capitalism, BoA CEO Brian T. Moynihan suggested that the WEF's prerogatives will not be satisfied with ESGs as a "sidecar" for investors.[30] On top of investments in ESGs, "six trillion dollars" must be "aligned" with stakeholder capitalism "every single year." Moynihan argued that the "whole economy" must be revamped in terms of stakeholder capitalism and not merely with ESG investments. BoA is working to bring this alignment about. Those companies that fall below the stakeholder "bar" are not worthy of investments, said Moynihan. They should wither on the vine. The median turnover of a large corporate CEO is five years,[31] while less than one in

29 Madeleine Hillyer, "Global Business Leaders Support ESG Convergence by Committing to Stakeholder Capitalism Metrics," World Economic Forum, January 26, 2021, https://www.weforum.org/press/2021/01/global-business-leaders-support-esg-convergence-by-committing-to-stakeholder-capitalism-metrics-73b5e9f13d/.

30 "Global ESG Standards: Are We There Yet?" World Economic Forum, May 25, 2022, https://www.weforum.org/events/world-economic-forum-annual-meeting-2022/sessions/global-esg-standards-are-we-there-yet.

31 Amanda Schulhofer, Dan Marcec, and Kyle Benelli, "CEO Tenure

five lasts more than 10 years.[32] Moynihan has been at the helm for over 12 years, with "no plans to leave."[33] Thus, his unyielding insistence that capitalism must become stakeholder capitalism is quite significant.

All the top-10 asset management firms are on board with stakeholder capitalism and ESG investing. Curiously, nine of the top-10 asset management companies are also WEF partners. The Vanguard Group is the world's second-largest asset manager with more than $7.50 trillion in AUM as of 2021. Although not currently listed as an official WEF partner, Vanguard forcefully promotes ESG indexing for investments, declaring on its website: "Most of our funds are indexed and *follow an exclusionary strategy that omits companies that don't meet certain ESG criteria*" (emphasis mine)[34]—providing further evidence that ESGs are a demarcation device to reward the woke and penalize the unwoke.

· The WEF's list of ESG-abiding companies is outstripped only by the United Nations Environment

Rates," The Harvard Law School Forum on Corporate Governance, February 12, 2018, https://corpgov.law.harvard.edu/2018/02/12/ceo-tenure-rates/.

32 PricewaterhouseCoopers, "CEO Turnover at Record High; Successors Following Long Serving CEOS Struggling According to PWC's Strategy& Global Study," PwC, 2019, https://www.pwc.com/gx/en/news-room/press-releases/2019/ceo-turnover-record-high.html.

33 Elizabeth Dilts Marshall and Jessica DiNapoli, "Analysis: Bank of America Leaves Wall Street Wondering about next CEO," *Reuters*, June 15, 2021, https://www.reuters.com/business/bank-america-leaves-wall-street-wondering-about-next-ceo-2021-06-10/.

34 "ESG Funds That Reflect What Matters Most to You," The Vanguard Group, accessed June 30, 2022, https://investor.vanguard.com/investment-products/esg.

Program's (UNEP) consortia of investment, banking, and insurance firms. These are aligned with its Principles for Responsible Investment[35] and/or the subsidiary Principles for Responsible Banking and Principles for Sustainable Insurance. The six Principles for Responsible Investment read as follows:

> **Principle One:** We will incorporate ESG issues into investment analysis and decision-making processes.
>
> **Principle Two:** We will be active owners and incorporate ESG issues into our ownership policies and practices.
>
> **Principle Three:** We will seek appropriate disclosure on ESG issues by the entities in which we invest.
>
> **Principle Four:** We will promote acceptance and implementation of the Principles within the investment industry.
>
> **Principle Five:** We will work together to enhance our effectiveness in implementing the Principles.
>
> **Principle Six:** We will each report on our activities and progress towards implementing the Principles.

Notice that for signatories, ESG indexing pervades every aspect of business, including what com-

---

35 "What Are the Principles for Responsible Investment?," PRI, December 1, 2017, https://www.unpri.org/about-us/what-are-the-principles-for-responsible-investment.

panies they invest in (principles 1 and 3), how they adhere to ESG metrics themselves (principles 2 and 6), and how they cooperate with competitors to promote ESGs (principles 4 and 5). Thus, the goal of the principles is to universalize ESG investing.

In fact, over 4,700 asset management firms, asset owners, and asset service providers have signed onto the UN's six Principles for Responsible Investment. The list of signatories reads like a who's who of financial companies and investors and includes the world's largest asset managers, asset owners, and asset service companies.[36] Thus, the principles represent a complete overhaul of the investment industry in line with ESGs and stakeholder capitalism. Clearly, failure to meet ESG requirements will eventually exclude a vast number of companies currently on the stock markets, depriving them of investment capital.

Given that the banking and insurance industries have adopted versions of the principles, ESG scoring will also determine whether their customers are eligible for loans and insurance, thus driving many more firms out of business. The Principles for Responsible Banking explicitly state that signatory banks must align their practices and strategies with "the vision society has set out for its future in the Sustainable Development Goals (SDGs) and the Paris Climate Agreement."[37] "Society" has supposedly agreed that the UN's SDGs and the Paris Climate Agreement must be followed by banks and their cus-

---

36 "Signatory Directory," PRI, accessed June 30, 2022, https://www. unpri.org/signatories/signatory-resources/signatory-directory.

37 Adam Garfunkel, "Communicating the Principles for Responsible Banking," Junxion, n.d., https://junxion.com/insights/communicating-the-principles-for-responsible-banking/.

tomers, although "society" never voted on such measures. Rather, the UN, in conjunction with the WEF and other "stakeholders," have determined what society wants and what society will pay for it.

"ESG Is a Scam"

The ESG Index is a means of assembling a woke monopolistic cartel. But as it turns out, membership in this cartel is not primarily based on the environmental performance of companies. In fact, after a recent rebalancing, the S&P 500's ESG Index included Exxon Mobil and J.P. Morgan Chase among its top ten ESG performers and excluded Tesla entirely.[38] J.P. Morgan is the world's largest investor in oil producers[39] and Exxon Mobil ranks first among them.[40] Meanwhile, Tesla has produced more electric vehicles than any other manufacturer in the world, and yet it was excluded from the S&P's ESG Index altogether. The inclusion of Exxon Mobil and J.P. Morgan among top performers and the exclusion of Tesla led its CEO, Elon Musk, to declare, correctly, that "ESG is a scam."[41]

---

38 S&P Dow Jones Indices, "The (Re)Balancing Act of the S&P 500 ESG Index," *Seeking Alpha*, June 27, 2022, https://seekingalpha.com/article/4512804-rebalancing-act-of-sp-500-esg-index.

39 John Csiszar, "If Your Money Is in These Banks, You Might Be Invested in Oil and Gas," *GOBankingRates*, November 3, 2021, https://www.gobankingrates.com/investing/strategy/if-your-money-is-in-these-banks-you-might-be-invested-in-oil-gas/.

40 N. Sönnichsen, "Biggest Oil Companies 2021," *Statista*, April 14, 2022, https://www.statista.com/statistics/272709/top-10-oil-and-gas-companies-worldwide-based-on-market-value/.

41 Elon Musk, "Exxon Is Rated Top Ten Best in World for Environment, Social & Governance (ESG) by S&P 500, While Tesla Didn't Make the LIST! ESG Is a Scam..." Twitter, May 18, 2022, https://twit-

The reasons given for axing Tesla from the index also prove that ESG indexing is political to the core. Writes Margaret Dorn of *Indexology Blog*:

> A few of the factors contributing to its 2021 S&P DJI ESG Score were a decline in criteria level scores related to Tesla's (lack of) low carbon strategy and codes of business conduct. In addition, a Media and Stakeholder Analysis, a process that seeks to identify a company's current and potential future exposure to risks stemming from its involvement in a controversial incident, identified two separate events centered around claims of racial discrimination and poor working conditions at Tesla's Fremont factory, as well as its handling of the NHTSA investigation after multiple deaths and injuries were linked to its autopilot vehicles. Both of these events had a negative impact on the company's S&P DJI ESG Score at the criteria level, and subsequently its overall score. While Tesla may be playing its part in taking fuel-powered cars off the road, it has fallen behind its peers when examined through a wider ESG lens.[42]

What we see through this "wider ESG lens" is a political spectacle. ESG grading, notes *Bloomberg*, is, after all, a measure of public relations imagery, not environmental performance.[43] MSCI Inc., the

---

ter.com/elonmusk/status/1526958110023245829.

42 Margaret Dorn, "The (Re)Balancing Act of the S&P 500 ESG Index," *Indexology Blog*, SP Dow Jones Indices, May 17, 2022, https://www.indexologyblog.com/2022/05/17/the-rebalancing-act-of-the-sp-500-esg-index/.

43 Cam Simpson, Akshat Rathi, and Saijel Kishan, "The ESG Mirage," *Bloomberg*, December 10, 2021, https://www.bloomberg.com/

world's largest ESG indexing company, openly admits that it does not measure the impact of companies on the Earth and society. Indeed, "they gauge the opposite: the potential impact of the world on the company and its shareholders." Rather than measuring the environmental impacts of company practices, the largest ESG ranking company measures potential threats to companies and stockholders posed by environmental regulations, environmental activism, the community, and lack of natural resources. BlackRock is MSCI's biggest customer, proving that BlackRock's touting of sustainability is mere bluster and "mirage."

Meanwhile, Tesla has been besmirched with bad press regarding supposed racial discrimination, and Musk's South African provenance is used to support such allegations. In 2018, *Business Insider* claimed that Musk was a beneficiary of an apartheid emerald mine worked by black South Africans and owned by his father, Errol Musk.[44] Twitter mobs and other media outlets have continued to repeat the allegation, despite Musk's convincing refutation.[45]

---

graphics/2021-what-is-esg-investing-msci-ratings-focus-on-corporate-bottom-line/.

44 Phillip de Wet, "Elon Musk's Family Once Owned an Emerald Mine in Zambia - Here's the Fascinating Story of How They Came to Own It," *Business Insider*, February 28, 2018, https://www.businessinsider.co.za/how-elon-musks-family-came-to-own-an-emerald-mine-2018-2.

45 Elon Musk, "This Is a Pretty Awful Lie. I Left South Africa by Myself When I Was 17 with Just a Backpack & Suitcase of Books. Worked on My Mom's Cousin's Farm in Saskatchewan & A Lumber Mill in Vancouver. Went to Queens Univ with Scholarship & Debt, Then Same to UPenn/Wharton & Stanford," Twitter, December 28, 2019, https://twitter.com/elonmusk/status/1211071324518531072.

Many other criticisms have been leveled against Elon Musk—that he's part of the elite, that Tesla has been the beneficiary of government handouts and exemptions, that his transhumanist Neuralink is a brain-data-mining operation. Yet, his planned purchase of Twitter, his supposed free speech absolutism, and his subsequent renunciation of the Democratic Party as "the party of division and hate"[46] have put Musk squarely in the crosshairs of the woke cartel.

Tesla and Musk have thus been subjected to the "S" in ESG—the "social" or "social justice" quotient. "Diversity, equity, and inclusion" means exclusion of the politically incorrect. This applies to corporations as much as it does to individuals. Musk has been deemed a deplorable, and thus his company does not pass "social justice" muster.

As such, Musk has exposed the contradictions within the woke cartel's measurement apparatus. Anything that can be used against a company, or its owners, will be used—when the target runs afoul of the woke arbiters, that is. That's because the ESG is an impressionistic, qualitative metric that exposes companies to the whims of a woke dictatorship.

I'm not suggesting that Musk is a free-market hero or a lowercase libertarian, nor am I suggesting that anyone should feel sorry for the billionaire. But there is little doubt that he's become corporate ene-

---

46 Elon Musk, "In the Past I Voted Democrat, Because They Were (Mostly) the Kindness Party. But They Have Become the Party of Division & Hate, so I Can No Longer Support Them and Will Vote Republican now. Watch Their Dirty Tricks Campaign against Me Unfold ..." Twitter, May 18, 2022, https://twitter.com/elonmusk/status/1526997132858822658.

my number one for the woke cartel. The battle shaping up between Musk and the regime will prove to be an important one, if only because it pits the power of the latter against a high-visibility manufacturer and the reputed "richest man in the world." We will learn how powerful the woke cartel is and just how far it will go to infringe property rights and eradicate any remaining legitimate (consumer-based) market criteria—no matter how much its moves reek of hypocrisy or how obvious its vendetta.

In today's political economy, satisfying shareholders, employees, and customers to earn profits has become less important for corporations than ingratiating the woke cartel and the governments that support it. Corporate fealty to wokeness, state dictates, and state narratives can be explained in terms of a fully politicized economy. Woke corporatism is what happens when social democracy or democratic socialism grows to such proportions as to make profiting nearly impossible without political approval. Unfortunately, Elon Musk has already learned a great deal about woke political capitalism.[47]

There is a worldwide trend to make the ESG Index universal, global, and mandatory for corporations.[48] But there are also indications that official political pushback in the U.S. may be forthcoming.[49] In

47 Randall G Holcombe, "Political Capitalism," Cato Institute, *Cato Journal*, 2015, https://www.cato.org/sites/cato.org/files/serials/files/cato-journal/2015/2/cj-v35n1-2.pdf.

48 Ryan Nelson, "Examining the State of Worldwide Mandatory ESG Disclosures," *Conservice ESG*, November 16, 2021, https://www.gobyinc.com/examining-worldwide-mandatory-esg-disclosures/.

49 Michael Ginsberg, "'It's a Scam': House Republicans Prepare Next Salvo in War on Woke Capital," *The Daily Caller*, July 20, 2022, https://dailycaller.com/2022/07/19/house-republicans-esg-investing-

the meanwhile, ESG compliance will reduce overall productivity and abridge property rights. But a compliant market economy of sorts will exist, a kind of "actually existing socialism," where the bulk of the spoils go to the compliant and the elite. To adopt and alter the academic phrase "publish or perish," the new mantra is "belong or perish."

Yet, the woke cartel's *multi-pronged attacks* on society are by no means restricted to mega-corporations. ESGs may soon be applied to individuals, replete with carbon allowances and social credit scores. Meanwhile, formal education has been deeply compromised by wokeness, and Hollywood, America's producer of cultural icons, has long since become an avid woke promoter. We are no longer surprised by superheroes like Green Arrow fighting a battle to protect the environment from evil, profit-making corporations.

Stakeholder capitalism is not a grassroots movement. It's a multi-pronged, well-funded, and unipolar assault on property rights and individual liberty by leftist elites.

Woke Corporatism, or Economic Fascism

As I have noted, to promote stakeholder capitalism, arch stakeholder proponent Klaus Schwab erects the straw man of "neoliberalism," or what amounts for Schwab to the free market. Stakeholder capitalism is opposed to free-market capitalism.

But in blaming the free market, Schwab and company are complaining about the wrong thing.

---

woke-capital-jim-banks-andy-barr/.

Corporatism,[50] and not fair and free competition, is the real source of what Schwab and his ilk seemingly decry. Corporatism—otherwise known as "economic fascism"[51]—involves the politicization of the economy and the coordination of production and the running of society by a consortium of dominant interest groups, just like the one that the WEF establishes. Woke corporatism, or economic fascism, allows nominal private ownership but effectively puts corporations under the pressures of the woke cartel and the eventual control of legislation promulgated by the state. Aided by the Fourth Estate, the Fifth Estate of the WEF and its corporate partners apply extra-governmental pressure on corporate and individual behavior. If anything, stakeholder capitalism is a form of corporatism or economic fascism. Contrary to Larry Fink's assertion, the corporatism he promotes involves the exercise of corporate power, in advance of state sanctions, to achieve a particular ideological and political agenda. That agenda is wokeness.

Stakeholder capitalism also involves corporations in undertaking what are otherwise state functions. Corporations also become "stakeholders" in government. The corporate stakeholder model of the Great Reset spills into its governance and geopolitical model: states and favored corporations in "public-private partnerships" in control of governance.

---

50 Thomas J. DiLorenzo, "The Rise of Economic Fascism in America," Mises Institute, August 27, 2021, https://mises.org/wire/rise-economic-fascism-america.

51 Thomas J. DiLorenzo, "Economic Fascism," FEE Freeman Article, Foundation for Economic Education, June 1, 1994, https://fee.org/articles/economic-fascism/.

The configuration yields a corporate-state hybrid largely unaccountable to the constituents of national governments.

The cozy relationship between multinational corporations and governments has even aroused the scorn of a few academics.[52] Some note that the UN-WEF partnership and the governance model of the WEF represent at least the partial privatization of the UN's Agenda 2030, with the WEF bringing corporate partners, money, and supposed expertise on the Fourth Industrial Revolution (4-IR) to the table. And the WEF's governance model extends well beyond the UN, affecting the constitution and behavior of governments worldwide. This usurpation has led political scientist Ivan Wecke to call the WEF's governmental redesign of the world system "a corporate takeover of global governance."[53]

This is true, but the WEF model also represents *the governmentalization of private industry.* Under Schwab's stakeholder capitalism and the multistakeholder governance model, governance is not

52 Steven Umbrello, "Should We Reset?"; Steffen Roth, "The Great Reset. Restratification for Lives, Livelihoods, and the Planet," *Technological Forecasting and Social Change* 166 (February 3, 2021): 1-8, https://doi.org/10.1016/j.techfore.2021.120636; Alexander Trauth-Goik, "Repudiating the Fourth Industrial Revolution Discourse: A New Episteme of Technological Progress," *World Futures* 77, no. 1 (2020): 55–78. https://doi.org/10.1080/02604027.2020.1788357; Kasper Schiølin, "Revolutionary Dreams: Future Essentialism and the Sociotechnical Imaginary of the Fourth Industrial Revolution in Denmark," *Social Studies of Science* 50, no. 4 (2019): 542–66, https://doi.org/10.1177/0306312719867768.

53 Ivan Wecke, "Conspiracy Theories Aside, There Is Something Fishy About The Great Reset," *openDemocracy,* August 16, 2021, https://www.opendemocracy.net/en/oureconomy/conspiracy-theories-aside-there-something-fishy-about-great-reset/.

only increasingly privatized, but also and more importantly, corporations are *deputized* as major additions to governments and intergovernmental bodies. The state is thereby extended, enhanced, and augmented by the addition of enormous corporate assets. These include funding directed at "sustainable development" to the exclusion of the non-compliant as well as the use of Big Data, AI, and 5G to monitor and control citizens. In the case of the covid vaccine regime, the state has granted Big Pharma monopoly protection and indemnity from liability in exchange for a vehicle to expand its powers of coercion. As such, corporate stakeholders become what I have called "governmentalities"[54]—otherwise "private" organizations wielded as state apparatuses, with no obligation to answer to pesky constituents.

Woke capitalism is thus more accurately called woke corporatism. Fink, Schwab, Moynihan, and others use the rhetoric of "sustainability" and "social justice" as a cover for their economic fascism.

ESGs Favor Totalitarianism

While weakening the investment positions of non-ESG-compliant companies in the U.S. and elsewhere, ESG-minded investors have strengthened the financial positions of companies in authoritarian countries. This is particularly the case in China, where top-down governmental controls over corporate behavior either force Chinese companies to abide by ESG standards, or else to misrepresent their compliance. Indeed, Morgan Asset Management notes that ESG reporting from China is unreli-

---

54 Michael Rectenwald, "The Google Election," *Mises Wire*, November 10, 2020, https://mises.org/wire/google-election.

able: "The content of ESG reports in China is highly qualitative. Quantifiable metrics, which are vital for investment analysis, are limited. The transparency of the methodology and the consistency of disclosure are additional concerns for investors."[55]

Yet, Wei Li, chief investment strategist at the BlackRock Investment Institute (BII), recommended that investors triple their exposure to Chinese equity and bond markets, given that "China is under-represented in global investors' portfolios but also, in our view, in global benchmarks."[56] To the delight of Fink, BlackRock received Chinese approval for the first wholly owned foreign asset management firm in the country: "We are honored to be in a position in which we can support more Chinese investors, access financial markets and build portfolios that can serve them throughout their lives," he remarked.[57]

How or whether Chinese companies meet ESG criteria is a curiosity. China, it would seem, fails miserably in terms of all three ESG measures. As Marion Smith of the Common Sense Society notes, investment firms like BlackRock "tout their work to save the world while investing in perhaps the worst violator of environmental, social, and corporate-governance standards" in the world.[58]

55 "Sustainable Investing," J.P. Morgan Asset Management, accessed June 30, 2022, https://am.jpmorgan.com/us/en/asset-management/institutional/investment-strategies/sustainable-investing/.

56 Steve Johnson, "BlackRock Calls for Investors to Lift Allocations to China's Markets," *Financial Times*, August 17, 2021, https://www.ft.com/content/f876fb63-1823-4f4b-a28f-faa7797aa49c.

57 Thomas Hale, "BlackRock Wins Chinese Approval for Mutual Fund Business," *Financial Times*, June 11, 2021, https://www.ft.com/content/5bb13be2-68da-4e53-8d32-5340b67ef82f.

58 Marion Smith, "BlackRock's Hypocrisy Highlights ESG's Short-

The economic, geopolitical, and humanitarian significance of investment strategies favoring Chinese companies cannot be overstated, especially given China's military expansionism and BlackRock's investment in companies whose military and surveillance technologies have been linked to human rights abuses, including efforts to target China's ethnic and religious minority populations in Xinjiang.[59] More importantly, ESG investing in China threatens market capitalism itself by abetting companies that bolster a communist authoritarian-totalitarian regime.

comings," *National Review*, February 3, 2022, https://www.nationalreview.com/2022/02/blackrocks-hypocrisy-highlights-esgs-shortcomings/.

59 Ryan Morgan, "Reports: US Firm BlackRock Investing in Chinese Military, Spy Companies Tied to Human Rights Abuses," *American Military News*, October 29, 2021, https://americanmilitarynews.com/2021/10/reports-us-firm-blackrock-investing-in-chinese-military-spy-companies-tied-to-human-rights-abuses/.

CHAPTER SEVEN

Woke Ideology

I'VE DISCUSSED the Great Reset and introduced several ways of understanding the economics. The stakeholder capitalism of the Great Reset can be thought of as "capitalism with Chinese characteristics," neo-feudalism, corporate socialism, and economic fascism.

Here I consider the ideological aspect of the Great Reset. Just how do the planners mean to establish the reset ideologically? That is, how would a reset of the mass mind come to pass that would allow for the many elements of the Great Reset to be put into place—without mass rebellion, that is? After all, if the Great Reset is to take hold, some degree of conformity on the part of the population will be necessary—despite the enhanced, extended, and more precise control over the population that transhumanist technology and a centralized digital currency would afford.

This is the function of ideology. Ideology, as the Marxist historian of science Richard Lewontin has argued, works "by convincing people that the society in which they live is just and fair, or if not just and fair then inevitable, and that it is quite useless to resort to violence."[1] Ideology establishes the "social legitimation" that Lewontin sees as necessary for gaining the assent of the ruled. "The battleground is in people's heads, and if the battle is won on that ground then the peace and tranquility of society are guaranteed."[2] Ideology on this account is not exactly the same as worldview. It is rather the mental programming necessary for domination and control short of the use of force. Ideological indoctrination is easier, less messy, and less expensive than state and state-supported violence.

Some may argue that the ideology of the Great Reset is simply socialist-communist ideology. After all, in many respects, socialist-communist ideology supports what the Great Reset promises to deliver. And this may work for some. There are those who would welcome, on socialist grounds, the "fairness," "equality," or "equity" that the Great Reset promises. Socialists might overlook or excuse the oligarchical control of society because of the supposed fairness, equality, or equity among the mass of the population, and on the presumption that the oligarchy will be overthrown in the not-so-distant future. Socialism embeds a levelling predisposition that puts a premium on "equality" among the visible majority, even when that equality comes as a great loss for many otherwise "middle-class" subjects. In fact, when I briefly entertained the rantings of members of the Revolutionary Communist Party, USA, including its

---

1   R.C. Lewontin, *Biology as Ideology: The Doctrine of DNA*, New York: HarperPerennial, n.d., page 6.

2   Ibid., page 7.

leader, Bob Avakian, they admitted to me that world-wide socialism would mean reduced standards of living for much of the world, especially in the United States. They had no problem with this; in fact, they seemed to relish the prospect. No doubt, as Friedrich Nietzsche suggested, socialism is fueled, at least in part, by *ressentiment*—by resentment and envy of the property owner. Much could be said about socialists' apparent approval, or at least conditional and temporary acceptance, of big monopolistic oligarchical corporatists and their preference for big business over small.[3] Socialists see monopolization under capitalism as inevitable, as necessary for producing a more consolidated target to be overthrown, and as a sign of the imminent collapse of capitalism and the coming socialist-communist apocalypse.

Likewise, many socialists will be amenable to the Great Reset on principle—especially those who accept its rhetoric at face value. But for all its newfound popularity, socialism-communism still doesn't represent the majority. While popular among millennials and other millennialists, socialism-communism remains unsavory for many. It is regarded as alien, obscure, and loosely connotes something negative. But more importantly, for reasons that I'll give below, socialist-communist ideology is not the ideology that best fits the goals of the Great Reset. This is where wokeness comes in.

What, exactly, is wokeness? As I write in *Beyond Woke*:

---

3 Matt Bruenig, "Small Businesses Are Overrated," *Jacobin*, January 16, 2018, https://jacobinmag.com/2018/01/small-businesses-work-ers-wages.

According to the social justice creed, being "woke" is the political awakening that stems from the emergence of consciousness and con-scientiousness regarding social and political injustice. Wokeness is the indelible inscription of the awareness of social injustice on the con-scious mind, eliciting the sting of conscience, which compels the newly woke to change their beliefs and behaviors.[4]

This is as close to a definition of wokeness as I can manage, gleaning it as I have from the assertions of those who embrace it. Of course, the etymology of the word "woke," and how it became an adjective describing those who are thus awakened into con-sciousness of social and political injustice, is another matter. I discuss the etymology in *Google Archipelago*:

"Woke" began in English as a past tense and past participle of "wake." It suggested "having become awake." But, by the 1960s, woke began to function as an adjective as well, gaining the figurative meaning in the African American community of "well-informed" or "up-to-date." By 1972, the once modest verbal past tense be-gan to describe an elevated political conscious-ness. In 2017, the Oxford English Dictionary (OED) recognized the social-conscious aware-ness of woke and added the definition: "alert to racial or social discrimination and injustice."[5]

4 Michael Rectenwald, *Beyond Woke*, Nashville, TN: New English Review Press, 2020, pages 7-8.

5 Michael Rectenwald, *Google Archipelago: The Digital Gulag and the Simulation of Freedom*, Nashville, TN: New English Review Press, 2019, page 42.

Yet, there are as many definitions of wokeness as people who've heard of it, as is the case with most anything the least bit controversial. I'm sure that others can and will add to the definition or suggest that wokeness should be defined altogether differently. But the above definition and historical-semantical renderings are sufficient for our purposes. According to adherents, then, wokeness is enhanced awareness of social and political injustice and the determination to eradicate it.

But what could wokeness have to do with the Great Reset? As a corrective, wokeness is not aimed at the sufferers whose complaints, or imagined complaints, it means to redress. Wokeness works on the majority, the supposed beneficiaries of injustice. It does so by making the majority understand that it has benefited from "privilege" and preference—based on skin color (whiteness), gender (patriarchy), sexual proclivity (heteronormativity), birthplace (colonialism, imperialism, and first worldism), gender identity (cis gender privilege), and the domination of nature (speciesism/anthropocentrism)—to name some of the major culprits. The list could go on and is emended, seemingly by the day. This majority must be rehabilitated, as it were. The masses must understand that they have gained whatever advantages they have hitherto enjoyed because of the unfair treatment of others, either directly or indirectly, and this unfair treatment is predicated on the circumstances of birth. The "privilege" of the majority has come at the expense of those minorities designated as the beneficiaries of wokeness, and wokeness is the means for rectifying these many injustices.

And what are the effects of being repeatedly reprimanded as such, of being told that one has been the beneficiary of unmerited "privilege," that one's relative wealth and well-being have come at the expense of oppressed, marginalized, and misused Others? Shame, guilt, remorse, unworthiness. And what are the expected attitudinal and behavioral adjustments to be taken by the majority? They are to expect less. Under woke ideology, one will be expected to forfeit one's property rights, because even these rights, nay, especially these rights, have come at the expense of others.

Thus, wokeness works by habituating the majority to the reduced expectations of the Great Reset. It does this by instilling a belief in the unworthiness of the majority to thrive, prosper, and enjoy their lives. Wokeness indoctrinates the majority into the propertyless future (for them, at least) of the Great Reset, while gratifying the Left, its main ideological propagators, with a sense of moral superiority, even as they too are scheduled to become bereft of prospects.

One question remains. Why is wokeness more suited to the objectives of the Great Reset than socialist-communist ideology? To answer this question, we must recall the selling points of socialism-communism. Despite the levelling down that I mentioned above, socialism-communism is promissory. It promises benefits, not deficits. It does not operate by promising the majority that they will lose upon the establishment of socialism-communism. Quite to the contrary, socialism-communism promises vastly improved conditions—yes, fairness, equality, or equity—but also prosperity for the mass of humanity, prosperity that has been denied under capitalism.

The workers of the world are called to unite, not under the prospect of reduced expectations, but based on great expectations—not, according to Marx, to establish utopia, but at least to destroy and replace the current dystopia with a shared cornucopia. We know, of course, how this promise is kept: with an iron fist. But it is nevertheless still proffered and believed by all too many in our midst.

We have seen, on the other hand, the subtractive character of woke ideology. Wokeness demands the forfeiture of advantages on moral grounds. Unlike socialism-communism, it does not offer empowerment or advocate the takeover of the means of production and the state by political means. Wokeness is a form of recrimination that compels the abdication, not the acquisition, of goods.

Woke ideology, I contend, has tilled the soil and planted the seeds for the harvest that the Great Reset represents to the ruling elite. Was wokeness intentionally crafted for this purpose? Not necessarily, but it nevertheless can and is being appropriated for these ends, just as other ideological formations have been used for other ends. The ruling elite appropriates the available means at its disposal to effect its plans, including available ideologies. Woke ideology was available and ready for appropriation and application. Wokeness serves the Great Reset best, and thus we see the language of wokeness in the books and other literature devoted to its establishment: fairness, inclusion, etc.

Naturally, wokeness will not work on everyone. But the demand has been made universal so that unapologetic, noncompliant dissenters are figured as regressive, reactionary, racist, white supremacist, and more, and are dismissed, if not punished, on those grounds. Wokeness has thus attained dominance. Countering it will be a major requirement for challenging the Great Reset.

Part II

The Anatomy of the Great Reset

In addition to these pragmatic goals, the powers
of financial capitalism had another far-reaching
aim, nothing less than to create a world system
of financial control in private hands able to dom-
inate the political system of each country and the
economy of the world as a whole. This system
was to be controlled in a feudalist fashion by the
central banks of the world acting in concert, by
secret agreements arrived at in frequent private
meetings and conferences. The apex of the system
was to be the Bank for International Settlements
in Basle, Switzerland, a private bank owned and
controlled by the world's central banks which were
themselves private corporations. Each central
bank, in the hands of men like Montagu Norman
of the Bank of England, Benjamin Strong of the
New York Federal Reserve Bank, Charles Rist of
the Bank of France, and Hjalmar Schacht of the
Reichsbank, sought to dominate its government by
its ability to control Treasury loans, to manipulate
foreign exchanges, to influence the level of econom-
ic activity in the country, and to influence coopera-
tive politicians by subsequent economic rewards in
the business world.

—Carrol Quigley

CHAPTER EIGHT

The Round Table Roots of the Great Reset

T HE GREAT RESET is the culmination of the efforts of numerous organizations that have fostered and contributed to the World Economic Forum (WEF) and its agenda over decades. These include not only the United Nations (UN) but also a network of NGOs founded on the same principles as the WEF and sharing members with it. It's not as if the WEF appeared out of the thin blue air and began issuing edicts on the global economy and global governance. Rather, the WEF is heir to a long line of globalist ideas and policies that extend back to the early twentieth century.

In fact, the WEF is modeled after the Rhodes Society, founded in 1903. It derives from successors to Lord Alfred Milner's Round Tables. These successors include the Royal Institute of International Affairs (RIIA, otherwise known as Chatham House, founded in 1920), the Council on Foreign Relations (CFR, founded in 1921), the Bilderberg Group (founded in

1954), and the Club of Rome (founded in 1968). The WEF is essentially a fraternal twin of the Trilateral Commission (founded in 1973).

We can, in fact, trace a direct line of succession from each organization to the next. Each of these organizations convenes meetings of prominent government officials, business leaders, media moguls, and academics. Each organization drafts international political treaties and global governance policies and draws up plans for the global economy. And many of these organizations—although the WEF is somewhat of an exception here—hold their meetings under the Chatham House Rule. This rule of secrecy stipulates that "[w]hen a meeting, or part thereof, is held under the Chatham House Rule, participants are free to use the information received, but neither the identity nor the affiliation of the speaker(s), nor that of any other participant, may be revealed."[1] That is, the ideas discussed during meetings can be disseminated, but their sources and those party to them must remain undisclosed.

Of these organizations, the WEF represents the most public face of globalism to date. Unlike its forebears, it exhibits a relative openness. As an organization, the WEF outstrips its ancestors in terms of reach, penetration, and "success." While leaders in these earlier and coterminous groups have been instrumental in shaping some of the most historically significant geopolitical policies worldwide, the organizations themselves have not had the impact that the WEF has enjoyed. The "success" of the WEF is

---

1 "Our History," Chatham House – International Affairs Think Tank, March 28, 2022, https://www.chathamhouse.org/about-us/our-history.

primarily due to its enrollment of corporations (as partners), government officials (as members and contributors), civil society groups, and prominent individuals. Also significant is its partnership with the UN.

In a sense, the WEF represents the "pragmatic" application of the ideational work done in older globalist organizations. To analogize, we might say that the WEF is to these earlier organizations what Lenin was to Marx. Like Marx, Lenin was a theorist. But unlike Marx, Lenin was also a "practical" revolutionary. Likewise, the WEF theorizes but also administers and coordinates practical applications with immense global consequences. Nevertheless, Lenin would not have been Lenin without Marx and the WEF would not have been the WEF without these earlier Round Table groups.

The WEF's relative openness explains, at least in part, its notoriety. We may speculate about the WEF's decision to "go public" with its formal agenda. One might argue that the WEF's annual meetings are out in the open because the globalists have become confident that their plans can no longer be resisted. Another explanation might be that the globalists have become desperate to have their policies and prescriptions enacted. Perhaps they believe their own rhetoric regarding climate change and other imminent environmental catastrophes. The prospect of doom requires that they make their plans known. Another possible explanation is that with the WEF, the globalist rhetoric has finally been honed to make the public rollout of the agenda feasible. (More on rhetoric in the following chapter.) Finally, there is the possibility that the WEF's agenda is not entirely open.

In fact, we should not overstate the case for the WEF's openness. Based on their four-year ethnographic study of the WEF, anthropologist Christina Garsten and sociologist Adrienne Sörbom concluded that the WEF operates as a "half-secret" organization.[2] While its official program is public, its annual events include private programs and invitation-only secret meetings, where the Chatham House Rule is strictly observed.[3] Based on extensive exposure to the WEF through interviews of staff (including Klaus Schwab), attendance at several annual meetings, and the divulgences of annual meeting invitees, the authors conclude that the WEF's modus operandi is one of "discretionary governance," with all of the connotations that attend to the word discretionary: discrete, free to do what one deems best in a situation (as opposed to being bound by rules), revealing the right information to the right people, and withholding it from the wrong people.

The authors of the ethnographic study describe a particular secret meeting to which they managed to gain admission. The topic of conversation was "what to do with the Arctic"—which revealed the hubris of the attendees, considering their assumed capacity to control an entire land mass. The attendees included the prime minister of a Nordic country, members of the Arctic Council, a scientist, and CEOs or top executives of corporations with interests in the region.

---

2 Christina Garsten and Adrienne Sörbom, "Discretionary Governance," *Global Governance: A Review of Multilateralism and International Organizations* 27, no. 4 (2021): 540–60, https://doi.org/10.1163/19426720-02704006, page 552.

3 Ibid., page 553.

The meeting was held under the Chatham House Rule, which applies to all such secret meetings and private programs at the Davos conference.[4]

Furthermore, "[t]he organization itself is committed to holding its events so that critical topics can be discussed without media attention or other forms of leakage." A managed secrecy and an invitation-only policy shrouds much of the WEF's agenda in mystery, even though it is not strictly speaking a secret society. "What is not on display is the invitation-only part of the program. The internet displays are, in some respects, mystifiers posing as demystifiers."[5] That is, the open aspect of the agenda masks the secret aspect and deflects attention from it.

Likewise, the WEF is not so different from the earlier Round Table groups. It also shares with them an extensive roster of members, contributors, and affiliates. WEF members overlap with memberships in the Rhodes Society, the RIIA, the CFR, the Bilderberg Group, the Club of Rome, and the Trilateral Commission. Some WEF members and associates overlap with multiple Round Table-based groups. Furthermore, the WEF's Young Global Leaders (YGL) program recruits members and contributors as ambassadors of its globalist agenda, essentially in the same way that the Rhodes Scholarships recruited academics as ambassadors of the British Empire. The same may be said of its Global Shapers program, discussed in a subsequent chapter. And, several YGLs have also been Rhodes Scholars.

Meanwhile, many of these overlapping Round Table memberships also coincide with concurrent

4   Ibid.
5   Ibid., pages 552-553.

memberships in global governance institutions, including the UN, the World Bank, the International Monetary Fund (IMF), the Organization for Economic Cooperation and Development (OECD), and the World Health Organization (WHO). These Round Table organizations (and their UN, World Bank, IMF, OECD, and WHO counterparts) promulgate similar if not identical policies and prescriptions for economic globalization, "sustainable development," and technological innovation, policies and prescriptions that are integral to the WEF's Great Reset and the vaunted Fourth Industrial Revolution.

To recap, the Round Table roots of the WEF are evidenced by:

1. a historical line of succession from Milner's Round Tables, to the RIIA, to the CFR, to the Bilderberg Group, to the Club of Rome, to the WEF and the Trilateral Commission;

2. the parallels between the WEF's Young Global Leaders program and the Rhodes Scholarships;

3. the overlapping memberships across the WEF, its predecessor Round Table organizations, and their UN, World Bank, IMF, OECD, and WHO counterparts;

4. the similar if not identical globalist policies of these organizations (both presently and historically);

5. a degree of secrecy and at least a situational adherence to the Chatham House Rule.

The Rhodes Society and the WEF

The history of these Round Table groups before the recent incarnations has been told by others. While the term "Round Table" as applied to these groups was coined by Lord Alfred Milner, the structural model and globalist agenda of Milner's Round Tables derive from the Rhodes Trust, which manages Oxford University's Rhodes Scholarship program. According to the late Georgetown University Professor Carroll Quigley—whose "Development of Civilization course was cited by the university's Foreign Service alumni from 1941 to 1969 as the most influential course in their undergraduate studies"[6]—Cecil Rhodes and Lord Milner, and the trustees and executives of the Rhodes Trust, formed a "Rhodes Society" and began to develop Round Table organizations. In Quigley's *Tragedy and Hope*, we are told that Milner's Round Table groups soon emerged from the Rhodes Society. These groups were followed, in the wake of World War I, by successive globalist Round Table NGOs, including the RIIA and the CFR.[7] The Bilderberg Group, the Club of Rome, the Trilateral Commission, and the WEF followed World War II.

I am not alleging, as Robert I. Rotberg suggests in his criticism of Quigley's "conspiratorial" claims, that the Rhodes-sponsored early Round Tables "launched a successful cabal that effectively ran much of Britain and British possessions overseas

---

6 "Carroll Quigley Dies, GU Professor," archive.ph, accessed August 14, 2022, https://archive.ph/20210118230440/https://www.washingtonpost.com/archive/local/1977/01/06/carroll-quigley-dies-gu-professor/304f0138-cdef-4d37-ab30-a9ad320e9b52/.

7 Carroll Quigley, *Tragedy and Hope: A History of the World in Our Time*, San Diego, CA: Dauphin Publications, 2014.

from at the least the 1890s to the 1940s" (emphasis in original).[8] I am merely claiming that the Round Tables themselves were successfully launched, regardless of how much control they ultimately wielded over the British commonwealth and its colonies.

The Rhodes Trust, Rhodes Scholarship, and the Round Table Groups

Inspired by John Ruskin and financed by the fortune of Cecil Rhodes, the Rhodes Trust[9] was formally established in 1903—to induct intellectuals into British culture so that they would help advance the British Empire across the globe.[10] According to Quigley, "Rhodes left part of his great fortune to found the Rhodes Scholarships at Oxford in order to spread the English ruling class tradition throughout the English-speaking world as Ruskin had wanted."[11] Lord Milner was "[a]mong Ruskin's most devoted disciples." Milner was a trustee of the Rhodes Trust and an executive member of the secret Rhodes Society:

[O]n February 5, 1891...Rhodes and [William

---

8   Robert I Rotberg, "Did Cecil Rhodes Really Try to Control the World?," *The Journal of Imperial and Commonwealth History* 42, no. 3 (2014): 551–67, https://doi.org/10.1080/03086534.2014.934000.

9   "Launch of Global Rhodes Scholarships - Rhodes Trust," Rhodes House - Home of The Rhodes Scholarships, February 19, 2018, https://www.rhodeshouse.ox.ac.uk/news-events/latest-news/news/2018/february/launch-of-global-rhodes-scholarships/.

10   Philip Ziegler, "Legacy: Cecil Rhodes, the Rhodes Trust and Rhodes Scholarships," The Association of American Rhodes Scholars: Book Review of Legacy, May 11, 2008, https://www.american-rhodes.org/news-113.html.

11   Quigley, *Tragedy and Hope*, page 131.

T.] Stead organized a secret society of which Rhodes had been dreaming for sixteen years. In this secret society Rhodes was to be leader; Stead, Brett (Lord Esher), and Milner were to form an executive committee; Arthur (Lord) Balfour, (Sir) Harry Johnston, Lord Rothschild, Albert (Lord) Grey, and others were listed as potential members of a "Circle of Initiates"; while there was to be an outer circle known as the "Association of Helpers" (later organized by Milner as the Round Table organization)...Thus the central part of the secret society was established by March 1891. It continued to function as a formal group, although the outer circle [of Milner's Round Tables] was, apparently, not organized until 1909-1913. This group was able to get access to Rhodes's money after his death in 1902 and also to the funds of loyal Rhodes supporters like Alfred Beit (1853-1906) and Sir Abe Bailey (1864-1940). With this backing they sought to extend and execute the ideals that Rhodes had obtained from Ruskin and Stead.[12]

The Rhodes Scholarship program has since shifted from inducting recipients into an Anglophile globalism promoting the political-economic aims of British imperialism to inducting recipients into a multicultural, multilateral globalism that is committed to "social justice" and "the world's diversity:"

The two new Global Scholarships are part of a wider geographic expansion of the Rhodes Scholarships. In recent years, the total number of Scholarships awarded each year has increased from 83 to over 100, including new

---

12   Ibid.

Scholarships in China, East and West Africa, Israel, Jordan, Lebanon, Malaysia, Palestine, Singapore, Syria and the United Arab Emirates. This increases the number of Rhodes Scholars studying at the University of Oxford at any one time to more than 250. The expansion to include the two new Global Scholarships (with this number set to increase in future years) marks a historic moment for the Rhodes Trust, and further strengthens the reach of the Scholarship around the world.[13]

Thus, the Rhodes Scholarship fosters the same "diversity, equity, and inclusion" values as the UN and the WEF. But while the Rhodes Trust and Rhodes Scholarship no longer emphasize Anglocentric imperialism, a kind of economic imperialism through planned globalization is still the agenda. Like the UN and the WEF, the Rhodes Trust and Scholarship uses "diversity, equity, and inclusion" as a cover for an elite-centered globalism.[14] The elite's "inclusion" of "diversity" within its ranks equals "equity" and works as a scrim to mask its elitist power gambits to the exclusion of the vast majority in decision-making. To justify and disguise its cultural, economic, and political imperialism, this elite network has reconstituted itself with women and people of

13 "Launch of Global Rhodes Scholarships - Rhodes Trust," Rhodes House - Home of The Rhodes Scholarships, February 19, 2018, https://www.rhodeshouse.ox.ac.uk/news-events/latest-news/news/2018/february/launch-of-global-rhodes-scholarships/.

14 See the "United Nations Declaration on the Rights of Indigenous Peoples" for an example of this tactic. "United Nations for Indigenous Peoples | Indigenous Peoples," United Nations, accessed August 14, 2022, https://www.un.org/development/desa/indigenouspeoples/.

color, and with people of different ethnicities, and from different regions. This charade explains why we find so many "exotic" representatives admitted to its inner circle. (See Table 2.1.) Likewise, after changing its name from the European Management Forum to the World Economic Forum in 1987, the WEF pivoted from an explicitly Eurocentric to a multicultural and multilateral globalism. Despite this new emphasis, the WEF has maintained its commitment to the advancement of an elite-planned world economy implemented through corporate-socialist stakeholder capitalism.

The WEF's YGL program also emulates the Rhodes Scholarship's recruitment methods. In 2017, at a John F. Kennedy School of Government event, David Gergen, a member of the Bilderberg group, interviewed WEF founder and chairman Klaus Schwab. He asked Schwab about the "governance" impacts of the YGL's "executive education" program. Schwab's reply is telling:

> [T]here's this notion to integrate young leaders as part of the World Economic Forum since many years [sic]. And I have to say when I mention now names like Mrs. [Angela] Merkel, even Vladimir Putin, and so on, they all have been Young Global Leaders of the World Economic Forum. But what we are very proud of now, the young generation, like Prime Minister [Justin] Trudeau, president of Argentina, and so on, that we penetrate the cabinets...And I know that half of his [Trudeau's] cabinet, or even more than half of his cabinet, are actually Young Global Leaders of the World Economic Forum...It's true in Argentina, and it's true in

France now...What is important for me is those Young Global Leaders have an opportunity to come here, and we have established a course now since several years. And I think this corporation [WEF] has a tremendous impact because, being here for a week, really creates a strong community" (emphasis mine).[15]

The parallels between the WEF's YGL program and the Rhodes Scholarships extend even further. Many WEF members, contributors, and YGLs have also been Rhodes Scholars. The list of WEF members, contributors, and YGLs who are or have been Rhodes Scholars is extensive. (See Table 2.1.) One notable example is Rhodes Scholar Chrystia Freeland. While never a YGL, Freeland is a WEF member[16] and a member of the WEF Board of Trustees.[17] She was educated at Harvard University before continuing her studies on a Rhodes Scholarship at the University of Oxford. Freeland is currently Canada's Deputy Prime Minister and Minister of Finance. Before that, she served as Deputy Prime Minister of Canada and Minister of Intergovernmental Affairs. In this capacity, "she led Canada's united [and draconian] response to the COVID-19 pandemic."[18] It was Freeland, as Deputy Prime Minister and Minis-

---

15 skellycat9, "Klaus Schwab/Harvard Talk/ Trudeau Cabinet & Others 'Penetrated,'" YouTube, January 26, 2022, https://www.youtube.com/watch?v=b4cDNyvrP40.

16 "Chrystia Freeland," World Economic Forum, accessed August 28, 2022, https://www.weforum.org/people/chrystia-freeland.

17 "Leadership and Governance," World Economic Forum, accessed September 13, 2022, https://www.weforum.org/about/leadership-and-governance.

18 Ibid.

ter of Finance, who was responsible for freezing the bank accounts of those who participated in or donated money to the Canadian truckers' convoy protest and laughed when she was asked about it during a press conference.[19]

Several other WEF members/Rhodes Scholars are also members of other Round Table NGOs, including the CFR, the Bilderberg Group, and the Trilateral Commission. These include such notables as former U.S. President Bill Clinton,[20] who has attended Bilderberg meetings.[21] Curiously, in his speech at the 1992 Democratic National Convention that nominated Al Gore as its vice presidential candidate, Clinton acknowledged his intellectual debt to Carroll Quigley:

> As a teen-ager I heard John Kennedy's summons to citizenship. And then, as a student at Georgetown, I heard that call clarified by a professor named Carroll Quigley, who said to us that America was the greatest nation in history because our people have always believed in two things: that tomorrow can be better than today, and that every one of us has a personal, moral

19 Yanky, "Watch: Chrystia Freeland Laughed When She Announced That She Was Freezing Canadians' Bank Accounts for Protesting the Trudeau Liberals' Tyrannical Lockdowns," Twitter, August 28, 2022, https://twitter.com/Yanky_Pollak/status/1563699261006651392.

20 "William J. Clinton," World Economic Forum, accessed August 15, 2022, https://www.weforum.org/people/william-j-clinton.

21 Jessica Hartogs, "Bilderberg: World's Most Powerful Flock to Annual Secret Meeting," CNBC, June 8, 2016, https://www.cnbc.com/2016/06/08/bilderberg-worlds-most-powerful-flock-to-annual-secret-meeting.html.

responsibility to make it so.[22]

As we shall see, Quigley was sympathetic to the globalist plans of this elite.

Other WEF YGLs who were Rhodes Scholars and members of other Round Table Groups include Clinton's Deputy Secretary of State Strobe Talbott,[23] who has been a member of the CFR and has served on the North America Executive Committee of the Trilateral Commission; Robert B. Reich,[24] Clinton's Secretary of Labor (who blocked me on Twitter);[25] Richard N. Haass,[26] who has served as the President of the CFR; Jared Cohen,[27] who has served as a member of the CFR, the Trilateral Commission, and the Bilderberg Group;[28] as well as several other members

22 "Transcript of Speech by Clinton Accepting Democratic Nomination," *The New York Times*, July 17, 1992, https://www.nytimes.com/1992/07/17/news/their-own-words-transcript-speech-clinton-accepting-democratic-nomination.html.

23 Strobe Talbott," World Economic Forum, accessed August 15, 2022, https://www.weforum.org/people/strobe-talbott.

24 "Robert Reich," Robert Reich | Faculty & Affiliated Academics | Faculty and Impact | Goldman School of Public Policy | University of California, Berkeley, April 15, 2021, https://gspp.berkeley.edu/faculty-and-impact/faculty/robert-reich; "Robert Reich - Agenda Contributor," World Economic Forum, accessed August 15, 2022, https://www.weforum.org/agenda/authors/robert-reich/.

25 Michael Rectenwald, "Proudest Moment of My Life," Twitter, August 22, 2022, https://twitter.com/TheAntiWokeProf/status/1561564509990522880.

26 "Richard N. Haass," World Economic Forum, accessed August 15, 2022, https://cn.weforum.org/agenda/authors/richard-n-haass.

27 Jared Cohen," World Economic Forum, accessed August 15, 2022, https://www.weforum.org/people/jared-cohen.

28 "List of Participants 2018," Bilderberg Meetings, accessed August 15, 2022, https://bilderbergmeetings.org/meetings/meeting-2018/

of the CFR, namely Peter Blair Henry,[29] James Manyika,[30] Dan Esty,[31] Brett House,[32] and Sylvia Mathews
Burwell.[33] Burwell is also a former CFR board member and has worked as the Chief Operating Officer of
the Bill & Melinda Gates Foundation. House has also
served as a principal adviser to the executive office
of the Secretary-General of the UN, a policy adviser
to the UN Development Program (UNDP), an economist for the IMF, and an analyst for the World Bank.

Additionally, like House, several other WEF
members/Rhodes Scholars have worked for or collaborated with the UN, the WHO, the IMF, and the
World Bank. (See Table 2.1.) Notables include the
following:

- Dr. Leana Wen:[34] Wen is a CNN medical analyst and a Washington Post columnist. One of the
most vocal proponents of draconian policies throughout the covid crisis, Wen suggested on CNN that the
unvaccinated should be quarantined and should not

participants-2018.

29 "Peter Blair Henry," World Economic Forum, accessed August
15, 2022, https://www.weforum.org/people/peter-blair-henry.

30 "James Manyika," World Economic Forum, accessed August 15,
2022, https://www.weforum.org/people/james-manyika.

31 Dan Esty - Agenda Contributor," World Economic Forum, accessed August 15, 2022, https://www.weforum.org/agenda/authors/
dan-esty.

32 "Brett House," World Economic Forum, accessed August 15,
2022, https://www.weforum.org/people/brett-house.

33 "Sylvia Mathews Burwell," World Economic Forum, accessed August 15, 2022, https://www.weforum.org/people/syl-
via-mathews-burwell.

34 "Leana Wen," World Economic Forum, accessed August 14,
2022, https://www.weforum.org/people/leana-wen.

be allowed to go outside.[35] She also declared on CNN that the unvaccinated should be banned from interstate travel.[36] Wen has been the President of Planned Parenthood, where she soon failed,[37] and is a consultant with the WHO, the Brookings Institution, and the China Medical Board. Wen is a WEF YGL. A native of China, her apparent totalitarian sympathies have been scrutinized.[38]

• Elizabeth Cousens:[39] Cousens is the United Nations Foundation's third President and Chief Executive Officer.[40] At the UN, she's also served as a Principal Policy Adviser and Counsellor to the Permanent Representative of the United States (Susan

---

35 Paul Joseph Watson, PrisonPlanet Live, "We Were Right," YouTube, August 28, 2022, https://www.youtube.com/watch?v=hDaqN-gOsw6M.

36 Cristina Laila, "Doctor on CNN: Americans Who Wish to Have Privileges Need to Get Vaccinated: 'Having the Right to Travel Interstate, It's Not a Constitutional Right' (Video)," *The Gateway Pundit*, September 10, 2021, https://www.thegatewaypundit.com/2021/09/doctor-cnn-americans-wish-privileges-need-get-vaccinated-right-travel-interstate-not-constitutional-right-video/.

37 Sarah Kliff and Shane Goldmacher, "Why Leana Wen Quickly Lost Support at Planned Parenthood," *The New York Times*, July 18, 2019, https://www.nytimes.com/2019/07/17/us/politics/planned-parenthood-wen.html.

38 "Covid Communism: CNN Lead Propagandist, 'Doctor' Leana Wen, Says Unvaccinated People Should Not Be Allowed to Travel in US from State to State (Op-Ed)," *Survive the News*, December 20, 2021, https://www.survivethenews.com/covid-communism-cnn-lead-propagandist-doctor-leana-wen-says-unvaccinated-people-should-not-be-allowed-to-travel-in-us-from-state-to-state-op-ed/.

39 "Elizabeth Cousens," World Economic Forum, accessed August 29, 2022, https://www.weforum.org/people/elizabeth-cousens.

40 "Elizabeth Cousens," unfoundation.org, December 23, 2021, https://unfoundation.org/who-we-are/our-people/elizabeth-cousens/.

Rice), as a US Ambassador to the UN Economic and Social Council (ECOSOC), and as an Alternate Representative to the UN General Assembly. She has worked to implement the Sustainable Development Goals of Agenda 2030 and "helped build public-private partnerships to solve global challenges at scale."[41] In other words, in line with the WEF's agenda, Cousens has been working to establish stakeholder capitalism worldwide.

• Guido Schmidt-Traub:[42] Schmidt-Traub has served as executive director of the UN Sustainable Development Solutions Network, which operates under the auspices of the UN Secretary-General to support the implementation of the Sustainable Development Goals and the Paris Agreement. Schmidt-Traub also managed the Millennium Development Goals (MDGs) Support Team at the UNDP (2006-2008) and served as policy advisor and then as associate director of the UN Millennium Project in New York, which was tasked with developing an action plan to achieve the MDGs. Schmidt-Traub also advised countries around the world on their implementation of the MDGs. That is, he is a promoter of "sustainable development" and likewise of Agenda 2030.

• Zia Qureshi:[43] Qureshi is an agenda contributor for the WEF. He has served as a director of strategy and operations in the Office of the Senior Vice

41 Ibid.

42 "Guido Schmidt-Traub," World Economic Forum, accessed August 29, 2022, https://www.weforum.org/people/guido-schmidt-traub.

43 "Zia Qureshi - Agenda Contributor," World Economic Forum, accessed August 29, 2022, https://www.weforum.org/agenda/authors/zia-qureshi.

President and Chief Economist of the World Bank. Qureshi has also served as executive secretary of the Joint World Bank-IMF Development Committee, and he is the lead author of the World Bank reports prepared for the G-20 summits in Toronto, Seoul, and Cannes. In addition, he has led the World Bank's work for the G-20 Growth Framework and Mutual Assessment Process, and he has led teams on several flagship publications on global issues, including the joint World Bank-IMF Global Monitoring Report and the World Bank report on Global Economic Prospects. In short, Qureshi is a globalist banker developing World Bank and IMF policies and promoting them within the WEF.

• Jane Nelson:[44] Nelson is an agenda contributor for the WEF. She has worked with UN Global Compact preparing the UN Secretary-General's report for the General Assembly on cooperation between United Nations and the private sector, as such facilitating links between the UN-WEF and their corporate partners to extend stakeholder capitalism. Nelson has also served on the WEF Food Systems Stewardship Board, and she is also the co-author of five of the WEF's global corporate citizenship reports. She has also worked as an adviser to the Clinton Global Initiative. Nelson is thus a key player in advancing the WEF globalism.

• Mark Suzman:[45] Suzman is a WEF agenda

---

44 "Jane Nelson - Agenda Contributor," World Economic Forum, accessed August 29, 2022, https://www.weforum.org/agenda/authors/jane-nelson-ceda7004-b979-4522-9746-b57d24ea9277.

45 "Mark Suzman - Agenda Contributor," World Economic Forum, accessed August 29, 2022, https://www.weforum.org/agenda/authors/mark-suzman-b9d95f6f-1f0f-4eaf-8669-bf9f39d49c78.

contributor and the CEO of the Bill & Melinda Gates Foundation. He has served as the policy director of the Office of the Administrator at the UN Development Program (UNDP) and as a senior adviser on Policy and Strategic Communications for the Office of the UN Secretary-General, as a director of Global Development Policy, Advocacy and Special Initiatives, and as chief strategy officer and president of Global Policy & Advocacy.

It is also worth noting here that like Suzman, Trevor Mundel, another WEF contributor, is also a Rhodes Scholar. He has worked for the Gates Foundation. WEF member Marc Tessier-Lavigne, who is also a Rhodes Scholar, has worked as the president of The Rockefeller University.[46]

Noteworthy WEF associates who were not Rhodes Scholars but who have affiliations with other Round Table NGOs include Ashok Khosla,[47] Alan AtKisson,[48] and Kate Raworth.[49] All three are Club of Rome members, have worked in various roles at the UN, and are prominent environmentalists. Khosla was the president of the Club of Rome and an adviser and consultant for the World Bank. AtKisson was voted into the international Sustainability Hall of Fame in 2013. And Raworth co-authored the Human Development Report for the UNDP. Other WEF

---

46 Individual pages for these WEF members can be found by going to https://www.weforum.org and searching for each name.

47 "Ashok Khosla," World Economic Forum, accessed August 17, 2022, https://www.weforum.org/people/ashok-khosla.

48 "Alan AtKisson," World Economic Forum, accessed August 17, 2022, https://www.weforum.org/people/alan-atkisson.

49 "Kate Raworth," World Economic Forum, accessed August 17, 2022, https://www.weforum.org/people/kate-raworth.

associates who are also Club of Rome members include Chandran Nair[50] and Tasneem A. Siddiqui.[51]

What do these and other overlapping memberships tell us? First, they expose the incestuous nature of these globalist organizations. But moreover, they illustrate that these Round Table groups and international governance bodies are kindred organizations who share personnel and philosophical outlooks. They reveal the WEF's deep roots in these older Round Table groups and suggest that the WEF is buttressed by them. They demonstrate that the Great Reset project is not an orphan but rather grew out of these older Round Table organizations and has their implicit endorsement—plus the backing of the UN, the World Bank, and the IMF, etc. Finally, these philosophical and organizational connections make clear that the Great Reset has been in the making for many years, if not decades.

Tracing the Round Table Roots of the RIIA, the CFR, and the WEF

In this section, I show the connection between Milner's Round Table Groups and subsequent NGOs—the earliest precursors of the WEF, namely, the RIIA and the CFR. I also show the overlapping memberships among these NGOs and international governance bodies. Here we see the roots of Klaus Schwab's governmental multi-stakeholderism, or the association of statespersons, corporate heads, and leaders in international governance bodies and

---

50 "Chandran Nair," World Economic Forum, accessed August 17, 2022, https://www.weforum.org/people/chandran-nair.

51 "Tasneem A. Siddiqui," World Economic Forum, accessed August 17, 2022, https://www.weforum.org/people/tasneem-a-siddiqui.

their assertion of global governance. All these NGO Round Table-based "ginger groups,"[52] as Quigley called them, espouse a global governance model wherein various stakeholders set policies and prescriptions meant to be enacted by states in conjunction with these architects of global governance. Nowhere do we see an electorate represented as such. What Christina Garsten and Adrienne Sörbom write about the WEF is applicable to this entire network: "representation is fundamentally wanting, and there is no mechanism for representation."[53] Rather, these connected coteries mean to set governance policies, beyond the reach of democratic processes.

Branching out from the Rhodes Society, Milner's Round Table Groups established a generic NGO model that would serve as the structural and ideological basis for the RIIA, the CFR, the Bilderberg Group, the Club of Rome, the Trilateral Commission, and the WEF. The RIIA and the CFR are direct heirs to Milner's Round Tables. In *Tragedy and Hope*, Quigley writes:

> In 1919 they [Milner's Roundtable Groups] founded the Royal Institute of International Affairs (Chatham House)...Similar Institutes of International Affairs were established in the chief British dominions and in the United States (where it is known as the Council on Foreign Relations).[54]

The RIIA was set up in 1920 by Lionel Curtis,

---

52 Quigley, *Tragedy and Hope*, page 950.

53 Garsten and Sörbom, "Discretionary Governance," page 548.

54 Quigley, *Tragedy and Hope*, page 132.

who was a leader of Milner's Round Table Groups. The RIIA website notes:

> On the sidelines of the Paris Peace Conference, the British diplomat Lionel Curtis advocate[d] the creation of an institute for the study of international affairs. His vision is to foster mutual understanding between nations and for the institute to propose solutions to the biggest challenges facing the world.[55]

Quigley elaborates:

> At the end of the war of 1914, it became clear that the organization of this [Round Table] system had to be greatly extended. Once again the task was entrusted to Lionel Curtis who established, in England and each dominion, a front organization to the existing local Round Table Group. This front organization, called the Royal Institute of International Affairs [or the Chatham House], had as its nucleus in each area the existing submerged Round Table Group. In New York it was known as the Council on Foreign Relations, and was a front for J. P. Morgan and Company in association with the very small American Round Table Group.[56]

Both the RIIA and the CFR—the latter of which was set up in 1921 as the American counterpart to the former[57]—were founded by participants in the post-

---

55 "Our History," Chatham House – International Affairs Think Tank, March 28, 2022, https://www.chathamhouse.org/about-us/our-history.

56 Quigley, *Tragedy and Hope*, pages 951-952.

57 Priscilla Roberts, "Chatham House, the Council on Foreign Rela-

WWI Versailles Peace Conference, where the League of Nations was also hatched.[58] In fact, the RIIA and the CFR were formed as private NGO counterparts to the global governance arm of the League of Nations. That is, the Versailles Peace Conference germinated new globalist Round Table-based NGOs, whose globalism, it was thought, was justified by the war, and who used the war as a pretext for their globalist ambitions.

Not only were the RIIA, the CFR, and the League of Nations born out of the Paris Peace Conference and Milner's Round Table movement but also they have been financed by Rockefeller philanthropies, including funds from the Rockefeller Foundation.[59]

On top of bankrolling the League of Nations, the Rockefeller dynasty has consistently played a dominant role in CFR policymaking. In 1930, John D. Rockefeller III became a CFR member.[60] From 1949-1985, David Rockefeller served as chairman of the

---

tions, and China policy during the Korean war, 1950–1953," *Journal of Transatlantic Studies* 18, 36–58 (2020), https://doi.org/10.1057/s42738-019-00039-5.

58 "CFR at 100: Reaching out to New Communities," Council on Foreign Relations, accessed August 19, 2022, https://www.cfr.org/celebrating-a-century/reaching-out/.

59 "Royal Institute of International Affairs 2022," The Rockefeller Foundation, August 9, 2022, https://www.rockefellerfoundation.org/grant/royal-institute-of-international-affairs-2022/; "Council on Foreign Relations," The Rockefeller Foundation, August 19, 2022, https://www.rockefellerfoundation.org/grantee/council-on-foreign-relations-2/; Martin Morse Wooster, "John Rockefeller Jr.," *Philanthropy Roundtable*, January 28, 2022, https://www.philanthropyroundtable.org/resource/john-rockefeller-jr/.

60 "CFR at 100: A Changing Membership," Council on Foreign Relations, accessed August 20, 2022, https://www.cfr.org/celebrating-a-century/changing-membership/.

board of the CFR.[61] Today, John D. ("Jay") Rockefeller IV is a distinguished fellow of the CFR[62]. Other Rockefellers who are currently CFR members include David Rockefeller, Jr., Sharon P. Rockefeller,
Steven C. Rockefeller, Susan Cohn Rockefeller, and
Valerie Rockefeller.[63]

The Rockefeller Foundation collaborates with
and funds the WEF.[64] Rockefeller philanthropy,
however, is not the only thread connecting the CFR,
the League of Nations, and the WEF. WEF members
and contributors are (or were) also members of the
CFR, several of whom were Rhodes Scholars as well.
Some WEF-CFR members also hold memberships
in other Round Table NGOs, such as the Trilateral
Commission and the Bilderberg Group. Noteworthy are Paula J. Dobriansky and Adam Posen, who
are members of the Trilateral Commission; Thomas
Donilon, who is a member of the Trilateral Commis-

61 "Historical Roster of Directors and Officers," Council on Foreign Relations, accessed August 20, 2022, https://www.cfr.org/historical-roster-direc-
tors-and-officers.

62 "John D. Rockefeller IV," Council on Foreign Relations, accessed
August 20, 2022, https://www.cfr.org/expert/john-d-rockefeller-iv.

63 "Membership Roster," Council on Foreign Relations, accessed
August 20, 2022, https://www.cfr.org/membership/roster.

64 Govind Shivkumar, Mariana Mazzucato, Rajiv Shah, Sara Farley,
Sara Scherr, and Naveen Rao, "Rockefeller Foundation," World Economic Forum, accessed August 19, 2022, https://www.weforum.org/
organizations/the-rockefeller-foundation; "World Economic Forum
2021," The Rockefeller Foundation, August 9, 2022, https://www.
rockefellerfoundation.org/grant/world-economic-forum-2021-4/;
"Claudia Juech, the Rockefeller Foundation - Economic Opportunities in the 21st Century," Global Strategic Foresight Community,
accessed August 19, 2022, https://reports.weforum.org/global-stra-
tegic-foresight/claudia-juech-the-rockefeller-foundation-econom-
ic-opportunities-in-the-21st-century/.

sion and a "Distinguished Fellow" of the CFR; and David M. Rubenstein, who is a member of the Bilderberg Group,[65] the chairman of the board of the CFR,[66] and a co-founder and co-chairman of the Carlyle Group.[67] (See Table 2.1.)

At the same time, other WEF-CFR members have also worked or collaborated with global governance institutions, such as the UN and the World Bank. These include Jack Leslie, who has served as USA Chairman of United Nations High Commissioner for Refugees; Stephen Rhinesmith, a consultant for the World Bank, who also "conducted a session on global leadership for the Young Global Leaders at the World Economic Forum in Davos"; and C. Fred Bergsten, a senior fellow of the CFR and member of the Executive Committee of the Trilateral Commission, who has also served on the Bretton Woods Commission, which set up the World Bank and the IMF.[68] Similarly, several WEF members and contributors are (or were) also members of the RIIA. (See Table 2.1.)

The Bilderberg Group, the Club of Rome, and the Trilateral Commission

The Bilderberg Group was established in 1954

---

65 "Participants 2017," Bilderberg Meetings, accessed August 20, 2022, https://www.bilderbergmeetings.org/meetings/meeting-2017/participants-2017.

66 "Annual Report," Council on Foreign Relations, accessed August 20, 2022, https://www.cfr.org/annual-report-2021.

67 "The Carlyle Group," David M. Rubenstein, The Carlyle Group, accessed August 23, 2022, https://www.davidrubenstein.com/the-carlyle-group.html.

68 Individual pages for these WEF members can be found by going to https://www.weforum.org and searching for each name.

as a next-generation Round Table NGO.[69] The founder[70] and chairman[71] of the Bilderberg Group was Prince Bernhard of the Netherlands, who had been a Nazi Storm Trooper[72] and was an "honorary sponsor" of the third annual WEF meeting in 1973.[73] The group was founded after the establishment of the World Bank, the IMF, and the UN—which had its headquarters built on land donated by Rockefeller philanthropy. The prince later became the first president of the World Wildlife Fund.

David Rockefeller was a founding member of the Bilderberg Group.[74] He was simultaneously the chairman of the board of the CFR.[75] Another founder of the Bilderberg Group, which follows the Chatham House Rule of Secrecy,[76] was its Honorary Secretary

69 "Brief History," Bilderberg Group, accessed August 20, 2022, https://bilderbergmeetings.org/background/brief-history.

70 David Rockefeller, *Memoirs*, New York, NY: Random House Trade Paperbacks, 2003, page 410.

71 "Former Steering Committee Members," Bilderberg Group, accessed August 20, 2022, https://bilderbergmeetings.org/background/steering-committee/former-steering-committee-members.

72 "Obituary: Prince Bernhard," *The Guardian*, December 3, 2004, https://www.theguardian.com/news/2004/dec/03/guardianobituaries.monarchy.

73 "The Davos Manifesto – 1973," World Economic Forum, accessed August 20, 2022, https://widgets.weforum.org/history/1973.html.

74 Rockefeller, *Memoirs*, pages 410-411.

75 "Historical Roster of Directors and Officers," Council on Foreign Relations, accessed August 20, 2022, https://www.cfr.org/historical-roster-directors-and-officers.

76 "About Bilderberg Meetings," Bilderberg Meetings, accessed August 20, 2022, https://bilderbergmeetings.org/.

General,[77] Joseph Retinger,[78] who collaborated with the Polish Socialist Party.[79]

This mixture of corporatists, fascists, and socialists involved in the founding of the Bilderberg Group corroborates Quigley's claim that the Round Table Groups have allied themselves with autocratic regimes of all kinds. It also helps to explain the corporate-socialist-fascist economics of the Great Reset. In *Tragedy and Hope*, Quigley states:

> There does exist, and has existed for a generation, an international Anglophile network which operates, to some extent, in the way the radical Right believes the Communists act. In fact, this network, which we may identify as the Round Table Groups, has no aversion to cooperating with the Communists, or any other groups, and frequently does so. I know of the operations of this network because I have studied it for twenty years and was permitted for two years, in the early 1960's, to examine its papers and secret records. I have no aversion to it or to most of its aims and have, for much of my life, been close to it and to many of its instruments.[80]

The Bilderberg Group's blend of corporatists and so-

---

77 "Former Steering Committee Members," Bilderberg Group.

78 Andrzej Pieczewski (2010) "Joseph Retinger's conception of and contribution to the early process of European integration," *European Review of History: Revue européenne d'histoire*, 17:4, 581-604, DOI: 10.1080/13507486.2010.495766.

79 M. B. Biskupski, "Spy, Patriot or Internationalist? The Early Career of Jozef Retinger, Polish Patriarch of European Union," *The Polish Review* 43, no. 1 (1998): 23–67, http://www.jstor.org/stable/25779031.

80 Quigley, *Tragedy and Hope*, page 950.

cialists has been recapitulated by the RIIA:

> During the 1970s Chatham House begins An-
> glo-Soviet roundtable meetings, an early ini-
> tiative in track-two diplomacy. The aim (con-
> troversial for some) is to develop structures for
> East-West cooperation by cultivating relations
> with Soviet reformers.[81]

This conjunction of corporatists, fascists, and socialists has also been mirrored by the WEF, which has collaborated with Western capitalists along with oligarchs from the Communist regimes of China and the former USSR. Its connections with Nazism—vis-à-vis Klaus Schwab's father[82] and Prince Bernhard—completes the triangle.

Schwab studied at Harvard's International Seminar,[83] the executive director of which was Rockefeller protégé Henry Kissinger,[84] who is a member of the Bilderberg steering committee,[85] a member of

81   "Our History," Chatham House – International Affairs Think Tank.

82   Johnny Vedmore, "Schwab Family Values," *Unlimited Hangout*, February 20, 2021, https://unlimitedhangout.com/2021/02/investiga-tive-reports/schwab-family-values/.

83   Johnny Vedmore, "Dr. Klaus Schwab or: How the CFR Taught Me to Stop Worrying and Love the Bomb," *Unlimited Hangout*, March 10, 2022, https://unlimitedhangout.com/2022/03/investiga-tive-reports/dr-klaus-schwab-or-how-the-cfr-taught-me-to-stop-worrying-and-love-the-bomb/.

84   "The Nobel Peace Prize 1973," NobelPrize.org, accessed August 20, 2022, https://www.nobelprize.org/prizes/peace/1973/kissinger/biographical/.

85   "Steering Committee," Bilderberg Group, accessed August 20, 2022, https://bilderbergmeetings.org/background/steering-commit-tee/steering-committee.

the CFR Board of Directors,[86] a founding member of the Trilateral Commission,[87] and a member of the WEF.[88] The origin of the WEF is entangled with eminent Bilderbergers, as Kissinger's influence on Schwab, and Prince Bernhard's honorary sponsorship of the third annual WEF meeting, make clear.

Several WEF members and contributors are (or were) also members of the Bilderberg Group, a few of whom have been identified in the previous sections as Rhodes Scholars. Others are CFR members and/or Trilateral Commission members as well. In addition to Kissinger, three WEF members have also served on the Bilderberg Steering Committee: Eric Schmidt, Peter Thiel, and Alex Karp. Other WEF-Bilderbergers include Etienne Davignon, Mark Tucker, Reid Hoffman, Wilbur Ross, and Niall Ferguson, the last of whom won the CFR's Arthur Ross Prize. Bilderberger Peter Sutherland, who has served on the Foundation Board of the WEF, has also served as the chairman of the Trilateral Commission, a special representative of the Secretary-General of the UN, and "Director-General, GATT, WTO."[89]

---

86 "Henry A. Kissinger Chair for U.S. Foreign Policy," Council on Foreign Relations, accessed August 20, 2022, https://www.cfr.org/henry-kissinger-chair-us-foreign-policy.

87 Henry A Kissinger, "Henry Kissinger: My Friend David Rockefeller, a Man Who Served the World," *The Washington Post*, March 30, 2017, https://www.washingtonpost.com/opinions/henry-kissinger-my-friend-david-rockefeller-a-man-who-served-the-world/2017/03/30/bd4789b0-13f6-11e7-ada0-1489b735b3a3_story.html.

88 "Henry A. Kissinger," World Economic Forum, accessed August 20, 2022, https://www.weforum.org/people/henry-a-kissinger/.

89 Individual pages for these WEF members and contributors can be found by going to https://www.weforum.org and searching for

At the 1973 WEF annual meeting, where Bilderberger Prince Bernhard was an honorary sponsor, Aurelio Peccei gave a speech on the Club of Rome's 1972 Limits to Growth (discussed in the next chapter). One of its authors was Dennis Meadows, who is also a member of the WEF. In fact, Peccei co-founded the Club of Rome in 1968 with Alexander King.[90] In 1974, Pierre Trudeau, Justin Trudeau's father, attended the Club of Rome meeting in Salzburg.

The WEF was founded in 1971, three years after the establishment of the Club of Rome. In 1972, the UN set up its Environmental Program (UNEP), under the leadership of Maurice Strong, who was also its first executive director.[91] Strong was a WEF Foundation Board member and an advisor to the president of the World Bank.[92] He was not a member of the Club of Rome. But he collaborated on global environmentalist projects with Soviet leader Mikhail Gorbachev, who was a Club of Rome member.[93] In fact, it was Bilderberger Prince Bernhard's daughter, Bilderberger Queen Beatrix of the Netherlands, who brought Strong and Gorbachev together to work on

---

each name.

90 "Our History," Chatham House – International Affairs Think Tank.

91 "UNEP@50: Our Leaders Through the Years," UNEP, accessed August 20, 2022, https://www.unep.org/unep-50-leaders-through-years/maurice-strong.

92 Written by Klaus Schwab, Founder and Executive Chairman, "Maurice Strong: An Appreciation," World Economic Forum, accessed August 20, 2022, https://web.archive.org/web/20201211002249/https:/www.weforum.org/agenda/2015/11/maurice-strong-an-appreciation/.

93 "Gorbachev, Mikhail," Club of Rome, accessed August 20, 2022, https://www.clubofrome.org/member/gorbachev-mikhail/.

environmentalist projects. One of these projects was the Earth Charter.[94] Natalie Grant (Wraga), who was a U.S. State Department Sovietologist and expert in Soviet disinformation,[95] wrote that Strong's Earth Council collaborated with the Soviet-sponsored communist front group called Green Cross International, headed by Gorbachev.[96] The collaboration led to the Earth Charter, which would "provide a 'new mode of life' based upon radical 'principles for the whole of humanity.'"[97] Grant claimed that Green Cross was utterly infiltrated by communists. The entire environmental movement, Grant wrote, "has all the traits of a Soviet disinformation operation."[98]

Altogether, these chronological and organizational overlaps suggest that the origins of the Great Reset's SDG agenda can be traced to coordinated efforts between the WEF, the Club of Rome, and the UNEP. At the same time, collaborations between Gorbachev, the Club of Rome, Queen Beatrix, and Maurice Strong validate Quigley's statement: "This network, which we may identify as the Round Table Groups, has no aversion to cooperating with the Communists, or any other groups, and frequently does so."

Coordinated environmentalist efforts between

---

94 Natalie Grant, "Green Cross: Gorbachev and Global Enviro-Communism," *The Resister* 4, no. 3 (1998): 58–62.

95 Adam Bernstein, "Natalie Grant Wraga Dies at 101," *The Washington Post*, November 15, 2002, https://www.washingtonpost.com/archive/local/2002/11/15/natalie-grant-wraga-dies-at-101/8b23d8ce-cb4a-4c6e-9778-937baa780d62/.

96 Grant, "Green Cross: Gorbachev and Global Enviro-Communism," page 59.

97 Ibid., page 60.

98 Ibid., page 62.

158 The Great Reset and the Struggle for Liberty

the WEF, the Club of Rome, and the UN are further evidenced by the fact that several WEF members and contributors are (or were) also members of the Club of Rome and/or the UN. (See Table 2.1.) Many of these work on SDGs. WEF members who hold high rank at the Club of Rome include Sandrine Dixson-Declève, who has served as the co-president of the Club of Rome, and Chandran Nair, who has served on the executive committee of the Club of Rome.[99]

On top of these overlapping memberships, the Club of Rome has directly contributed to the publishing of important WEF white papers. For instance, the WEF's Global Risks Report 2020 gives "[t]hanks... to members of the Club of Rome (George Biesmans, Sandrine Dixson-Declève, Gail Whiteman) for their contributions [to the Report]."[100] In another WEF white paper entitled "Paving the Way: EU Policy Action for Automotive Circularity," which was published "[i]n Collaboration with SYSTEMIQ," the WEF endorses the Circular Cars Initiative[101]—as part of the circular economy that it peddles—which likewise partners with SYSTEMIQ, which partners with the Club of Rome.

It is also important to note the WEF's connections to the Trilateral Commission. Although it was

---

99 Individual pages for these WEF members can be found by going to https://www.weforum.org and searching for each name.

100 "Acknowledgements," Global Risks Report 2020, accessed August 21, 2022, https://reports.weforum.org/global-risks-report-2020/acknowledgements/.

101 "Paving the Way: Eu Policy Action for Automotive Circularity," accessed August 21, 2022, https://www3.weforum.org/docs/WEF_Circular_Cars_Initiative_Paving_the_Way_2021.pdf.

founded by David Rockefeller and Zbigniew Brzezinski two years after the formation of the WEF,[102] it is yet another Round Table NGO with similar objectives. Many members of the Trilateral Commission are (or were) also members of the WEF, including several who have already been identified above as Rhodes Scholars and/or members of the CFR and/or the Bilderberg Group.

We learn from this exposé that a vast network of globalist organizations stemming from the Round Table movement has drafted a global corporate and political talent pool to provide the ideological and organizational conditions for establishing the Great Reset. The NGO structure of the WEF derives from earlier Round Table groups and retains their elitist character. This elitism remains intact despite its new "diversity," and stems directly from the Rhodes Trust and its Rhodes Scholarship. It holds that the elite should direct global affairs and control the global economy.

We should note, however, especially in the case of these Round Table-based NGOs, that nothing they advocate is binding on any governments, unless their prescriptions are adopted by nation states and/or regional governance bodies. But the WEF has managed to bypass legislation through its enrollment of corporate partners, which have adopted stakeholder capitalism and integrated it into their operations. Moreover, like the earlier Round Table NGOs, and to a greater extent, the WEF has infiltrated governments. The Great Reset is ushered in under various guises, such as "Build Back Better" in the U.S., and in

---

102 "About Us." The Trilateral Commission, June 5, 2022, https://www.trilateral.org/about/.

policies the world over.

I turn next to the enviro-neo-Malthusian roots of the Great Reset, which all these Round Table groups share, and which underwrites their individual and collective vision and actions.

Table 2.1
WEF Member/Rhodes/Round Table/Other Cross Affiliations

WEF member (*=YGL) (**Board member)	Rhodes Scholar	RIAA	CFR	Bilderberg	Club of Rome	UN	WHO	IMF	World Bank	Gates Fndn	Carlyle Group	OECD	Rockefeller Fndn
Tony Abrahams	■												
Alan AtKisson					■								
Katinka Barysch*		■											
C. Fred Bergsten			■					■	■				
George Biesmans					■								
François Bonnici	■						■						
Luciana Borio			■										
Joy Buolamwini	■						■						
Sylvia Mathews Burwell	■									■			
Rachel Carrell	■												
Clayton Christensen	■												
Amrita Cheema	■												
Bill Clinton	■			■									
Jared Cohen	■		■										
Steven Crown	■												
Elizabeth Cousens	■					■							
Etienne Davignon			■										
Sandrine Dixson-Declève					■								
Paula J. Dobriansky			■										
Thomas Donilon			■										
Dan Esty	■												
Nial Ferguson				■									

WEF member (*YGL) (**Board member)	Rhodes Scholar	RIAA	CFR	Bilder-berg	Club of Rome	UN	WHO	IMF	World Bank	Gates Fndn	Carlyle Group	OECD	Rocke-feller Fndn
Brad Henderson*	■												
Peter Blair Henry	■												
Cameron Hepburn	■												
Reid Hoffman				■									
Brett House	■					■		■	■				
Miles Jackson													
Malavika Jayaram		■										■	
Alex Karp				■									
Marc Kielburger	■					■							
Nikolas Kirby	■												
Henry Kissinger			■	■									
Nicholas D. Kristof	■												
Ashok Khosla					■				■				
Marc Tessier-Lavigne	■					■							
Bernice Lee		■				■							■
Jack Leslie			■			■							
Heather Long	■												
Kopano Matlwa Mabaso	■												
Trudi Makhaya	■												
Robert Malley	■												
John H. McCall MacBain	■												
Dennis Meadows					■								
Trevor Mundel	■									■			

WEF member (*=YGL) (**Board member)	Rhodes Scholar	RIAA	CFR	Bilder-berg	Club of Rome	UN	WHO	IMF	World Bank	Gates Fndn	Carlyle Group	OECD	Rocke-feller Fndn
Robert Reich	■												
Stephen Rhinesmith			■						■				
Mariame McIntosh Robinson	■												
Wilbur Ross				■									
David M. Rubenstein			■								■		
Pardis Sabeti	■												
Prashant Sarin	■												
Eric Schmidt				■									
Guido Schmidt-Traub	■					■							
Tasneem A. Siddiqui					■								
Dhananjayan Sriskandarajah	■												
Walter Stahel					■								
Richard Stengel	■												
Maurice Strong**						■			■				
Peter Sutherland**			■			■							
Mark Suzman	■									■			
Strobe Talbott	■		■										
Peter Thiel				■									
Mark Tucker				■									
Malcolm Turnbull	■												
David Alexander Walcott*	■					■		■					
Leana Wen*							■						

CHAPTER NINE

The Enviro-Neo-Malthusian Roots of the Great Reset

A THOROUGH UNDERSTANDING of the Great Reset would be incomplete without a treatment of its environmentalist and neo-Malthusian roots. The Great Reset project emerged from a long line of enviro-neo-Malthusian catastrophism deriving from earlier Round Table NGOs and the United Nations (UN). The Great Reset is utterly premised on this catastrophism. There would be no need for establishing stakeholder capitalism, for promoting and mandating the ESG Index, or for the Great Reset's institutionalization of either, if not for the supposed looming environmental and population crises.

This chapter traces the narrative and organizational history that ultimately led to the Great Reset's launch. In the course of this exploration, we will see a shift in approaches—from blatant Malthusianism and neo-Malthusian interventionism to rhetoric subtly addressing the environment and population in terms of "human rights" and "gender equality"

163

and finally to the rhetoric of "sustainable develop-ment." Throughout these rhetorical and method-ological stages, an enviro-neo-Malthusian substra-tum subsists.

Malthusianism and neo-Malthusianism

In his *Essay on Population*, first published in 1798,[1] Thomas Malthus argued that human popula-tion, when left unchecked, tends to grow exponen-tially (2, 4, 16...), while the resources that humans depend on for sustenance tend to grow arithmetical-ly (2, 3, 4...). Thus, he argued, without empirical ev-idence or theoretical justification, that human popu-lation inevitably bumps up against natural limits and that only by curbing its population can humankind reduce misery. As a Christian conservative, Malthus recommended that the poor practice sexual restraint and abstinence. An English cleric, Malthus appar-ently missed the Bible verse in which God directed human beings to "be fruitful and multiply" (Genesis 1:28).

The difference between Malthusianism and neo-Malthusian is that the latter adopts the Malthu-sian population principle but recommends active measures to address the tendency, especially con-traception but also sterilization and other methods. With neo-Malthusianism, the theory crosses from the political Right to Left and is wedded to progres-sive ideology and policy. It was adopted by such pro-gressives as Margaret Sanger, for example.

The history of the transmutation from Malthu-sianism to neo-Malthusianism began with the ear-

---

1 Thomas Robert Malthus, *An Essay on the Principle of Population*, London: J. Johnson, 1798.

liest known pro-birth-control pamphlet in English. Entitled *Every Woman's Book, Or, What is Love?*, it was written and published in 1826 by the artisanal radical freethinker, Richard Carlile. This provocative little book advocated free love accompanied by birth control methods to prevent "the undesired and often mischievous and unhappy consequences of female impregnation."[2]

Dr. Charles Knowlton soon followed Carlile and published *Fruits of Philosophy, or the Private Companion of Young Married People*, in 1832, in Massachusetts.[3] The pamphlet was a pro-birth-control manual detailing the physiology of human sexuality and how couples could limit the size of their families. In the "Philosophical Proem" introducing the text, Knowlton argued that sex was a physiological and moral necessity; he reasoned from Benthamite utilitarian principles that any moderate expression of sexual passion that did not result in misery added a net pleasure to the world and thus was to be encouraged. Furthermore, the sexual instinct would not be curbed in the mass of humanity, according to Malthus's recommended abstention. Only practical measures to limit procreation—new methods of contraception—could solve the predicament resulting from the sexual instinct on the one hand and the

---

2 Richard Carlile, *Every Woman's Book, Or, What Is Love?: Containing Most Important Instructions for the Prudent Regulation of the Principle of Love, and the Number of a Family*, London: Printed and Published by R. Carlile, London: R. Carlile, 1828, page iii.

3 Charles Knowlton, Charles Bradlaugh, and Annie Besant, *Fruits of Philosophy: An Essay on the Population Question*, Rotterdam: v.d. Hoeven & Buys, 1877.

tendency of overpopulation on the other.[4] (Carlile and Knowlton advocated voluntary methods of birth control. They were much more "libertarian" than their neo-Malthusian successors.)

Thus, progressive neo-Malthusianism was born and would be developed throughout the remainder of the nineteenth century and through the twentieth century. But, when stemming from an elite, it would become decidedly interventionist and coercive, involving the imposition of reproductive restraints on the masses.

Neo-Malthusians who recommend control over the reproduction of others are very unpopular among the majority, no doubt because these misanthropes seem to suggest that the majority shouldn't exist in the first place. Yet, we rarely if ever learn of neo-Malthusians volunteering to commit suicide to reduce the supposed overpopulation problem. Likewise, we are loath to think that such advocates can be found among world leaders, whether elected or not. Even though Malthus was wrong in his assertion that human population naturally outstrips the resources for human sustenance—he gave no consideration to technological innovations, for one, and history has proven him wrong—Malthusian population "ethics" have persisted, and the population principle has been adopted as an unexamined premise in the machinations of numerous thinkers.

A particularly egregious example of neo-Malthusianism, written in 1971, the year that the World Economic Forum was founded, can be found in the *Proceedings of the Eighth Annual Symposium of the Eugenics Society*, which included a series of ar-

---

4 Ibid., pages 9-11.

ticles entitled *Population and Pollution.* In the introductory essay, entitled "Ethics and the Population Increase," Eliot Slater remarked regarding the near extinction of blue whales:

> The cost of this cosmic crime is beyond calculation. We are offered, in the economics of the slaughterhouse, an equivalence between populations of 60 thousand whales and 3 million human beings. But we must be more realistic than that. *Whales are valuable, and human beings are not*...It would have been worth while saving those 60 thousand whales at almost any cost in human lives. At 3 million lives it would have been an excellent bargain, and better still at 30 million. It [sic] we could have kept the whales and pruned the human population by 300 million, we should have made a substantial contribution to human welfare (emphasis mine).[5]

Slater also stated blankly: "Because there are too many of us, a man does his neighbour more harm than good, just by staying alive."[6] Slater blamed Christianity for the plague of over-population, because the Christian religion "banned the human checks of abortion and infanticide."[7] He argues further: "As human birth takes on a negative value for society, human death takes on a positive one. In time we shall probably have to allow easy ways out [eu-

---

5 Eliot Slater, "General Introduction: Ethics and the Population Increase," *Population and Pollution: Proceedings of the Eighth Annual Symposium of the Eugenics Society*, London, 1971, Eds. Peter R. Cox and John Peel, London: Academic Press, 1972, page 2.

6 Ibid., page 3.

7 Ibid., page 4.

thanasia] for those who badly need them."[8] Slater's views can righty be characterized as genocidal.

Paul Ehrlich is best known for his catastrophist 1968 environmental treatise entitled *The Population Bomb*. In this bomb-throwing book, Ehrlich wrongly predicted global catastrophes—famine, pestilence, and plague—before the dawn of the twenty-first century. In exploring possible bulwarks against catastrophe owing to overpopulation, Ehrlich proposed spiking drinking water and food supplies with sterilizing agents:

> Many of my colleagues feel that some sort of compulsory birth regulation would be necessary to achieve such control [of population growth]. One plan often mentioned involves the addition of temporary sterilants to water supplies or staple foods. Doses of the antidote would be carefully rationed by the government to produce the desired population size.[9]

Ehrlich also argued: "Abortion is a highly effective weapon in the armory of population control."[10] The goal of population control, he maintained, is to stabilize the human population at a planetary optimum: "Obviously we need a stable world population with its size rationally controlled by society."[11]

In 1977, Ehrlich touted the same population control methods in *Ecoscience: Population, Resources,*

---

8 Ibid.

9 Paul R. Ehrlich, *The Population Bomb*, Binghamton, NY: Ballantine, 1968, page 121.

10 Ibid., page 79.

11 Ibid., page 149.

Environment, which he co-authored with Anne Holdren, and Obama's White House science czar, John P. Holdren. Here, the authors advocated poisoning drinking water and food supplies with sterilizing additives, in combination with "compulsory abortion" laws.[12] They also fantasized about a new birth control technology:

> The development of a long-term sterilizing capsule that could be implanted under the skin and removed when pregnancy is desired opens additional possibilities for coercive fertility control. The capsule could be implanted at puberty and might be removable, with official permission, for a limited number of births.[13]

The authors stressed the need for a world government managed by the United Nations Environment Programme (UNEP) and United Nations (UN) "population agencies" to enforce population control laws:

> Perhaps those agencies [the United Nations Conference on Trade and Development and a United Nations Conference on Science and Technology], combined with UNEP and the United Nations population agencies, might eventually be developed into a Planetary Regime—sort of an international superagency for population, resources, and environment. Such a comprehensive Planetary Regime could con-

---

12 Paul R. Ehrlich, Anne H. Ehrlich, and John P. Holdren, *Ecoscience: Population, Resources, Environment*, San Francisco: W. H. Freeman and Co., 1977, pages 786-788.

13 Ibid., page 787.

trol the development, administration, conservation, and distribution of all natural resources, renewable or nonrenewable."[14]

Ehrlich is a supporter of the neo-Malthusian-eugenicist World Wildlife Fund (WWF) and the WEF, and the support is mutual.

Misanthropy and control freakishness underlie all enviro-neo-Malthusian discourse, although it is usually more muted in rhetoric and tone. Misanthropy is typically expressed in terms that sound humanitarian on their face. Population must be controlled for human well-being, human rights, and for preserving the environment on which humans depend. (Controlling one's reproduction is considered a "human right," while reproduction itself is not.) In the process, the environment becomes elevated to a status on par with that of human beings and is considered an entity that deserves rights of its own. This becomes evident by the time we reach Agenda 21, and its descendent, Agenda 2030. Thus, in Agenda 21, we find such tortured statements as the following:

> The growth of world population and production combined with unsustainable consumption patterns places increasingly severe stress on the life-supporting capacities of our planet. These interactive processes affect the use of land, water, air, energy and other resources. Rapidly growing cities, unless well-managed, face major environmental problems...The human dimensions are key elements to consider in this intricate set of relationships and they

---

14 Ibid., page 943.

should be adequately taken into consideration in comprehensive policies for sustainable development. Such policies should address the linkages of demographic trends and factors, resource use, appropriate technology dissemination, and development. Population policy should also recognize the role played by human beings in environmental and development concerns.[15]

The Great Reset agenda is rooted in such enviro-neo-Malthusian population "ethics." The enviro-neo-Malthusianism of the WEF stems from a long line of prescriptions and policies from such globalist organizations as the League of Nations, the UN, the Club of Rome, and numerous non-profit corporations and NGOs. As the principal orchestrator of the Great Reset, the WEF has adopted the sustainable development goals (SDGs) of the UN's Agenda 2030. Agenda 2030 "affirms" the Programme of Action of the UN's 1994 International Conference on Population and Development, which evolved from four prior UN conferences on world population and the League of Nations' seminal World Population Conference.

The UN's melding of environmental and population policy, discussed below, was paralleled by the Club of Rome, whose members penned its notorious neo-Malthusian treatise of environmental catastrophism, *The Limits to Growth: A Report of the Club of Rome's Project on the Predicament of Man-*

---

15 "Agenda 21: Sustainable Development Knowledge Platform," United Nations, 1991, https://sustainabledevelopment.un.org/outcomedocuments/agenda21/, Chapter 5, point 5.3.

kind, in 1972.[16] *Limits to Growth* was published in the same year that the United Nations Environment Programme (UNEP) was established and one year after the WEF was founded. *Limits to Growth* drew on research from several UN branches and studies published by neo-Malthusian-eugenics non-profit corporations and NGOs. Dennis Meadows was a key author of *Limits to Growth* while Maurice Strong played the lead role in establishing UNEP. Both were WEF contributing members, and Maurice Strong was a Foundation Board member of the WEF.

Limits to Growth addressed what its authors deemed the most pressing problems facing humanity: accelerating industrialization, rapid population growth, widespread malnutrition, depletion of non-renewable resources, and a deteriorating environment. We find in this report a core set of concerns that have animated the UN's and the WEF's population and environmental catastrophism. The authors draw three conclusions: 1) the present rate of growth is unsustainable and will lead to a collapse within the next hundred years, 2) a course correction is still possible, 3) the sooner the world's people address these crises, the better their chances of success. The authors identify the usual Malthusian concern—exponential growth. Except now exponential growth applied not only to population but also to food production, industrialization, pollution, and consumption of nonrenewable natural resources. At the core of this exponential growth lay exponential

16   Donella H. Meadows, Dennis L. Meadows, Jorgen Randers, and William W. Behrens III, *The Limits to Growth: A Report of the Club of Rome's Project on the Predicament of Mankind*, New York, NY: Universe Books, 1972.

population growth. *Limits to Growth* recommended a "great transition—the transition from growth to global equilibrium."[17]

As I mentioned in the previous chapter, two years after the WEF was founded, Aurelio Peccei, the Club of Rome co-founder, presented the findings of *Limits to Growth* at the 1973 WEF third annual meeting. The WEF has been arguing for limits to growth consistently ever since.[18]

Then, in 1974, the United States Agency for International Development (USAID) circulated its "National Security Study Memorandum 200 (NSSM 200)," issued by Henry Kissinger, another WEF member. NSSM 200 explored "Research to Improve Fertility Control Technology" and laid out strategies for global population control measures, including sterilization and abortion programs.[19] USAID funds the WHO.[20]

---

17 Ibid., page 24.

18 For recent examples, see: Steve Howard and Usha Rao-Monari, "We Can Decide to Live within the Limits of Our Planet," World Economic Forum, February 2, 2019, https://www.weforum.org/agenda/2019/02/we-can-decide-to-live-within-the-limits-of-our-planet/; Anitra Nelson and Brian Coffey, "Everything You Need to Know about Ecological Economics," World Economic Forum, November 19, 2019, https://www.weforum.org/agenda/2019/11/ecological-economics-sustainability-climate-change-environment; and Alessio Terzi, "Is Infinite Economic Growth Possible on a Finite Planet?," World Economic Forum, November 19, 2021, https://www.weforum.org/agenda/2021/11/green-economy-new-technology-climate-change/.

19 "National Security Study Memorandum NSSM 200 - United States Agency for International Development," U.S. Agency for International Development, December 10, 1974, https://pdf.usaid.gov/pdf_docs/PCAAB500.pdf.

20 Shejal Pulivarti, "Deputy Administrator Coleman's Meeting with World Health Organization Europe Regional Director Dr.

Beginning in 1992 and under the leadership of WEF members, the UN and the Club of Rome jointly launched a new era of environmental neo-Malthusianism. The Club of Rome published its sequel to *Limits of Growth*, entitled *Beyond the Limits: Confronting Global Collapse, Envisioning a Sustainable Future.*[21] This histrionic treatise reiterated and amplified the concerns of its precursor and added climate change to what the Club of Rome called "the global problematique," the interlocking set of dire conditions facing humanity. *Beyond the Limits* argued that economic contraction and decreased population growth were necessary to avert catastrophe. The authors revised the three conclusions of *Limits to Growth*. The new conclusions were: 1) that humans had already surpassed the limits of sustainability and a reduction of material and energy inputs was essential to avoid an "uncontrolled decline in per capita food output, energy use, and industrial production," 2) the decline was not inevitable, but two changes would be necessary—"a comprehensive revision in policies and practices that perpetuate growth in material consumption and in population," and a dramatic increase in efficiency of materials use, and 3) a sustainable society was still possible, but it required "an emphasis on sufficiency, equity,

---

Hans Kluge: Readout," U.S. Agency for International Development, August 2, 2022, https://www.usaid.gov/news-information/press-releases/aug-2-2022-deputy-administrator-coleman-meeting-world-health-organization.

21 Donella H. Meadows, Dennis L. Meadows, and Jorgen Randers, *Beyond the Limits: Confronting Global Collapse, Envisioning a Sustainable Future*, Post Mills, Vermont: Chelsea Green Publishing Company, 1992.

and quality of life rather than quantity of output."²²

Also in 1992, Maurice Strong launched UN Agenda 21. Among other things, Agenda 21 established the UN's Millennium Development Goals (MDGs), which included the "sustainable development" goal (MDG 7), later blown up into Agenda 2030 (discussed in "Translating Agenda 2030").

Beyond the Limits and Agenda 21 mark the Club of Rome and the UN's public adoption of "sustainable development," the term coined in the 1987 "Brundtland Report," or "Our Common Future."²³ Commissioned from the World Commission on Environment and Development by the UN's Maurice Strong, its principal author was Jim MacNeil, who was the Secretary General of the World Commission.²⁴ The phrase "sustainable development" was used 197 times in the seminal 300-page document. Sustainable development was defined as development that "meets the needs of the present without compromising the ability of future generations to meet their own needs."²⁵ To curb population growth, unequivocally figured as the primary obstacle to sustainable development, the report stated: "Developing countries will also have to promote direct measures to reduce fertility, to avoid going radically beyond the productive potential to support their

---

22 Ibid., pages xv-xvi.

23 Gro Harlem Brundtland, Report of the World Commission on Environment and Development: "Our Common Future," New York, NY: United Nations, 1987.

24 As noted in Jim MacNeill, Pieter Winsemius, and Taizo Yakushiji, *Beyond Interdependence*, Trilateral Commission, 1991.

25 Ibid., I.3.27.

populations."[26] The Brundtland Report is thought by at least one author to be "the operational blueprint for implementing sustainable development worldwide." It defines "a process which is supposed to encompass all aspects of human life and all beings existing on planet Earth."[27]

In 1995, at the WEF's "silver anniversary" annual meeting, the forum announced its aim of "ensuring sustainability in an overpopulated world."[28] Thus, the WEF did not differ in principle from its Round Table kin or its UN partner. Population "ethics" has been an underlying value of the WEF for decades. Environmentalist neo-Malthusianism must be understood as integral to the Great Reset agenda.

World Population Conferences

The Malthusian roots of the United Nations' population policies can be traced to the League of Nations and its First World Population Conference, held in 1927. This conference led to the formation of the International Union for the Scientific Study of Population, which helped organize the UN's First World Population conference in 1954. Four more World Population Conferences followed, each roughly a decade apart—in 1965, 1974, 1984, and 1994. The report from of the last of these conferences, the UN International Conference on Population and Devel-

---

26 Ibid., III.4.51.

27 Branko Malić, "Agenda 21: An Introduction," *21st Century Wire*, August 17, 2016, https://21stcenturywire.com/2016/05/08/agenda-21-an-introduction/.

28 "Overcoming Indifference with the 'Davos Secret,'" World Economic Forum, accessed August 25, 2022, https://widgets.weforum.org/history/1995.html.

opment in Cairo,[29] was endorsed in the Agenda 2030 report.

The League of Nations First World Population Conference, held in 1927,[30] was organized with the help of Margaret Sanger, who explicitly advocated for neo-Malthusian and eugenics policies aimed at controlling population growth.[31] According to *The Lancet*, "The conference proper opened with a paper by Prof. RAYMOND PEARL upon the *Biology of Population Growth*" (emphasis in original).[32] Pearl, who was funded by the Rockefeller Foundation,[33] studied under biometrics pioneer, Karl Pearson,[34] a close colleague of Francis Galton, the founding father of eugenics.[35] Although Pearl became critical of eugenics around the time of the World Population

---

29 "Conferences | Population," United Nations, accessed August 25, 2022, https://www.un.org/en/conferences/population.

30 "The World Population Conference, Rome 1954 - Jstor.org," accessed August 25, 2022, https://www.jstor.org/stable/41218450.

31 "Round the World for Birth Control, 1920-1966," The Margaret Sanger Papers Project, accessed August 25, 2022, https://marii.hosting.nyu.edu/sanger/publications/volume_iv/.

32 "The World Population Conference at Geneva: August 31st-Sept. 3rd, 1927," *The Lancet*. Elsevier, September 23, 2003, https://www.sciencedirect.com/science/article/abs/pii/S0140673601312254.

33 Sharon Kingsland, "Raymond Pearl: On the Frontier in the 1920's: Raymond Pearl Memorial Lecture, 1983," *Human Biology* 56, no. 1 (1984): 1–18. https://www.jstor.org/stable/41463546.

34 "Raymond Pearl," Johns Hopkins Bloomberg School of Public Health, accessed August 25, 2022, https://publichealth.jhu.edu/departments/biostatistics/about/history/raymond-pearl; John Aldrich, "Karl Pearson's 'Biometrika': 1901-36," *Biometrika 100*, no. 1 (2013): 3–15, https://www.jstor.org/stable/43304536.

35 Jeffrey M. Stanton (2001), "Galton, Pearson, and the Peas: A Brief History of Linear Regression for Statistics Instructors," *Journal of Statistics Education*, 9:3, DOI: 10.1080/10691898.2001.11910537.

Conference, *Johns Hopkins Magazine* reported that "he did not extend his criticism to the racism and anti-Semitism at the heart of so much eugenics research and policies."[36]

The first UN World Population Conference was held in Rome in 1954.[37] This conference was convened in collaboration with the UN Food and Agriculture Organization (FAO), along with the United Nations Educational, Scientific and Cultural Organization (UNESCO), the World Health Organization (WHO), and the International Bank for Reconstruction and Development (IBRD).[38] This last organization is a division of the World Bank.

The proceedings of the Rome conference reiterated the standard Malthusian refrain regarding the pressures of human population growth on food and other resources:

> It has often been feared that the means of subsistence cannot be found for mankind's increasing numbers...Though it may now be difficult to imagine that very much larger numbers will inhabit the earth in the future, it cannot be proved that this is impossible. Without doubt, the increase of populations has raised severe problems and will raise new problems in the future.

36 Melissa Hendricks, "Raymond Pearl's 'Mingled Mess,'" *Johns Hopkins Magazine*, April 2006, https://pages.jh.edu/jhumag/0406web/pearl.html.

37 "Proceedings of the World Population Conference, Rome, 31 August-10 September 1954," United Nations, accessed August 25, 2022, https://digitallibrary.un.org/record/3926459.

38 "World Population Conference, 1965," United Nations, accessed August 25, 2022, https://digitallibrary.un.org/record/735531.

The second UN World Conference on Population was held in Belgrade in 1965.[39] It was financed by the IBRD, the Rockefeller Foundation, and the Population Council. The Population Council is an international NGO that promotes Malthusian-eugenic population control programs. The Population Council, meanwhile, was founded by John D. Rockefeller III[40] and has been financed by the David and Lucile Packard Foundation.[41] David Packard was the founder of Hewlett Packard, which partners with the WEF.[42]

The summary report from this second UN World Conference considered both neo-Malthusian and non-Malthusian (non-population-related) theories but ultimately synthesized the two prongs. The report made 15 references to "birth control," 18 references to "fertility control," three references to "population control," 15 references to "sterilization," 76 references to "abortion," 102 references to "contraception," and 25 references to "Malthusianism" (including "Malthusian control").[43] According to the UN web-

39 "Conferences | Population," United Nations, accessed August 25, 2022, https://www.un.org/en/conferences/population.

40 "Timeline | Population Council," Population Council, accessed August 25, 2022, https://www.popcouncil.org/about/timeline.

41 "Population Council," The David and Lucile Packard Foundation, accessed August 25, 2022, https://www.packard.org/grants-and-investments/grants-database/population-council-10/.

42 Luiz Avelar, Anna Collard, and Pedro Ahlers, "Partners," World Economic Forum, accessed August 25, 2022, https://www.weforum.org/partners#H; Antonio Neri, Paul Sheeran, Gilles Thiebaut, Peter Ungaro, and Jennifer Temple, "Hewlett Packard Enterprise," World Economic Forum, accessed August 25, 2022, https://www.weforum.org/organizations/hewlett-packard-enterprise.

43 Ibid.

site: "The conference was held at a time when expert studies on demographics of development coincided with the start of population programs funded by the United States Agency for International Development (USAID)." USAID's *Population Program Assistance* is cited in *Limits to Growth.*

In 1974, the UN convened the third UN World Conference on Population in Bucharest.[44] It built on the neo-/non-Malthusian synthesis launched at the previous conference. As a result of this conference, the UN issued the World Population Plan of Action, which stipulated "among other principles, that the essential objective is the social, economic and cultural development of countries, that demographic variables [population size, and age and sex distribution] and development are interdependent and that policies and demographic targets are an integral part of socio-economic development policies."[45] In other words, population must be factored into any consideration of development, and vice versa. In a notable shift from strict neo-Malthusianism, this report recommended a "reduction of *involuntary sterility, subfecundity, defective births and illegal abortions*" (emphasis mine).[46] Note that the report called only for a "reduction" of involuntary sterility and illegal abortions, not for their elimination. This qualification recognized that earlier proposals had called for involuntary sterility and illegal abortions. The report called for population reduction policies to avert the

---

44 "Conferences | Population," United Nations.

45 "Report of the United Nations World Population Conference, 1974, Bucharest, 19-30 August 1974," United Nations, 1975, https://documents-dds-ny.un.org/.

46 Ibid.

classical Malthusian catastrophe of famine:

> In some developing countries additional population growth could contribute to the planned development of national resources while in others with acute resource problems and inadequate institutional and social structures, *a policy designed to reduce present rates of population growth should constitute an integral part of national programmes for social and economic advancement.* In the view of some representatives the absence of such policies could well lead to serious crises including acute food shortages and consequent rises in mortality and morbidity rates (emphasis mine).[47]

In 1994, the UN International Conference on Population changed its name to the UN International Conference on Population and Development (ICPD).[48] By adding "development" to the title, the UN signaled its new commitment to a synthesis of neo-Malthusian and non-Malthusian policies. At the conference, a new Programme of Action was adopted:

> This new agenda for action has emphasized the indissoluble relationship between population and development and focuses on meeting the needs of individuals within the framework of universally recognized human rights standards rather than simply responding to demographic goals.[49]

---

47 Ibid.

48 Ibid.

49 "International Conference on Population and Development

The UN now placed a new emphasis on managing population and economic and technological development as "human rights" initiatives, especially in terms of "family planning" and "gender equality." The ICPD recognized that the problems of population growth and resource management could be addressed through "gender equality" initiatives that provide women more access to education, employment, and healthcare, especially family planning services. The new strategy meant that women could *voluntarily* forgo pregnancy in pursuit of their education and careers. In cases of pregnancy, "reproductive healthcare" should be available. As such, gender-based "human rights" initiatives substituted for coercive methods of neo-Malthusian population control, like involuntary sterilization and abortion. *"Gender equality" is coded language for reproductive control on different terms.* Although the ICPD Programme of Action stressed voluntary population interventions in the name of "human rights," the methods were still aimed at mitigating population growth to avert the resource shortages forecasted by the Malthusian analyses of prior UN conferences.

The ICPD also represented a watermark UN global population conference because it was the first to situate population policies in terms of "sustainable development." The Programme of Action mentioned "sustainability" 143 times and "sustainable development" 85 times and included an explicit call "to implement sustainable population and reproductive health programmes." Principle 6 of the ICPD

Programme of Action," United Nations Population Fund, 2014, https://www.unfpa.org/publications/international-conference-population-and-development-programme-action.

Programme of Action stated:

> Sustainable development as a means to ensure human well-being, equitably shared by all people today and in the future, requires that *the interrelationships between population, resources, the environment and development* should be fully recognized, properly managed and brought into harmonious, dynamic balance. To achieve sustainable development and a higher quality of life for all people, States *should reduce and eliminate unsustainable patterns of production and consumption and promote appropriate policies, including population-related policies* (emphasis added).[50]

Notice that "sustainable development" meant development that leads to resources "equitably shared by all people." Development becomes unsustainable when equity is not achieved. Sustainable development thus leads to the equitable distribution of resources, and vice versa. Production and consumption that do not tend toward equity must be variably reduced, while population must also be regulated in line with production. Sustainable development therefore defines a system of managing resource production and consumption relative to population size while all three must be calibrated in terms of the environment (climate change, etc.) and equity. This "harmonious, dynamic balance" of resources relative to population, the environment, and equity represented a new enviro-neo-Malthusian paradigm under which environmental resources are finite, but only because development must be cali-

---

50 Ibid.

brated to population, whose growth must be strictly regulated. Technological innovations cannot lift the ceiling on those limits if lifting said limits would lead to unsustainability. Likewise, resources and population must be controlled through human (state and other stakeholder) interventions. Like the ICPD's gender-based population policies, its sustainable development policies were ultimately neo-Malthusian in principle, despite differences in methodology and rhetoric (and circular logic). Indeed, the Programme of Action declares the following:

> Never before has the world community had so many resources, so much knowledge and such powerful technologies at its disposal which, if suitably redirected, could foster sustained economic growth and sustainable development. None the less, the effective use of resources, knowledge and technologies is conditioned by political and economic obstacles at the national and international levels. Therefore, although ample resources have been available for some time, their use for socially equitable and environmentally sound development has been seriously limited.[51]

That is, technological innovation could lead to sustainable development but only if it is properly directed (by, we may assume, the UN). Without environmental and social justice policies in place, development becomes inequitable and unsustainable. The ICPD's gender-equity and social-justice initiatives were thereby conceived as sustainable development goals. The UN explicitly connected the ICPD

---

51 Ibid.

Programme of Action, gender equity, and the SDGs:

> The United Nations reports on the progress made in fulfilling the mandate of the ICPD Programme of Action. At the annual Commission on Population and Development, the UN reviews the state of sexual and reproductive health and rights around the world. This includes progress made, or ground lost, in efforts to empower women, educate girls, and eliminate gender-based violence and harmful practices.
>
> Population data are crucial for measuring progress in achieving the Sustainable Development Goals (SDGs). Data from the UN Population Division underpin the calculation of roughly a third of the indicators used currently for the global monitoring of the SDGs[52]

If population data accounted for one-third of the indicators used for monitoring the SDGs, then production, consumption, and equity amounted to the other two-thirds.

The preamble to the 2030 Agenda "reaffirm[ed]" the outcomes of all major United Nations conferences and summits, including the Programme of Action of the International Conference on Population and Development. Furthermore, SDG 5.6 (Goal 5.6) of Agenda 2030 "ensures universal access to sexual and reproductive health and reproductive rights as agreed in accordance with the Programme of Action of the International Conference on Population and Development...and the outcome documents of

---

52 "Conferences | Population," United Nations.

their review conference."[53] "Reproductive rights," of course, does not mean the right to reproduce but rather the right *not* to reproduce and the right to access the means to prevent reproduction.

The Great Reset can be understood, in part, as the "public-private partnership" project launched to help the UN achieve its Agenda 2030 SDGs. UN Agenda 2030 is based on Agenda 21 and the International Conference on Population and Development (ICPD). The ICPD evolved out of a series of UN and League of Nations global population conferences steeped in Malthusian and neo-Malthusian policies. Likewise, the Great Reset is neo-Malthusian at base.

Globalist Environmentalism

The 1970s marked the rise of globalist environmentalism, which began with the UN's process of rebranding its neo-Malthusian population policies in terms of "green" conservation and stewardship. By the 1990s, the UN's population control policies had been thoroughly rebranded in terms of sustainable development. Sustainable development took in both population and environmental concerns, including climate change.

The 1972 UN Conference on the Environment in Stockholm[54] and the 1992 UN Conference on En-

---

53 "Transforming Our World: The 2030 Agenda for Sustainable Development | Department of Economic and Social Affairs," United Nations, accessed October 27, 2021, https://sdgs.un.org/2030agenda, page 20.

54 "United Nations Conference on the Human Environment, Stockholm, 1972," United Nations, accessed August 30, 2022, https://www.un.org/en/conferences/environment/stockholm1972.

vironment and Development[55] were convened in the same years as the publication of the Club of Rome's *Limits to Growth* and *Beyond the Limits*. The UN Environment Program (UNEP) emerged from the 1972 conference and Agenda 21 emerged from the 1992 conference. Agenda 21 has been the prime driver of the UN's sustainable development projects and is the precursor and basis of Agenda 2030.

The 1987 World Commission on Environment and Development, where the term "sustainable development" was coined, fell between these conferences. The 1972 and 1992 conferences were led by Maurice Strong, who became the first Executive Director of UNEP and a Commissioner of the 1987 World Commission.[56] Strong played lead roles in coining "sustainable development" and launching both the UNEP and Agenda 21. He was a Foundation Board member of the WEF.

The timing of these conferences and projects, along with their policy overlaps, points to coordination between the UN, the Club of Rome, and the WEF. Such coordination is further evidenced by the fact that *Limits to Growth*, which was co-authored by Dennis Meadows (WEF), cites several UN agencies and Malthusian NGOs, including the Population Council and the Population Reference Bureau.

The UNEP website states the following:

---

55 "United Nations Conference on Environment and Development, Rio de Janeiro, Brazil, 3-14 June 1992," United Nations, accessed August 30, 2022, https://www.un.org/en/conferences/environment/rio1992.

56 "UNEP@50: Our Leaders Through the Years," UNEP, accessed August 30, 2022, https://www.unep.org/unep-50-leaders-through-years/maurice-strong.

Since its inception in 1972, the United Nations Environment Programme (UNEP) has been the global authority that sets the environmental agenda, promotes the coherent implementation of the environmental dimension of sustainable development within the United Nations system and serves as an authoritative advocate for the global environment.[57]

The UNEP also declares that it "works closely with its 193 Member States and representatives from civil society, businesses, and other major groups and stakeholders to address environmental challenges through the UN Environment Assembly, the world's highest-level decision-making body on the environment."[58] The stakeholder rhetoric derives directly from Klaus Schwab and the WEF.

Like all the UN branches, the UNEP addresses population concerns in tandem with the mitigation of environmental damage and sustainable development. In a 1995 white paper entitled "Environmental Information: Issues and Sources of Information," the UNEP asserts:

Man. Potentially the most serious of all threats to the environment. Several of the examples already given are the result of man's activities but there are less direct influences, for example the enormous consumption of energy and materials, particularly in World's richer countries, and the effects of overpopulation.[59]

---

57 "About UN Environment Programme," UNEP, accessed August 30, 2022, https://www.unep.org/about-un-environment.

58 Ibid.

59 John M. Sweeney, ed., "Environmental Information — Issues

Here we see the usual lament about the supposed excessive patterns of consumption in the developed world in connection with overpopulation. The two are treated as inextricably wed. Consumption, especially in the developed world, must be reduced, and as such, so must population growth. There is no doubt that the UNEP has deemed "First World" overconsumption and overpopulation to be a scourge on the planet that must be addressed. The reduction of consumption and population growth in the developed world is the sine qua non of environmental catastrophism.

---

and Sources of Information," United Nations Environment Programme, October 1995, https://wedocs.unep.org/bitstream/handle/20.500.11822/28854/Environmental_Information.pdf, page 7.

CHAPTER TEN

The Tentacles of the WEF

B ORN OF AN ACTUAL INSURRECTION, the United States of America has for almost 250 years enjoyed an independent spirit coursing through its veins. The U.S. has, for all its many faults, stood as a beacon of liberty. How, then, did the U.S., of all places, arrive at an era when Americans may soon see a group of faraway globalists determine their way of life? And it's not only Americans who are coming to terms with the prospect of invisible handlers, invisible rulers, and invisible overlords; so too is the entire world population.

A collectivist worldview, an incessant emphasis on "equality," climate catastrophism, and most recently, health emergencies have been marshaled by nation states and their agencies to pave the way for popular acceptance of these new overlords and their policies and plans. Many of these new overlords have been groomed and indoctrinated by the World Economic Forum (WEF), the latest and likely the most influential face of a century-long globalist agenda to date.

So, what is the WEF, and how has it managed to gain such influence and wield such power? This chapter begins to answer this vital question.

The WEF is an NGO, an international non-governmental and lobbying organization. Based in Cologny, outside Geneva, Switzerland, it was founded as the European Management Forum on January 24, 1971, by Klaus Schwab, a German engineer and "economist." The Forum is funded by public subsidies and by 1,000 corporate members and sees its mission as "improving the state of the world by engaging business, political, academic, and other leaders of society to shape global, regional, and industry agendas."[1]

With approximately 650 employees in its home office as of 2021, the WEF also has regional offices in Beijing, New York, San Francisco, and Tokyo. The highest governing body of the WEF is its Foundation Board, which consists of its most influential members, some of whom are drawn from its corporate funding partners.[2]

At its start, the WEF was funded by the European Commission and European industrial associations. After only two years, however, Schwab decided to cut ties with the Commission and to invite select politicians to its events.[3] By 1974, Schwab had shifted the emphasis of the European Management

---

1 "Our Mission," World Economic Forum, accessed July 31, 2022, https://www.weforum.org/about/world-economic-forum/.

2 Christina Garsten and Adrienne Sörbom, "Discretionary Governance," *Global Governance: A Review of Multilateralism and International Organizations* 27, no. 4 (2021): 540–60, https://doi.org/10.1163/19426720-02704006, page 548.

3 Ibid., page 547.

Forum from Eurocentric corporate management to global governance. According to the WEF:

> Events in 1973, namely the collapse of the Bretton Woods fixed exchange rate mechanism and the Arab-Israeli War, saw the Annual Meeting expand its focus from management to economic and social issues. Political leaders were invited for the first time to Davos in January 1974.[4]

The European Management Forum became the World Economic Forum in 1987. In 2015, the Swiss government formally recognized the Forum as an international organization, and the WEF now describes itself as "the International Organization for Public-Private Cooperation."[5]

The WEF has positioned itself as filling gaps between national, international, and transnational governance organizations, which it has deemed incapable of effective global governance, due to exclusive membership of state actors. The WEF aims to overcome what it considers to be the inertia of such international intergovernmental governance bodies as the United Nations (UN) by networking business, governmental, and civil society leaders.[6]

Corporate Partners
"Public-private cooperation" is the modus operandi of the WEF. Public-private partnerships entail the networking of corporations, states, NGOs, influ-

---

4 "History," World Economic Forum, accessed July 31, 2022, https://www.weforum.org/about/history.

5 Garsten and Sörbom, "Discretionary Governance," page 548.

6 Ibid., page 547.

ential individuals, and national and international governance bodies into what has become an effective global hegemon. While Schwab may be merely a front man for the WEF network, under his ostensible leadership, the organization has nevertheless managed to connect and coordinate a vast assemblage of partners, public and private, to the Davos Agenda. Its corporate partners include over 1,000 of the world's largest and most impactful business organizations while it incorporates leaders of the world's major nation states.[7]

The reach of the WEF into the corporate establishment is extensive and penetrating. For example, BCG (Boston Consulting Group) is proud to display its deep connections to the WEF. BCG consults clients in such industries as aerospace and defense, financial institutions, health care, oil and gas, power and utilities, principal investors and private equity, and technology, media, and telecommunications.

In 2022, BCG announced its partnership with the World Economic Forum. "Like our fellow members, BCG attends the Annual Meeting in Davos, the Annual Meeting of the New Champions in China, and many other regional gatherings." The consulting group boasts that 11 "[c]urrent and former BCGers have been selected as Young Global Leaders (YGL), a community of exceptional people under 40 years old." BCG is heavily invested in the WEF: "The World Economic Forum taps our people and insights for its collaborative projects, publications, and global communities to engage stakeholders, im-

---

7 Penelope Naas, Roger A. Grimes, and Duncan Jones, "Partners," World Economic Forum, accessed August 10, 2022, https://www. weforum.org/partners/.

prove policymaking, inform business decisions, and share best practices."[8]

In November 2021, *American Faith*'s Jon Fleetwood listed 10 banks partnering with the WEF and its Great Reset agenda. Among them: JP Morgan Chase & Co., Bank of America, Citi, and Goldman Sachs. Fleetwood also noted: "The WEF's Great Reset is referred to by the Transnational Institute as 'a silent global coup d'etat' to capture world dominance."[9]

As a trifling example of how the WEF enlists its key corporate and state partners, consider the former (and possibly future) Democratic presidential candidate, current Secretary of Transportation, and former WEF YGL, Pete Buttigieg. Buttigieg worked as a management consultant at McKinsey & Company, a WEF corporate partner.[10] A consultant firm, McKinsey has its hands in every imaginable industry. Its website boasts of its WEF partnership and drips with WEF-inflected rhetoric:

> As a strategic partner, McKinsey supports the World Economic Forum's mission of improving the state of the world. McKinsey collaborates with the Forum through multiple industry ac-

---

8 "BCG Partners with the World Economic Forum," BCG Global, accessed September 12, 2022, https://www.bcg.com/about/partner-ecosystem/world-economic-forum.

9 Jon Fleetwood, "10 Banks Partnered with Anti-American 'Great Reset' Agenda," *American Faith*, November 6, 2021, https://americanfaith.com/10-banks-partnered-with-anti-american-great-reset-agenda/.

10 Lucia Graves, "Buttigieg releases McKinsey client list but details fail to satisfy critics," *The Guardian*, December 13, 2019, https://www.theguardian.com/us-news/2019/dec/13/pete-buttigieg-mckinsey-client-details.

tion groups, research, and publications that help inform the relevant global conversation, and by participating in the annual meeting held in Davos, Switzerland.

Latest themes

Global cooperation | Economic rebalancing | Society & equity | Nature & climate | Industry transformation | Fourth Industrial Revolution.[11]

An October 2019 *Politico* article noted that Buttigieg chose to keep his term at the consulting firm shrouded in as much secrecy as the political climate would bear, no doubt because his work there had political implications:

> It's unclear exactly what Buttigieg did in those formative years in business before he launched his political career. The South Bend, Ind., mayor has previously said he worked on projects involving renewable energy, "war zone economic development" and grocery prices, but a shroud of confidentiality covers most of McKinsey's activities.[12]

One is led to wonder what is going on at McKinsey that Buttigieg had to keep under wraps. A recent New Hampshire poll taken concerning possible 2024 Democratic presidential candidates places

---

11 "McKinsey and the World Economic Forum," McKinsey & Company, accessed August 1, 2022, https://www.mckinsey.com/featured-insights/world-economic-forum/overview.

12 Daniel Strauss, "Buttigieg distances himself from his McKinsey consulting days," *Politico*, October 30, 2019, https://www.politico.com/news/2019/10/30/pete-buttigieg-mckinsey-consulting-061626.

Buttigieg at the top of the dirt heap.[13] Thus, as the WEF reached its fiftieth year in operation, it exerts influence on those aiming at the pinnacle of global power.

Young Global Leaders (YGLs)

The tentacles of the WEF have reached well beyond the U.S. Secretary of Transportation, however. The WEF's YGL program has been exerting enormous influence across the West and beyond.[14] In their responses to the covid "pandemic," for example, WEF YGLs, as national and regional political leaders, administrators, and public health officials, voted for and/or implemented some of the most stringent lockdown, masking, social distancing, and vaccination mandates in the world.

The results of a draft study on the correlation between the nationwide distribution of YGLs in several countries and the severity of non-pharmaceutical interventions (NPIs), such as lockdowns and other closures, found a positive correlation between the most stringent NPIs and the prevalence of WEF YGLs in those countries. These YGL-associated NPIs were most noticeable during the second wave of the pandemic, leading the researchers to conclude that the WEF served as an "echo chamber or amplifier for certain opinions and strategies that were formed and implemented during or before the first months

---

13 Caroline Vakil, "Buttigieg edges out Biden among Democrats in New Hampshire poll," *The Hill*, July 26, 2022, https://thehill.com/homenews/campaign/3574672-buttigieg-edges-out-biden-among-democrats-in-new-hampshire-poll/.

14 "The Forum of Young Global Leaders," World Economic Forum, accessed August 1, 2022, https://www.younggloballeaders.org/.

of the COVID-19 crisis."[15] Since NPIs were not asso-ciated with a reduction of covid-19-related deaths,[16] and since severe NPIs had significant negative con-sequences of their own, including a correlation with an increase in deaths,[17] the YGL program can be seen as a substantial source of what I have called the covid crisis—not the so-called pandemic itself, but the re-sponses to SARS-CoV-2 and the impact of the re-sponses on social and economic life.

Schwab launched the Forum of Young Global Leaders in 2005, with funding from the one-mil-lion-dollar, Israeli-based Dan David Prize.[18] The Fo-rum is reserved for leading prospects who are under

---

15   Rainer J. Klement and Harald Walach, "Is the Network of World Economic Forum Young Global Leaders Associated with COVID-19 Non-Pharmaceutical Intervention Severity?," Review copy, 2022, https://papers.ssrn.com/sol3/papers.cfm?abstract_id=4211288.

16   Q. De Larochelambert, Marc, A., Antero, J., Le Bourg, E., & Toussaint, J.-F. (2020), "Covid-19 Mortality: A Matter of Vulnerabil-ity Among Nations Facing Limited Margins of Adaptation," *Frontiers in Public Health*, page 8; R.J. Klement and H. Walach, "Low Vitamin D Status and Influenza Vaccination Rates are Positive Predictors of Early Covid-19 Related Deaths in Europe–A Modeling Approach," *Zenodo*, April 12, 2021.

17   T. Hale, N. Angrist, B. Kira, A. Petherick, et al., "Government responses and COVID-19 deaths: Global evidence across multiple pandemic waves," *PLoS One*, 16, July 9, 2021, e0253116.

18   Steve Nadis, "Next-Generation Leadership," Harvard Kennedy School - Next-Generation Leadership, originally published in *Har-vard Kennedy School Magazine*, Summer 2009, https://web.archive. org/web/20120531072135/http://www.hks.harvard.edu/news-events/ publications/hks-magazine/archives/summer-2009/next-gen-eration-leadership; "Young Global Leaders," Wikipedia, citing Next-Generation Leadership, Harvard: John F. Kennedy School of Government, 2009, archived from the original on 7 September 2009, accessed August 1, 2022, https://en.wikipedia.org/wiki/Young_Glob-al_Leaders.

40 years of age and show promise for global governance. The first class consisted of 237 members.[19] In 2021, the WEF reported that there were approximately 1244 YGLs, including 739 alumni.[20] WEF YGLs have included the following notable political leaders: Emmanuel Macron, President of France; Jacinda Ardern, Prime Minister of New Zealand; Alexander De Croo, Prime Minister of Belgium; Chrystia Freeland, Deputy Prime Minister of Canada; Sanna Marin, Prime Minister of Finland; Haakon, Crown Prince of Norway; and Tom Cotton, Republican Arkansas Senator, among others. YGLs also include numerous key figures in journalism, business, sports, and the arts.[21]

Maxime Bernier PC, the founder and leader of the People's Party of Canada (PPC), posted a 2017 video featuring Schwab at Harvard boasting of the WEF's penetration of governments worldwide.[22] He declared:

> Klaus Schwab in 2017 says he's proud [that] his World Economic Forum infiltrates governments and he personally knows more than half of Trudeau's cabinet. Just another conspiracy

---

19 "Young Global Leaders," Wikipedia, accessed August 1, 2022, https://en.wikipedia.org/wiki/Young_Global_Leaders.

20 "2020–2021 Young Global Leaders Annual Report: Responding to Adversity, Leading with Responsibility," World Economic Forum, accessed September 9, 2022, https://www3.weforum.org/docs/WEF_YGL_Annual_Repot_2020_2021.pdf.

21 Young Global Leaders," Wikipedia, accessed August 1, 2022, https://en.wikipedia.org/wiki/Young_Global_Leaders.

22 skellycat9, "Klaus Schwab/Harvard Talk/Trudeau Cabinet & Others 'Penetrated,'" YouTube, January 26, 2022, https://www.youtube.com/watch?v=b4cDNyvrP40.

theory of course, nothing to see here.
#TheGreatReset.

In a recent article, *The Spectator* (AU) asked whether the WEF is comprised of "heroes or villains." It listed recent YGL alumni and noted:

> Also associated with the WEF are famous names such as outgoing UK Prime Minister Boris Johnson, and a sizeable chunk of Tory MPs - most of which were contesting the leadership... The speaker list for the Davos Agenda 2021 and 2022 included the now former German Chancellor Angela Merkel, Chinese President Xi Jinping, Indian PM Narendra Modi, Israeli PM Naftali Bennett, Japanese PM Kishida Fumio, Indonesian PM Joko Widodo, UN Secretary-General Antonio Guterres, the Managing Director of the International Monetary Fund (IMF) Kristalina Georgieva, and our very own former Prime Minister Scott Morrison.[23]

The *Spectator* article also questioned the motives of the WEF:

> In 2022, their focus is on Climate Change, artificial intelligence, cybersecurity, education, employment, the Metaverse, manufacturing, the digital economy, digital identity, trade, investment, health, energy, diversity, inclusion and so on. This organization boasts that it has a plan to reshape every single aspect of society. To reset it. To build back better.[24]

---

23 Joel Agius, "The World Economic Forum: heroes or villains?," *The Spectator* (AU), July 27, 2022.
24 Ibid.

Klaus Schwab has claimed on several occasions that Russian President Vladimir Putin, Canadian Prime Minister Justin Trudeau, and former Chancellor of Germany Angela Merkel have been YGLs, although no evidence of their YGL memberships can be found on their individual WEF pages.[25]

This has led to some confusion, but it is largely owing to the fact that the YGL program was first named "Global Leaders for Tomorrow." Launched in 1992, the first class of Global Leaders for Tomorrow met in 1993 and included prospects who appeared destined to become world leaders: Angela Merkel, Chancellor of Germany; Tony Blair, UK Prime Minister; Gordon Brown, Blair's successor; Victor Orban, Prime Minister of Hungary; Nicolas Sarkozy, President of France; Lee Hsien-Loong, Prime Minister of Singapore; and José Manuel Barroso, President of the European Commission. The first class also boasted a slew of leaders in business and philanthropy, such as Bill Gates (Bill & Melinda Gates Foundation), Antony Leung (The Blackstone Group), Vladimir Dlouhy (Goldman Sachs), Plinio Musetti (JP Morgan), Michael S. Dell (Dell Inc.), and Roy Thomson (The Thomson Reuters Corporation). Other notables included George Stephanopoulos (*ABC News* correspondent), Lawrence H. Summers (President of Harvard University), and Wendy Kopp (Teach for All).[26]

---

25 skellycat9, "Klaus Schwab/Harvard Talk/ Trudeau Cabinet & Others 'Penetrated,'" op. cit.; "Klaus Schwab Brags Vladimir Putin, Tony Blair & Angela Merkel Belonged to WEF's Young Global Leaders," YouTube, February 25, 2022, https://www.youtube.com/watch?v=Vq6YaQNG05c.

26 "WEF/Global Leaders for Tomorrow/1993," Wikispooks, origi-

Johnny Vedmore has argued that the YGL program is a direct descendent and continuation of Henry Kissinger's International Seminar that was originally held at Harvard and was funded by the CIA. Kissinger influenced Schwab during the latter's time in Kissinger's International Seminar at Harvard. Kissinger was a board member of the Dan David Foundation when the Foundation granted Schwab the funding that enabled him to establish the YGL program. From this and other evidence, Vedmore concludes that the Global Leaders for Tomorrow-YGL program merely extends the same American imperialist objectives as Kissinger's long-lapsed seminar:

> Klaus Schwab became the heir to Henry Kissinger's most important project, the infiltration of individuals and organizations in countries around the world with the aim of creating globalist-aligned governments built within the framework of an outdated and soulless conceptualization of American imperialism.[27]

But this interpretation represents a misunderstanding of the YGL program and the WEF itself. Just as the Rhodes Scholarship shifted from a recruitment tool of Anglophile British imperialism into

---

nally published by World Economic Forum, accessed September 11, 2022, https://www.wikispooks.com/wiki/WEF/Global_Leaders_for_ Tomorrow/1993.

27 Johnny Vedmore, "The Unauthorized History of the WEF's Young Global Leaders Program," *Unlimited Hangout*, August 29, 2022, https://unlimitedhangout.com/2022/08/investigative-reports/the-kissinger-continuum-the-unauthorized-history-of-the-wefs-young-global-leaders-program/.

a tool of multilateral, multicultural globalism, so too did the WEF change its focus soon after its founding. (See Chapter 8.) The WEF YGL program does not hold to "an outdated and soulless conceptualization of American imperialism." Rather, it represents the exhaustion of this very paradigm, thanks in no small part to the WEF's own efforts in installing a new multilateral, multicultural globalism. What it retains from the earlier model is an elite-centered, elite-controlled agenda, but this agenda is neither British nor American imperialism. In fact, it represents the establishment of a new globalism, and aims at the end of American sovereignty to boot.

Global Shapers

Perhaps more important than the YGL program is the WEF's Global Shapers movement. With over 10,000 active "Shapers" and over 4,000 alumni, the Global Shapers have a presence in 500 city hubs and 150 countries. Established in 2011, the Global Shapers program is touted as a sort of training camp for young "changemakers" under 30 years old and serves as a method of recruitment into the YGL program.[28]

The WEF's recent-most publication on the Global Shapers lists six "impact areas" that Global Shapers address: protect the planet, strengthen civic engagement, improve health and well-being, deliver basic needs, reskill for the future, and create inclusive communities.[29]

---

28 Global Shapers, World Economic Forum, accessed September 10, 2022, https://www.globalshapers.org/.

29 "Global Shapers Annual Summit: Youth-Led Solutions for a More Equitable World," World Economic Forum, September 3, 2022,

From this list and the "humanitarian" efforts featured by the WEF Global Shapers' latest *Agenda Weekly* newsletter, one might be led to believe that the program amounts to nothing more than a league of benevolent do-gooders helping beleaguered communities to address natural disasters and food shortages, etc. But we must note that the program serves as an indoctrination camp and a means for funneling its alumni into positions of power, including as YGLs. The Shapers program also serves as a means by which the WEF's agenda is spread and insinuates itself into local communities and decision-making bodies throughout the world, under the innocuous cover of "youth." Moreover, like the semi-secret WEF annual meetings (see Chapter 8), the Global Shapers' summits are shrouded in semi-secrecy. Short of infiltrating the summits and observing Global Shapers meetings and activities, one finds it almost impossible to discover anything substantive about them. Likewise, we are left with the WEF's own pronouncements.

I return to the WEF's recent publication on the Global Shapers.[30] Under the first impact area, the desiderata to "reduce emissions" and promote "sustainable development" are named. The need to reduce emissions is, of course, premised on climate change as a legitimate threat, which is treated in Part III of this book. "Sustainable development" represents the UN's Agenda 2030 objectives.

Under the second impact area of civic engagement, inspiring young people to run for political of-

---

https://www.weforum.org/agenda/2022/09/global-shapers-annual-summit-youth-solutions-equitable-world/.

30 Ibid.

fice is specifically suggested. No doubt this means inspiring the Global Shapers themselves to seek political office.

Under the third impact area—improve health and well-being—addressing the covid-19 pandemic is mentioned. We can assume that Global Shapers are being treated to the same kinds of policy ideas as implemented by the YGLs. They are being taught that draconian lockdowns, masking, social distancing, and mandatory vaccinations represent the only viable means for responding to "pandemics."[31]

Under the fourth aspect, deliver basic needs— which should read "deliver services to address basic needs"—we find the UN objective of fighting poverty and supporting the world's most vulnerable communities. The means for fighting poverty never include industrial development in the developing world, as this would threaten the "sustainable development" goal mentioned under the first aspect. Likewise, fighting poverty is always figured in terms of aid from the developed world, or the development of other, "green" means of production that forever leave the developing world behind and under the threat of immiseration.

Under creating "inclusive communities," we find the same rhetoric that informs the "social justice" agenda of the WEF and the UN. This rhetoric suggests the WEF's multicultural, woke globalism is part of the Global Shapers' indoctrination.

We must conclude from the material provided by the WEF that the Shapers are indoctrinated into climate change catastrophism (see Part III), YGL-

---

31 "Themes," Global Shapers, accessed September 12, 2022, https://www.globalshapers.org/impact/themes/covid-19.

like pandemic responses, UN-style humanitarianism, and the WEF's overall geopolitical outlook. The Global Shapers represent the future of the Davos Agenda. Thus, we will want to keep an eye on the Shapers alumni as they shape-shift into YGLs and impact policy wherever they go.

UN-WEF Partnership

The WEF has banked on massive corporate funding to seed its success. But to gain trust from world leaders, the WEF needed the imprimatur of an international, intergovernmental organization, like the United Nations. In 2015, in celebration of its seventieth anniversary, the UN shared a version of its history:

> The United Nations is an international organization founded in 1945 after the Second World War by 51 countries committed to maintaining international peace and security, developing friendly relations among nations and promoting social progress, better living standards and human rights.[32]

The UN continues by describing its global reach and its supposedly laudable goals:

> *The work of the United Nations reaches every corner of the globe.* Although best known for peacekeeping, peacebuilding, conflict prevention and humanitarian assistance, there are many other ways the United Nations and its

---

32 "History of the UN," United Nations Seventieth Anniversary, United Nations, 2015, https://www.un.org/un70/en/content/history/index.html.

System (specialized agencies, funds and programmes) affect our lives and make the world
a better place (emphasis mine).[33]

This rhetoric barely masks the UN's totalitarian
desiderata. I examine the UN in subsequent chapters,
but suffice it to say for now that the UN's peacekeeping activities have been fruitless while the impacts
of its interventionist economic policies have mainly
served to thwart development, distort markets, and
influence member states to undertake interventionist policies destructive of the free market.

In 2019, the putative peacekeepers signed a
partnership agreement with the WEF as announced
in a WEF press release entitled "World Economic
Forum and UN Sign Strategic Partnership Framework."[34] The announcement noted that the signing
took place at United Nations headquarters between
UN Secretary-General António Guterres and World
Economic Forum Founder and Executive Chairman
Klaus Schwab. The aim of the agreement is "to accelerate the implementation of the 2030 Agenda for
Sustainable Development." This joint framework included six areas of focus: financing the 2030 Agenda, climate change mitigation, health, digital cooperation and governance, gender equality and the
empowerment of women, and education and skills,
all intended "to strengthen and broaden their com-

---

33 "History of the UN," United Nations Seventieth Anniversary,
United Nations, 2015, https://www.un.org/un70/en/content/history/
index.html.
34 "World Economic Forum and UN Sign Strategic Partnership Framework," World Economic Forum, June 13, 2019,
https://www.weforum.org/press/2019/06/world-economic-fo-
rum-and-un-sign-strategic-partnership-framework/.

bined impact by building on existing and new collaborations."

Combined, these "six areas of focus" are designed to affect every aspect of economic, social, political, and personal life. The interleaved agenda items amount to a stranglehold on the world's populations. The full framework suggests the power embodied in the alliance:

> Recognizing the ambition of the 2030 Agenda, the United Nations and the World Economic Forum seek to strengthen their partnership by focusing on jointly selected priorities and by pursuing a more strategic and coordinated collaboration, by leveraging their respective strengths and broadening their combined impact, building on existing and new collaborations by UN entities.[35]

The WEF's "strengths" include its vast network of Environmental, Social, and Governance (ESG)-abiding corporate partners, its collaboration with and coordination of digital giants, and its multistakeholder governance approach that includes its over 1,000 corporate partners. This networked cartel enforces the "stakeholder capitalism" model under which funding is directed at "sustainable development" to the exclusion of the non-compliant. At the same time, the UN and the WEF jointly exert their influence over worldwide governance systems. Networked together by the UN and the WEF, states and corporate stakeholders comprise a centralized

---

35 "UN WEF Partnership Framework," World Economic Forum, June 13, 2019, https://weforum.ent.box.com/s/rdlgipawkjxi2vdaid-w8npbtyach2qbt.

power grid unlike anything seen in history.

The UN-WEF memorandum of understanding (MOU) was signed at the United Nations in New York on June 13, 2019.[36] Its release led *openDemocracy*'s Harris Gleckman to observe: "Now the new WEF-UN agreement creates a second special place for multinational corporations inside the UN."[37] Gleckman further noted the lack of participation by member states as parties to the agreement:

> Were the Secretary-General convinced of the wisdom of a UN marriage with the WEF, he could have submitted the draft MOU for approval by the member states. Instead, the Secretary-General joined the WEF in declaring in effect that multistakeholder groups without any formal intergovernmental oversight are a better governance system than a one-country-one-vote system.[38]

In another *openDemocracy* column, political scientist Ivan Wecke detailed the plans of the WEF:

> Drafted by the WEF after the 2008 economic crisis, the initiative contains a 600-page report on transforming global governance. In the WEF's vision, "the government voice would be one among many, without always being the fi-

---

36 "UN and WEF Sign MOU on Strategic Partnership Framework for 2030 Agenda," News & Media Photo, United Nations, June 13, 2019.

37 Harris Gleckman, "How the United Nations is quietly being turned into a public-private partnership," *openDemocracy*, July 2, 2019, https://www.opendemocracy.net/en/oureconomy/how-united-nations-quietly-being-turned-public-private-partnership/.

38 Ibid.

nal arbiter." Governments would be just one stakeholder in a multi-stakeholder model of global governance.[39]

Wecke also noted some of the WEF's prominent corporate partners:

> WEF partners include some of the biggest companies in oil (Saudi Aramco, Shell, Chevron, BP), food (Unilever, The Coca-Cola Company, Nestlé), technology (Facebook, Google, Amazon, Microsoft, Apple) and pharmaceuticals (AstraZeneca, Pfizer, Moderna).[40]

And Wecke noticed a new wrinkle, which represents a tectonic shift in these public-private partnerships:

> Instead of corporations serving many stakeholders, in the multi-stakeholder model of global governance, corporations are promoted to *being* official stakeholders in global decision-making, while governments are relegated to being one of many stakeholders. In practice, corporations become the main stakeholders, while governments take a backseat role, and civil society is mainly window dressing (emphasis in original).[41]

Wecke suggested that the UN-WEF partnership and the governance model of the WEF represent

---

39 Ivan Wecke, "Conspiracy theories aside, there is something fishy about the Great Reset," *openDemocracy*, August 16, 2021, https://www.opendemocracy.net/en/oureconomy/conspiracy-theories-aside-there-something-fishy-about-great-reset/.

40 Ibid.

41 Ibid.

at least the partial privatization of the UN's Agenda 2030. This usurpation has led Wecke to call the WEF's governmental redesign of the world system "a corporate takeover of global governance."[42]

Corporations serve the state, and vice versa. For example, when word got out that covid cases and deaths are higher in countries with the highest vaccination rates, these "governmentalities" sprang into action. Big Tech removed, blocked, or shadow-banned news and views of users that ran counter to the official state narrative. Such news and views were deemed "misinformation" or "disinformation" and were squelched. Voices that would otherwise prove deleterious to the monolithic "health" goals of the CDC, the UN, the World Health Organization (WHO), and by extension, the WEF, are consigned to the digital dustbin of history. We learned that over fifty officials in a dozen agencies of the Biden regime corresponded and met with social media personnel to enforce the official covid narrative and to censor "misinformation."[43] In return, we may assume, these corporate assets are rewarded with preferential treatment by the state.

In 1999, *Forbes* interviewed Klaus Schwab in a Boston restaurant. By this time, Schwab's influence was already well known. "As president of the Geneva-based World Economic Forum (WEF), he

---

42 Ibid.

43 Zachary Stieber, "Over 50 Biden Administration Employees, 12 US Agencies Involved in Social Media Censorship Push – Documents," *CLG News/The Epoch Times*, September 7, 2022, https://www.legitgov.org/over-50-biden-administration-employees-12-us-agencies-involved-social-media-censorship-push-0; "Big Tech Used by US Govt to Shut Down Opposition," Odysee, *RT International*, September 2, 2022, https://odysee.com/@RT:fd/BIG-TECH-yt:a.

[Schwab] brings together once a year 1,000 chair-men and chief executives of the foremost global companies with another 1,000 world leaders, scientists and journalists," the magazine stated. *Forbes* revealed the following about the WEF head:

> When asked which great thinker influenced him, Schwab mentions Karl Popper, the An-glo-Austrian philosopher. Since financier George Soros also publicly espouses Popper as a visionary, we ask Schwab if Soros influenced him. Oops.
> "Soros learned at Davos," says Schwab, correcting the assumption.[44]

More insight was provided on Schwab from this 1999 interview: "At any rate, global companies do not fit behind neat national borders. The sovereign state has become obsolete," Schwab said. The *Forbes* article noted that in 1982, the Forum was a catalyst for the Uruguay Round of trade liberalization talks that ultimately led to the creation of the World Trade Organization.[45]

And finally, Klaus Schwab, the WEF, and the Great Reset have attained a significant British royal imprimatur. The Prince of Wales (now King of England) and the Duchess of Cornwall's website suggests that Prince Charles himself launched the Great Reset: "Today, through HRH's Sustainable Markets Initiative and the World Economic Forum, The Prince of Wales launched a new global initiative,

---

44 "Power broker," *Forbes*, November 15, 1999, https://www.forbes.com/global/1999/1115/0223108a.html.

45 Ibid.

The Great Reset." The royals' site acknowledges the centrality of corporate partners to the Great Reset project and equates the Great Reset and the "Build Back Better" initiative. It also calls the WEF meeting "a virtual roundtable," the significance of which was made clear in a previous chapter:

> The Great Reset, which was launched during a virtual roundtable today, aims to rebuild, redesign, reinvigorate and rebalance our world. It has been designed to ensure businesses and communities 'build back better' by putting sustainable business practices at the heart of their operations as they begin to recover from the coronavirus pandemic.[46]

The WEF also recognized the central role played by Prince Charles in the launching of the Great Reset.[47] Of course, "Prince Charles" stands not for the royals alone but also for "the City of London, Wall Street, and other financial centers; the Bank of England; and MI5, MI6, GCHQ—the intelligence centers."[48]

---

46   "#TheGreatReset," The Prince of Wales and The Duchess of Cornwall, June 3, 2020, https://www.princeofwales.gov.uk/thegreatreset.

47   Christopher Alessi, "'A golden opportunity' - HRH the Prince of Wales and other leaders on the Forum's Great Reset," World Economic Forum, June 3, 2020, https://www.weforum.org/agenda/2020/06/great-reset-launch-prince-charles-guterres-georgieva-burrow/. See also: Jon Fleetwood, "Globalist Great Reset Will Require 'Vast Military-Style Campaign': Prince Charles," *American Faith*, November 2, 2021, https://americanfaith.com/globalist-great-reset-will-require-vast-military-style-campaign-prince-charles/.

48   Richard Freeman, "The Global Reset: The Great Leap Backward," *Executive Intelligence Review* 48, no. 13 (March 26, 2021): 43–46,

With backing from and coordination of the largest transnational corporations, global financial institutions, the UN, world leaders, governmentalities, and even British royalty, it would appear that the Great Reset agenda is a fait accompli.

https://larouchepub.com/eiw/public/2021/eirv48n13-20210326/
eirv48n13-20210326_043-the_global_reset_the_great_leap.pdf, page
44.

Part III

Climate Catastrophism

In searching for a new enemy to unite us, we came up with the idea that pollution, the threat of global warming, water shortages, famine and the like would fit the bill. In their totality and in their interactions these phenomena do constitute a common threat which demands the solidarity of all peoples. But in designating them as the enemy, we fall into the trap about which we have already warned, namely mistaking symptoms for causes. All these dangers are caused by human intervention and it is only through changed attitudes and behaviour that they can be overcome. The real enemy, then, is humanity itself.
— Alexander King and Bertrand Schneider, the Club of Rome

We may get to the point where the only way of saving the world will be for industrialized civilization to collapse.
— Maurice Strong

The threat of environmental crisis will be the international disaster key to unlock the New World Order.
— Mikhail Gorbachev

CHAPTER ELEVEN

Climate Change Catastrophism

LIMATE CATASTROPHISM clearly was not in the cards as a defining issue when Al Gore stood as the Democratic presidential candidate in 2000. Gore had written *Earth in the Balance* in 1992 and his environmentalism was a signature prong of his presidential platform. He had labored to make George W. Bush's environmental record as governor of Texas a point of disqualification. He had helped to broker the Kyoto Protocol of 1997 and was a major proponent of its ratification. Yet, in the final days of his campaign, Gore found himself defending his environmental record on two fronts simultaneously—from the Green Party candidate Ralph Nader, who lambasted the Clinton administration as hypocritical, and from Bush, who portrayed him as a zealot for his positions on logging, oil drilling, and global warming. Thus, Gore was unable to unambiguously assert his environmentalist prerogatives without fac-

217

ing criticism from both the hard Left and the Right.[1]

Had the Supreme Court not stopped the counting of votes in Bush v. Gore, as a November 2021 letter to the *Los Angeles Times* suggested, the supposed climate emergency would have been addressed much earlier. "We might have dodged the bullet" and averted "a possible apocalypse."[2] Yet, the time was not fully ripe for climate catastrophism. Likewise, the requisite pressure was not applied by the establishment, and the Supreme Court, in a decision that it stated should not serve as precedent, summarily handed the presidency to Bush.

As I write, Democrats on Capitol Hill are pressuring the Biden administration to declare a climate emergency, voicing their doomsday predictions that without immediate action to curb and ultimately end our dependence on fossil fuels, "the planet" and, by implication, every living creature that inhabits it, will die. "If we don't really begin to lower emissions, this planet has no chance," said Representative Alan Lowenthal, a California Democrat. "We have a few years left and that's it. The planet is dying." This dire assessment and apocalyptic warning echoes Al Gore's 2006 book and documentary, *An Inconvenient Truth*, and his subsequent statements that climate inaction would cause the complete summer-

1   Douglas Jehl, "On a Favorite Issue, Gore Finds Himself on a 2-Front Defense," *The New York Times*, November 3, 2000, https://www.nytimes.com/2000/11/03/us/2000-campaign-environment-favorite-issue-gore-finds-himself-2-front-defense.html.

2   Roger Bell, "Letters to the Editor: Imagine Al Gore Won in 2000. Where Would We Be on Climate Change?," *Los Angeles Times*, November 1, 2021, https://www.latimes.com/opinion/story/2021-11-01/imagine-al-gore-won-in-2000-climate-change.

time meltdown of the North Pole ice by 2013.[3]

Even though such ridiculous predictions as Gore's have been put forth and falsified every time, it appears that thanks to the rise of "stakeholder capitalism" and the Environmental, Social, and Governance (ESG) Index, climate change catastrophism's heyday has finally arrived. It becomes necessary, therefore, to address it directly. This means evaluating the climate change science itself and subjecting the narrative to an unabashed critique. Forthright and highly qualified critics have raised the following issues, among many others, with climate change catastrophism:[4]

- the previously peddled "crises" of global *cooling*, acid rain, and ozone layer depletion,

---

3 Haris Alic, "Eight Years? Nine Years? Six Years Ago? A Climate Change Activist Guide to Doomsday," *Fox News*, July 26, 2022, https://www.foxnews.com/politics/climate-activists-embrace-doomsday-rhetoric-despite-falling-flat-in-previous-warnings.

4 See Bjørn Lomborg, *Cool It: The Skeptical Environmentalist's Guide to Global Warming*, London: Marshall Cavendish, 2010; Rupert Darwall, *The Age of Global Warming: A History*, London: Quartet Books, 2014; Bjørn Lomborg, *The Skeptical Environmentalist: Measuring the Real State of the World*, Cambridge: Cambridge University Press, 2016; István Markó, J. Scott Armstrong, William M. Briggs, Kesten Green, Hermann Harde, David R. Legates, Christopher Monckton of Brenchley, and Willie Soon, "To Put America First Is to Put Our Planet's Climate First," *Breitbart*, June 21, 2017. https://www.breitbart.com/politics/2017/06/16/america-first-climate/; Rupert Darwall, *Green Tyranny: Exposing the Totalitarian Roots of the Climate Industrial Complex*, New York: Encounter Books, 2019; S. Fred Singer, David R. Legates, and Anthony R. Lupo, *Hot Talk, Cold Science: Global Warming's Unfinished Debate*, Oakland, CA: Independent Institute, 2021; Alex Epstein, *Fossil Future: Why Global Human Flourishing Requires More Oil, Coal, and Natural Gas—Not Less*, New York: Portfolio/Penguin, 2022.

which proved to be unfounded;
- the complete dismissal of the benefits of fossil fuel use by climate activists;
- the failure to acknowledge that fossil-fuel-powered technologies significantly mitigate the effects of climate emergencies;
- the fact that deaths from extreme weather events have decreased dramatically during the so-called climate emergency;
- the fact that solar and wind energy technologies, after fifty-plus years of development and subsidies, are far from capable of replacing fossil fuels;
- the disingenuous use of the coldest period in the Holocene as the starting point for measuring rising temperatures;
- the manipulation of surface temperature readings to counter satellite readings, which show no significant recent warming;
- the exaggerated synthesis of scientific studies by the Intergovernmental Panel on Climate Change (IPCC) and the further exaggeration in disseminating synthesized findings to the public by designated "experts" and the media;
- the IPCC's hiding of its raw data and methodology, its blocking of outside investigations attempting to replicate its results, and its blocking of climate-change-skeptical scientists from publishing their findings in peer-reviewed journals ("Climategate");[5]
- the alteration of IPCC reports—after scientists had written and approved the final texts—to remove skepticism regarding claims that human activities are having a major impact on climate and global warming;

5   "Climategate 2.0," the Air Vent, July 2, 2012, https://noconsensus. wordpress.com/2011/11/22/climategate-2-0/.

- the fifteen-year period (1998–2013) of no significant warming, despite a seven percent rise in atmospheric CO_2 levels;
- the fact that the rate of global warming has decelerated since 1951, despite a 26 percent increase in CO_2 levels;
- the fact that the atmosphere cooled very slightly from 1950 to 1985 and again from 1997 to 2015, while during both periods, carbon dioxide levels rose dramatically;
- the fact that temperature reconstructions of the past show temperatures as high as recent temperatures in some regions (the Medieval Climatic Anomaly);
- the finding that during the Paleozoic and Mesozoic eras, there were long periods during which the levels of CO_2 were much higher than they are today while the temperatures were far colder;
- the recent IPCC estimates that the transient climate response (TCR, or the climate estimate for the remainder of the twenty-first century) falls within the range of natural climate variation over the past six million years;
- the research that shows no increases in droughts or tropical cyclone activity over the past forty years;
- the observation that the Antarctic sea ice extent *increased* between 1979 and 2012, contradicting global circulation models (GCMs);
- the fact that climate modeling has failed to predict climate trends accurately;
- the strong likelihood that warming is not necessarily negative at all but may, in fact, be positive;
- the well-known greening of the planet due to increased CO_2 levels and the benefits derived

thereof, including for agriculture;
• the fact that there is no known optimal or "natural" global temperature, even if global temperatures could be accurately measured, which is doubtful.

This is but the skeleton of a body of reasons for concluding that climate change catastrophism is overwrought and hyperbolic, if not based on outright fraud.

Meanwhile, a body of over 1,200 climatologists, environmental scientists, geologists, pollution meteorologists, and climate researchers from over 35 countries has signed the World Climate Declaration entitled "There Is No Climate Emergency." The document raises a few of the issues listed above and adds the following, conclusive comment:

> There is no climate emergency. Therefore, there is no cause for panic and alarm. We strongly oppose the harmful and unrealistic net-zero CO_2 policy proposed for 2050. If better approaches emerge, and they certainly will, we have ample time to reflect and re-adapt. The aim of global policy should be "prosperity for all" by providing reliable and affordable energy at all times. In a prosperous society men and women are well educated, birthrates are low and people care about their environment.[6]

Signatories include Nobel Laureate Norwegian-American Ivar Giaever as well as such nota-

---

6 "World Climate Declaration: There Is No Climate Emergency," *Clintel*, August 31, 2022, https://clintel.org/world-climate-declaration/.

bles as the American atmospheric physicist Richard Lindzen, and Jens Morten Hansen of the Geological Survey of Denmark and Greenland. The joint statement corroborates what S. Fred Singer et al. have argued:

> Contrary to some accounts of the history of the scientific debate, there was no gradually emerging "consensus" on the human role in climate change. Rather, politics quickly overtook science as environmental advocates and other interest groups recognized the utility of the climate change issue in advancing their own agendas.[7]

Much more can be said about "the science" behind climate change catastrophism. For example, James T. Moodey, a real-world gas physicist, has tested the claim that CO_2 retains heat long enough for the atmosphere to warm over time. Moodey and his team first isolated a mixture of vaporous (70 percent humidity) atmospheric air that included carbon dioxide. He then applied heat to the air-carbon dioxide mixture, which closely resembled atmospheric conditions. Once the heat source was discontinued, Moodey measured the rate of heat loss. He had already recorded temperature drops in the atmosphere over a period of a year at varying altitudes and in numerous climates. He noted that the atmosphere warms, on average, about 22 degrees every sunny or partly sunny day, regardless of the daytime high temperature. The vaporous air-carbon dioxide mixture that he tested cooled by 22 degrees in about

---

7 S. Fred Singer et al., *Hot Talk, Cold Science*, pages 70-71.

11 hours, 45 minutes. This, by no coincidence, closely matched the cooling rate of our atmosphere.

In the next series of tests, Moodey heated pure CO_2. The results varied by the type of container used, but he found that at the low end, the CO_2 lost all 22 degrees of heat in three minutes and 45 seconds. From these tests and his recordings of atmospheric temperatures, he concluded that carbon dioxide in the atmosphere cools as rapidly as vaporous air and the sun allow.[8] "Even the vaporous mixture cools faster than [in] 24 hours...In other words, *carbon dioxide is not a greenhouse gas*" (emphasis in original).[9]

Carbon dioxide is a heavy gas with a specific gravity of 1.62. It is 62 percent heavier than air. The CO_2 produced by emissions tends to fall to the Earth and its oceans and is absorbed, where it serves plants in the process of photosynthesis.

I asked Moodey how it is that climate scientists do not know these simple facts about carbon dioxide, or indeed about all so-called greenhouse gases (GHGs). He answered that when the money began to pour in for climate science research, it was directed entirely at academia, where the scientists learn theoretical gas physics to the exclusion of real-world gas physics.

Pedagogy surely explains, in part, the failure of climate scientists to reach reasonable conclusions about the properties of so-called GHGs. But only in part. Climate scientists are also incentivized by sta-

---

8 James Moodey, *The Ladder Out of Poverty: The Great Society Promised to End Poverty in America. It Did Not Work. Here is a Solution That Will Work*, Stairway Press, pages 113-114.

9 Ibid., page 114.

tus, research grants, and plum consultancies to repeat the dogma ad nauseum. And, added to pedagogy and the incentive system is the persecution of so-called deniers. Skeptics surely consider the certain and potentially career-ending inquisition that awaits the heretic. Although not (yet) faced with the literal internment that Galileo endured, climate scientists who publicly refute or even question "the science" are consigned to a prison of opprobrium, denunciation, and professional exclusion.

Yet, these observations merely beg the question: why is the establishment so hell-bent on climate change catastrophism? And what are these agendas that Singer and others have alluded to?

With deep roots in anti-capitalist and romantic ideology traceable to Nazism, the anti-U.S. peace movement, socialism-communism,[10] Soviet disinformation,[11] and the worship of nature, climate change catastrophism has been festering for over fifty years. But the evidence betrays the obvious: climate catastrophism cannot be primarily about the climate. If it were, then Germany, in the face of rising CO_2 emissions since its implementation of *Energiewende* (Energy Transition), would not have hastened the closure of its nuclear power plants, which provide the only reliable source of zero-emissions electricity, other than hydroelectric, which environmentalists also abjure. The same goes for California and New York.[12]

Philosophically, as Alex Epstein has made clear,

---

10 See: Darwall, *Green Tyranny*, op. cit.

11 Natalie Grant, "Green Cross: Gorbachev and Global Enviro-Communism," The Resister 4, no. 3 (1998): 58–62.

12 Darwall, *Green Tyranny*, page xxvi.

226 ᴄᴏ *The Great Reset and the Struggle for Liberty*

climate catastrophism is fueled by an "anti-impact framework," which hamstrings humanity by attempting to eliminate the human impact on the environment altogether. It is anti-human at base. The ideology ranks the wellbeing of "the environment" above human flourishing,[13] while denying that human beings are part of the environment.

The necessary outcome of climate change catastrophism is severely curtailed economic growth. This outcome is ironic, because the global elites at the World Economic Forum (WEF) and the United Nations (UN) regularly suggest that one of their objectives is to achieve "fairness" for people in underdeveloped countries. To date, this "fairness" has involved the de-industrialization of the West as well as wealth transfers from the developed to the developing world that amount to bribes for stemming further development, thus worsening their economies.

Climate change catastrophism boils down to renouncing and eliminating cheap and reliable energy and enriching climate alarmists like Al Gore—all in the interest of furthering a globalist political agenda. Most importantly, climate change catastrophism has to do with the vaunted "solidarity," "inclusivity," and "international cooperation" that the WEF, the UN, favored corporations, and their proxies in government deem necessary to mitigate the supposed crisis. These are code words that stand for a totalitarian regime under which a newly refurbished collectivism abrogates individual rights, curtails human freedom, and dismantles the engines of the economy. Because "the science" of climate change catastrophism is so obviously contrived and borderline fraudulent, one

---

13   Alex Epstein, *Fossil Future*, pages 74-105.

is forced to conclude that *the means* for "reversing climate change" must be *the ends* sought by climate change catastrophists, whether all the catastrophists know it or not. Likewise, rather than continuing our focus on "the science," our attention must be directed to these means/ends.

The Climate Change Catastrophism Complex

"The global climate change regime complex"—as academics David Coen, Julia Kreienkamp, and Tom Pegram unironically refer to the vast constellation of entities and actors responding to supposed anthropogenic climate change—is a set of "closely coupled regulatory regimes that may overlap, complement or conflict with each other."[14] It consists of international intergovernmental governance organizations, independent national advisory bodies, regions, cities, localities, and NGOs and other private sector actors comprising what has been called the Non-State Actor Zone for Climate Action (NAZCA).

Although these academics describe the global climate change regime complex as a non-hierarchical, overlapping, loosely associated assemblage lacking a "central core,"[15] it is ostensibly comprised of a uniform platoon marching in lockstep. Each of the marching soldiers wears a helmet, but the helmets are not artificially camouflaged. Rather, they are affixed with identical leafy branches, symbolizing devotion to the environment and obedience to the dic-

---

14 David Coen, Julia Kreienkamp, and Tom Pegram, *Global Climate Governance*, Cambridge, United Kingdom: Cambridge University Press, 2020, pages 3 and 53.

15 Ibid, page 2.

tates of their commander. The robotic soldiers gaze forward as they march, oblivious to the bystanders, some of whom are "climate deniers." The "climate deniers" view the marching platoon with a mix of wonder and terror, flummoxed at just how this army has been made to function so uniformly and under such discipline—especially considering the fraudulence that they perpetuate.

Disciplined messaging is what one finds when one reads the statements of academics, journalists, regime scientists, activists, or credulous laypersons. The Southern Poverty Law Center's rhetoric is virtually identical to that found almost anywhere climate change is mentioned:

> Despite the barrage of anti-science propaganda, there is virtually no doubt among climate scientists and others that we face huge challenges related to climate change, rising oceans, and resulting disastrous weather events — challenges that it seems certain can only be effectively met by multinational action.[16]

Such patent rhetoric is routinely repeated by all those enrolled in what I'll call the Climate Change Catastrophism Complex (CCCC). The central organ in the CCCC is of course the United Nations, and within the UN, the Framework Convention on Climate Change (UNFCCC), the central oversight agency.[17] As suggested previously, the body responsible

16 "Agenda 21: The UN, Sustainability and Right-Wing Conspiracy Theory," Southern Poverty Law Center, April 1, 2014, https://www.splcenter.org/20140331/agenda-21-un-sustainability-and-right-wing-conspiracy-theory.

17 United Nations Framework Convention on Climate Change,

for scientific publications is the IPCC, which was the joint creation of the United Nations Environment Program (UNEP) and the World Meteorological Organization (WMO). The IPCC operates under the aegis of the UNFCCC.

The UNFCCC establishes the foremost international environmental treaties governing national and global climate change policies encompassing a range of carbon-pricing schemes aimed at mitigating global warming. The first UNFCCC treaty was signed at the 1992 United Nations Conference on Environment and Development (UNCED), otherwise known as Earth Summit, in Rio de Janeiro. Five years later, the Conference of the Parties (COP) established the Kyoto Protocol in 1997.[18] Nineteen years later, COP21 replaced the Kyoto Protocol with the Paris Agreement,[19] otherwise known as the Paris Climate Accords, which went into force in November of 2016,[20] the same year that UN Agenda 2030 and its Sustainable Development Goals were launched.[21]

United Nations, accessed September 8, 2022, https://unfccc.int/files/essential_background/background_publications_htmlpdf/application/pdf/conveng.pdf.

18 "Kyoto Protocol to the United Nations Framework Convention on Climate Change – UNFCCC," United Nations, accessed September 8, 2022, https://unfccc.int/resource/docs/convkp/kpeng.pdf.

19 "Paris Agreement English - Unfccc.int," United Nations, accessed September 8, 2022, https://unfccc.int/sites/default/files/paris_agreement_english_.pdf.

20 "The Paris Agreement," Unfccc.int., accessed September 8, 2022, https://unfccc.int/process-and-meetings/the-paris-agreement/the-paris-agreement.

21 "World Economic Forum and UN Sign Strategic Partnership Framework," World Economic Forum, accessed October 27, 2021, https://www.weforum.org/press/2019/06/world-economic-forum-and-un-sign-strategic-partnership-framework/; "Transforming

Agenda 2030 updated Agenda 21 and the Millennium Development Goals. In 2021, the Paris Climate Accords were updated by the Glasgow Compact of COP26.[22]

The catastrophism of the IPCC reports has been progressively amplified with every iteration and has been adopted by the COPs, even as the evidence to support the IPCC's conclusions has been increasingly shown, even by the IPCC's own implicit admissions, to be sorely lacking. The catastrophism has been kept on life support, no matter the evidence. The tendentious arguments of the IPCC have clearly been decided in advance. S. Fred Singer et al. write regarding the IPCC:

> Politicians set the organization's agenda, name the scientists who are allowed to participate, and rewrite the all-important "Summaries for Policymakers" that the vast majority of policy makers and opinion leaders rely on to understand the thick and highly technical full reports.[23]

These reports feed into the COPs, which then feed into the UN's agenda proclamations. As stated above, the Paris Agreement of 2105 was followed by "The 2030 Agenda for Sustainable Development"

Our World: The 2030 Agenda for Sustainable Development | Department of Economic and Social Affairs," United Nations, accessed October 27, 2021, https://sdgs.un.org/2030agenda.

22   "Report of the Conference of the Parties Serving as the Meeting ... – UNFCCC," United Nations FCCC, March 8, 2022, https://unfccc.int/sites/default/files/resource/cma2021_10_add1_adv.pdf.

23   S. Fred Singer, David R. Legates, and Anthony R. Lupo, *Hot Talk, Cold Science*, page 72.

(Agenda 2030), launched in September of the same year. This project is the shorter-term, updated set of specific prescriptions for implementing the broader Agenda 21. Although neither document is legally binding on the member nations, these agenda documents nevertheless contain the climate change soldiers' marching orders, which many nation states and regions are enacting.

The influence of Agenda 2030 has been enormous. Nearly every mention of climate change includes "2030" as the ubiquitous refrain. The Great Reset is geared to 2030 as the target date for its completion. It is therefore necessary to translate its techno-bureaucratic euphemisms and doublespeak into accessible and forthright language, which I attempt to do next.

CHAPTER TWELVE

Translating Agenda 2030

W ITH ITS APPARENT concern for the universal "common good," leftist ideology provides the best cover for disguising totalitarian ambitions. Leftist totalitarians attempt to exert control over the world for the supposed welfare of the masses, the community, the disadvantaged, the developing world, women, children, the economy, and "the planet." Rightist totalitarianism, on the other hand, wears its totalitarian ambitions on its sleeve. It openly suggests that it must dominate for its own sake, because of some putative natural superiority. Such avowed supremacism does not represent a viable approach for achieving global hegemony. This explains why rightist totalitarianism is very rare, while leftist totalitarianism virtually dominated the twentieth century. (Nazism is a curious case. It was both socialist,[1] while also race supremacist.) Rightist totalitarianism, if it ever exists in pure form, offers

---

1 David Gordon, "Yes, the Nazis Were Socialists," Mises Institute, October 19, 2020, https://mises.org/wire/yes-nazis-were-socialists.

little opportunity for buy-in from the masses; its aim for domination is made too explicit. Leftist totalitarianism, on the other hand, poses as benign and clearly beneficial, as the de facto no-fault ideology whose moral probity is deemed unassailable. A supposed universal concern for "the common good" not only hides its totalitarian ambitions from the masses but also, perhaps, from the elites themselves.

As we have seen, when not avowedly socialist themselves, elites have allied themselves with communists, socialists, fascists, and other such political ideologues and their camps. Having the same object in view as the elites—a singular world system—these ideologues and camps serve the elite's totalitarian ambitions. This explains why globalist billionaires like George Soros routinely support leftist causes and groups while plebeian leftists essentially act as their unwitting foot soldiers and dupes.

As for the elites themselves, there is no sure way to know for sure—other than from confessions or Freudian slips—whether they consciously pursue totalitarianism or whether they believe the egalitarian ideology and rhetoric that they apparently embrace.

It is not as if the totalitarian ambition of leftist elites is anything new, however. In the context of the Great Reset, the roots of its globalist totalitarianism can be traced from the Rhodes Society to the Chatham House to the Council on Foreign Relations to the Bilderberg Group to the Club of Rome to the WEF and the Trilateral Commission. (See Chapter 8.)

Meanwhile, the totalitarian ambitions of the UN have long been descried and criticized. As the CATO Institute's Doug Bandow wrote in 1985:

[T]he UN has been actively promoting a comprehensive and totalitarian system of global management...The overriding UN ideology is one of international control of natural, financial, and informational resources, as well as the global regulation of economic and even cultural activities.[2]

Bandow goes on to state that "world socialism" is the UN's philosophy. This is illustrated in hundreds of UN reports and declarations. Consider these statements from the 1976 Vancouver Declaration on Human Settlements regarding land ownership, for example:

Land is an essential element in development of both urban and rural settlements. *The use and tenure of land should be subject to public control* because of its limited supply through appropriate measures and legislation including policies agrarian reform policies (emphasis mine).[3]

Land, because of its unique nature and the crucial role it plays in human settlements, *cannot be treated as an ordinary asset, controlled by individuals and subject to the pressures and inefficiencies of the market. Private ownership*

---

2 Doug Bandow, "Totalitarian Global Management: The UN's War on the Liberal International Economic Order," Cato Institute, October 24, 1985, https://www.cato.org/policy-analysis/totalitarian-global-management-uns-war-liberal-international-economic-order.

3 "Report of Habitat: United Nations Conference on Human Settlements," United Nations, 1976, https://documents-dds-ny.un.org/doc/UNDOC/GEN/N76/967/11/PDF/N7696711.pdf, page 8.

is also a principal instrument of accumulation and concentration of wealth and therefore contributes to social injustice; if unchecked, it may become a major obstacle in the planning and implementation of development schemes. Social justice, urban renewal, and development, the provision of decent dwellings and healthy conditions for the people can only be achieved if land is used in the interests of society as a whole...(emphasis mine).

Instead, the pattern of land use should be determined by the long-term interests of the community...

Public control of land use is therefore indispensable to its protection as an asset.[4]

I will add that the UN has apparently been informed by the Leninist notion that imperialism is late-stage capitalism (a conflation of political plunder and economic activity) and that the developing world is the proletariat exploited by wealthier nations.[5] This zero-sum thinking—premised on the false notion that the creation of wealth produces poverty for others and depends on it—informs the UN's many declarations and demands.

We have already seen that the UN's ideology is an elite-managed socialism. Bandow adds the following: "In addition to providing a forum for the

---

4   Ibid., page 61.

5   V.I. Lenin, "Imperialism, the Highest Stage of Capitalism," Marxists Internet Archive, accessed September 4, 2022, https://www. marxists.org/archive/lenin/works/1916/imp-hsc/. See publication information at website.

ideology of global management, the UN also helps underwrite the development and spread of redistributionist ideas."[6] That is, the UN's pronouncements, while not necessarily binding on member states, support the propensity of states to engage in centralized planning and management. Such planning and management grow the state and add to its powers. The UN thus works to undermine free market principles, thwarting the developing world's full participation in the free market and likewise cosigning on the developing world's poverty. This global management ideology does not yield to the self-direction of those it claims to serve but rather issues from an international elite whose power the UN represents and nurtures.

It is with such socialist, statist, and elitist inclinations in mind that we must read "Transforming Our World: The 2030 Agenda for Sustainable Development" (hereafter "Agenda 2030").[7]

While Agenda 2030 does not address climate change exclusively, the document is shot through with climate change catastrophism and an overall environmental alarmism. The belief that the planet is facing a climate emergency and worsening environmental degradation informs the entire agenda. The state of emergency is used as a pretext for exerting centralized control.

The words "sustainable," "sustainability," "sustainably," and "sustainable development" are used

---

6 Doug Bandow, "Totalitarian Global Management: The UN's War on the Liberal International Economic Order," op. cit.

7 "Transforming Our World: The 2030 Agenda for Sustainable Development | Department of Economic and Social Affairs," United Nations, accessed October 27, 2021, https://sdgs.un.org/2030agenda.

over 200 times in the 41-page document, including the word "sustainable" in the title, although the terms are never defined. The meaning of these cognate terms can be gleaned by tracing their historical roots.

Although he didn't use the term, the concept of "sustainable growth" dates to Thomas Malthus in his famous *Essay on Population*, first published in 1798.[8] As discussed in Chapter 9, Malthus argued that human population, when left unchecked, tends to grow exponentially, while the resources that humans depend on for sustenance tend to grow arithmetically. According to Malthus, human beings inevitably encounter natural limits to population growth (and happiness). He didn't provide an adequate explanation for why human population naturally outstrips that of the species on which it depends for its alimentary needs—except to point to the limits of space and nutriments imposed on other species and the (apparently insatiable) sex drive of human beings. But there is no reason to assume that human population grows exponentially while the population of the species it depends on grows arithmetically. The premise entirely discounts the power of human ingenuity to increase production. (This premise also led Malthus to deny the perfectibility of human beings and society and to inveigh against the "Poor Laws" in England, which provided the poor relief that he argued should be discontinued, because it only increased misery by encouraging excess reproduction.)

As discussed previously, Malthusianism was transmuted into neo-Malthusianism throughout the

---

8 Thomas Robert Malthus, *An Essay on the Principle of Population*, London: J. Johnson, 1798.

nineteenth and twentieth centuries, evolving into a progressive ideology whose adherents advocated (often coercive) birth control methods and family planning.

The Club of Rome, the neo-Malthusian association founded in 1968 in Italy, used the term "sustainable" six times in its first major publication, *The Limits to Growth* (1972)—in connection with panic around population growth, resource depletion, and environmental degradation.[9] These same associations attached to its frequent use of the word "sustainable" in *The First Global Revolution*, published in 1992, which added climate change to the Club of Rome's list of pressing and interlocking issues facing humanity ("the global problematique").[10] Published in the same year, the Club of Rome's *Beyond the Limits: Confronting Global Collapse, Envisioning a Sustainable Future* presents an even more dire picture of unfettered economic and population growth than its forebear, *The Limits to Growth*. It uses the word "sustainable" no less than 128 times.[11]

In the 1987 "Brundtland Report," also called "Our Common Future," the World Commission on Environmental Development (WCED)—an interna-

---

9   Donella H. Meadows, Dennis L. Meadows, Jorgen Randers, and William W. Behrens III, *The Limits to Growth: A Report of the Club of Rome's Project on the Predicament of Mankind*, New York, NY: Universe Books, 1972.

10   Alexander King and Bertrand Schneider, *The First Global Revolution: A Report by the Council of the Club of Rome*, London: Simon & Schuster, 1992.

11   Donella H. Meadows, Dennis L. Meadows, and Jorgen Randers, *Beyond the Limits: Confronting Global Collapse, Envisioning a Sustainable Future*, Post Mills, Vermont: Chelsea Green Publishing Company, 1992.

tional group of environmental "experts," politicians, and civil servants—coined the now ubiquitous term, "sustainable development."[12] Published at the behest of the General Assembly of the UN, with Maurice Strong as the leading commissioner, the UN report figures "sustainable development" as "intimately linked to the dynamics of population growth."[13] Population growth, the report argues, is more problematic in developed nations than in developing ones: "A child born in a country where levels of material and energy use are high places a greater burden on the Earth's resources than a child born in a poorer country."[14] This belief translates into the insistence that the developed world must reduce its consumption (and population), which connects to the WEF's economic model of reduced expectations and consumption for the majority in the developed world. The WCED used the term "sustainable development" a total of 197 times to describe the impacts of economic and population growth on traditional communities, "ecosystem conservation," resource depletion and degradation, "equity," food security, global warming, pollution, international conflicts, and in consideration of national sovereignty, the last of which is seen as an impediment to sustainable development.

From these neo-Malthusian documents, we may conclude that terms with the root word "sustain-

---

12 Gro Harlem Brundtland, *Report of the World Commission on Environment and Development: "Our Common Future,"* New York, NY: United Nations, 1987, https://sustainabledevelopment.un.org/content/documents/5987our-common-future.pdf.

13 Ibid., page 51.

14 Ibid.

able" point to the belief that the human population and the economy cannot continue to grow safely and "equitably." These texts represent neo-Malthusianism because they posit new limits to economic and population growth and new problems deriving from such growth. Further, we can conclude from the uses of terms with the root word "sustainable" that environmentalism, including climate change catastrophism, is inextricably connected with population control "ethics," or neo-Malthusianism.

The UN's Agenda 2030 draws directly on such neo-Malthusian roots. The report states: "We reaffirm the outcomes of all major United Nations conferences and summits which have laid a solid foundation for sustainable development," including "the Programme of Action of the UN's International Conference on Population and Development."[15] As discussed in Chapter 9, this Programme of Action builds on five previous international and world conferences on population, including four UN conferences and the League of Nations' seminal World Population Conference, which involved Malthusian-eugenicist, Margaret Sanger and eugenicist Raymond Pearl. (Pearl was funded by the Rockefeller Foundation.) The UN also promotes birth control, including abortion,[16] and advocates "gender equality,"[17] which, as

---

15 "Transforming Our World: The 2030 Agenda for Sustainable Development," page 8.

16 "USA: UN Experts Denounce Supreme Court Decision to Strike down Roe v. Wade, Urge Action to Mitigate Consequences," OHCHR, June 24, 2022, https://www.ohchr.org/en/press-releases/2022/06/usa-un-experts-denounce-supreme-court-decision-strike-down-roe-v-wade-urge.

17 "Transforming Our World: The 2030 Agenda for Sustainable Development," passim.

we have seen, amounts to the exclusive promotion of careerism for women, largely advanced to reduce reproduction. The UN also opposes unlimited, unfettered, and uncontrolled economic growth, which is intimately connected to population growth. The main pretext for problematizing economic growth for the UN is the protection of the environment, especially in connection with climate change. The enviro-neo-Malthusian preoccupation with unfettered growth, including population growth, is embodied in Agenda 2030. Furthermore, given its collectivist ethos, its penchant for advocating centralized control over the economy, and its climate catastrophism, the solutions are always top-down dictates. To avert disaster, a statist and "stakeholder" elite must steer the economy and manage/reduce world development and control population.

Agenda 2030 includes 17 Sustainable Development Goals (SDGs) and 169 targets. The SDGs are the successors to the UN's Millennium Development Goals (MDGs)[18] and UN Agenda 21,[19] the latter of which was launched as the result of the 1992 UN Conference on Environment and Development held in Rio de Janeiro and led by WEF board member Maurice Strong.[20]

---

18 "United Nations Millennium Development Goals," United Nations, accessed August 10, 2022, https://www.un.org/millennium-goals/bkgd.shtml.

19 "Agenda 21: Sustainable Development Knowledge Platform," United Nations, 1991, https://sustainabledevelopment.un.org/outcomedocuments/agenda21/.

20 "United Nations Conference on Environment and Development, Rio de Janeiro, Brazil, 3-14 June 1992," United Nations, Accessed August 10, 2022, https://www.un.org/en/conferences/environment/rio1992.

The 17 SDGs,[21] along with my translations, follow:

Goal 1: End poverty in all its forms everywhere.

Translation: Exert centralized government and stakeholder control using central banks, the International Monetary Fund (IMF), and the World Bank, possibly using central bank digital currencies (CBDCs; see Part IV) to rapidly redistribute wealth.

Goal 2: End hunger, achieve food security and improved nutrition and promote sustainable agriculture.

Translation: Exert centralized governmental and stakeholder control over agriculture with the consolidation of land ownership by the state or preferred owners; reduce/eliminate nitrates in fertilizers; eliminate pesticides in farming; introduce vertical urban farming; introduce new "sustainable" sources of protein (insects and synthetic meats); redistribute wealth to draw down consumption in the developed world.

Goal 3: Ensure healthy lives and promote well-being for all at all ages.

Translation: Redistribute health care with centralized governmental and stakeholder planning and control; promote mandatory vaccinations through the World Health Organization (WHO); possibly use technology to monitor organs and organ systems reporting to central databases (the Internet of Bodies, IoB; see Part IV).

---

21 "Do you know all 17 SDGs?," Department of Economic and Social Affairs, United Nations, April 20, 2018, https://sdgs.un.org/goals.

Goal 4: Ensure inclusive and equitable quality education and promote lifelong learning opportunities for all.

Translation: Exert centralized government and intergovernmental control over education; eliminate ideological opposition to UN objectives; promote collectivist ideology (propaganda and reeducation).

Goal 5: Achieve gender equality and empower all women and girls.

Translation: Promote careerism as the path for women as well as governmental and intergovernmental sponsored family planning through birth control (including abortion) to reduce population growth.

Goal 6: Ensure availability and sustainable management of water and sanitation for all.

Translation: Exert centralized governmental and stakeholder control over water resources; dictate acceptable access to and use of rivers and streams by controlling and/or eliminating unapproved industries that rely on water resources (such as fracking); privatize water with ownership in the approved hands, etc.

Goal 7: Ensure access to affordable, reliable, sustainable and modern energy for all.

Translation: Promote and legislate renewable energy to the exclusion of fossil-fuel-based energy; exercise centralized control of energy production and distribution using government sanctions, subsidies, taxes, and financial pressure on corporations

(ESGs); outmode/outlaw gasoline consumption and gas-driven locomotion; monitor and restrict carbon-based energy use with individual carbon footprint tracking (see Part IV); allow/encourage/mandate the purchase of carbon credits from the poor by the wealthy.

Goal 8: Promote sustained, inclusive and sustainable economic growth, full and productive employment and decent work for all.

Translation: Exert centralized control of the economy by governments and stakeholders using subsidies and sanctions to curtail/redirect growth in line with climate change catastrophist projections; provide state-based employment for the unemployed.

Goal 9: Build resilient infrastructure, promote inclusive and sustainable industrialization and foster innovation.

Translation: Exert centralized governmental and stakeholder control over infrastructure development to eliminate fossil-fuel-powered infrastructure with subsidies for renewables and sanctions and prohibitive taxes on fossil fuels.

Goal 10: Reduce inequality within and among countries.

Translation: Redistribute wealth by central planners within and especially between nation states; transfer wealth from the developed to the developing world to prevent development not in line with climate catastrophism and to fund sustainable development.

Goal 11: Make cities and human settlements inclusive, safe, resilient and sustainable.

Translation: Exert centralized governmental and stakeholder control over urban planning through government-backed architectural projects; limit living space through "smart" architectural designs and zoning laws; limit resource use through "smart" monitoring technologies and smart cities; locate populations within reach of public transportation to reduce/eliminate automobile use; overwrite zoning laws that prevent the building of high-rise housing in the suburbs.

Goal 12: Ensure sustainable consumption and production patterns.

Translation: Exert centralized governmental and stakeholder control over production and consumption to reduce/eliminate the use of fossil fuels and meat consumption and enforce the use of renewable energy in factories and plants through subsidies, sanctions, and taxes; implement and mandate ESGs across all sectors of the economy (the WEF helps here); exert governmental and stakeholder control over farming to reduce "greenhouse gas" emissions; introduce new "sustainable" sources of protein (insects and synthetic meats).

Goal 13: Take urgent action to combat climate change and its impacts.*

*Acknowledging that the United Nations Framework Convention on Climate Change is the primary international, intergovernmental forum for negotiating the global response to climate change.

Translation: Climate change catastrophism stemming from IPCC reports must dictate energy policies and all other resource use policies, which must be directed by the UN. All other sources of information must be deemed "misinformation" or "disinformation" and dismissed/condemned as climate change "denialism," akin to violent extremism.

Goal 14: Conserve and sustainably use the oceans, seas and marine resources for sustainable development.

Translation: Exert centralized governmental, intergovernmental, and stakeholder control over oceans and other large bodies of water; control access to oceans and bays; limit/outlaw drilling on ocean floors; control fishing rights, etc.

Goal 15: Protect, restore and promote sustainable use of terrestrial ecosystems, sustainably manage forests, combat desertification, and halt and reverse land degradation and halt biodiversity loss.

Translation: Exert centralized governmental and stakeholder control over land use; revert farmland to nature conservatories (see Chapter 14); induce states and/or approved stakeholders (private buyers) to accumulate and control land to prevent unsustainable/unwanted farming and development; reintroduce wild species and reduce the population of farm animals that putatively contribute to global warming.

Goal 16: Promote peaceful and inclusive societies for sustainable development, provide access to justice for all and build effective, accountable and inclusive institutions at all levels.

Translation: Peacekeeping must come from UN dictates; unapproved wars are "unsustainable," and states must be controlled by international law stemming from the UN; punish violators and "violent extremists," including those who resist UN dictates; use international bodies like NATO to pressure nations to abide by UN decrees; law becomes international by virtue of universal governmental adoption of UN policy recommendations.

Goal 17: Strengthen the means of implementation and revitalize the Global Partnership for Sustainable Development.

Translation: Turn policy recommendations into law; enroll corporate and state partners in the efforts to meet the SDGs (the WEF and its corporate partnerships apply here).

The meaning of Agenda 2030 comes into focus when we understand that consumption patterns in the developed world are considered harmful to the environment and are thought to exacerbate climate change. Redistributing wealth from the developed to the developing world thus reduces production and consumption in the developed world, where most of the damage to the environment is thought to take place. Likewise, equity—the redistribution of wealth—leads to sustainability, and vice versa. Thus, "equity" is not only supposed to help the poor but also is thought to mitigate negative environmental impacts. Further, population control is necessary so that increased production and consumption (growth) do not become sources of additional environmental damage, including exacerbated climate change. "Gender equality" must be understood in these terms. It represents the financial, medical, and sociopolitical encouragement of careerism and "reproductive health" (birth control) for women as a means for reducing population growth. Neo-Malthusian constraints are thus adopted "voluntarily." (See Chapter 9.)

Thus, Agenda 2030 promotes socialist redistribution, while relying on enviro-neo-Malthusianism. Underlying this vision is zero-sum thinking. According to this conception, wealth is necessarily represented as a static, fixed sum—not only because resources are regarded as finite but also because growth is considered environmentally unsustainable. Thus, "equity" can only be accomplished through wealth transfers from the developed to the developing world. Wealth transfers likewise amount to bribes to the developing world to inhibit or prevent "unsustainable" development. "Equity" not only averts the supposed looming environmental catastrophe by reducing consumption in the developed world and "unsustainable" development in the developing world but also allows the agenda to appear humanitarian even while leading to economic loss in the developed world and continued immiseration in the developing world. In short, the transfer of wealth is considered both environmentally essential and economically "fair." This is what is meant by the Great Reset's "fairer, greener future."[22]

On June 13, 2019, the WEF signed a memorandum of understanding with the UN to form a part-

---

22 Klaus Schwab and Thierry Malleret, *COVID-19: The Great Reset*, Geneva: Forum Publishing, 2020, p. 57.

nership centered on advancing Agenda 2030.[23] The WEF published the "United Nations-World Economic Forum Strategic Partnership Framework for the 2030 Agenda" shortly thereafter.[24] The WEF promised to help "finance" Agenda 2030. The framework also commits the WEF to helping the UN "meet the needs of the Fourth Industrial Revolution," including providing assets and expertise for "digital governance" (surveillance, etc.; see Part IV). Agenda 2030 appears to have been tailor-made to accommodate the UN-WEF partnership. It adopts the stakeholder concept introduced by Schwab decades earlier. The word "stakeholders" is used no less than 13 times in the 2030 resolution. The Great Reset, then, may be understood as the WEF's contribution to achieving the SDGs of Agenda 2030.

23 "World Economic Forum and UN Sign Strategic Partnership Framework," World Economic Forum, accessed October 27, 2021, https://www.weforum.org/press/2019/06/world-economic-forum-and-un-sign-strategic-partnership-framework/; "Transforming Our World: The 2030 Agenda for Sustainable Development," Department of Economic and Social Affairs, United Nations, accessed October 27, 2021, https://sdgs.un.org/2030agenda.

24 "The United Nations-World Economic Forum Strategic Partnership Framework for the 2030 Agenda," World Economic Forum, https://weforum.ent.box.com/s/rdlgipawkjxi2vdaidw8npbtyach2qbt.

CHAPTER THIRTEEN

The Great Leap Backward

Т HIS CHAPTER'S TITLE derisively refers to the notorious Great Leap Forward (1958-1961) as the Great Leap Backward. But China's Great Leap Forward is not the ultimate object of my scorn. That scorn is reserved for the contemporary project conducted by people, who, if they knew anything about history, or cared about its results, would never propose this treacherous and potentially world-devastating campaign called the Great Reset—unless their intentions are evil and not merely misguided.

Meanwhile, I'm not the first to think of this appellation in connection with Mao's Great Leap. That distinction may be held by a Soviet critic of Mao's quixotic strategies. In an article entitled "The Great Leap Backward," one A. Khan'kovskiy treated the Great Leap Forward as a major deviation from the "successful" Soviet socialist system that had followed "the Great October Socialist Revolution."[1]

---

1 A. Khan'kovskiy, "The Great Leap Backward," *Literaturnaya Gazeta*, no. 36 (September 6, 1967): 14–15. Pages in the retrieved document do not maintain the original pagination. I will refer to the page

According to the Soviet writer, Khan'kovskiy, the Soviets had undertaken their glorious revolution under unfavorable conditions. They had established a socialist state against "the united front of the imperialist powers."[2] (Meanwhile, the Soviets were launched and kept afloat by Western—especially U.S.—financing and technology.[3]) In spite of these difficulties, the Soviets had set the standard and vouchsafed to the Chinese a blueprint and model that it might follow. In the case of China, "[t]he gigantic might of the Soviet state was on its side." The Chinese benefitted from Soviet support as the Soviets treated the Chinese like a doting parent would its child. They had sent manpower, intelligence, material supplies, and money:

> Our country gave China economic and political aid: For many years an entire army of Soviet specialists—over 10,000 people—worked in China. They helped build factories, automotive vehicle, tractor and machine building plants, electric power stations, radio stations, mines, bridges (the famous bridge across the Yangtse) River, highways...[4]

Even American politicians had acknowledged the Soviet Union's largesse. According to Khan'kovskiy, a joint commission of the U.S. Congress wrote in a two-volume treatise on the Chinese economy:

numbers of the retrieved document.

2 Ibid., page 1.

3 Antony C. Sutton, *Wall Street and the Bolshevik Revolution*, Forest Row: Clairview, 2016; Antony C. Sutton, *National Suicide: Military Aid to the Soviet Union*, Dauphin Publications Inc., 2021.

4 Khan'kovskiy, "The Great Leap Backward," page 1.

"history is unaware of a similar example in which a country [the Soviet Union] would offer on a plate an entire industrial system."[5]

With Soviet assistance and funding, the Chinese began to trudge the road of happy destiny. In the first several years since the establishment of the Chinese People's Republic, Chinese economic output had increased by several factors. From 1949 to 1957, as noted by the U.S. congressional commission, the index of industrial production of the Chinese People's Republic rose by over 400 percent. China was on track to become another "successful" socialist state. For China, "[a]ll possibilities existed for a progress toward communism, following the true and tried way laid by the Great October Revolution."[6]

Mao's Early Career

In addition to the Soviet Union's aid to Communist China, Mao benefitted personally and politically from Western and Eastern European assistance. Mao had been supported in his early communist career by Yale University vis-à-vis Yale-in-China.[7] As Jonathan Spence, a professor of Chinese history, put it:

> In 1919, Mao, aged 26, was in Changsa, having his middle school education. He visited Peking and while there received his...serious introduction to communist theory in Li Ta-chao's Marxist Study Group. Now, if he was to develop

---

5 Ibid., page 2.

6 Ibid.

7 "Yale Group Spurs Mao's Emergence," *Yale Daily News*, February 29, 1972, page 1.

a reputation in socialist circles, he had to find a forum to propagate his views...At this crucial point the student union of Yale-in-China invited Mao to take over the editorship of their journal.[8]

The *Yale Daily News* noted that Mao accepted the offer. With Mao at the helm, the paper would now be refocused to include social criticism of contemporary issues and work toward "thought reorientation."[9]

After studying Marxist theory in Peking, Mao moved to Shanghai, where he met Ch'en Tu-hsiu, who later became the Communist Party leader. Ch'en instructed Mao to form an area branch of the party in Peking, but Mao found that he lacked the funds. Yale-in-China intervened again. Spence noted that "Yale-in-China agreed to rent him three rooms, which Mao named his 'culture bookshop.'" Business boomed as Mao rang up "high sales" with such titles in Chinese as *An Introduction to Marx's Capital, A Study of the New Russia*, and *The Soviet System in China*. Mao established branches of his bookstore and from the profits was able to establish several socialist youth corps and fund the Communist Party. Due to his success, Mao was chosen as one of the delegates to the 1st National Congress of the Chinese Communist Party at Shanghai in 1921. "From there it was only a small step to becoming one of the founders of the Communist movement in his country."[10]

Yale-in-China was not the only foreign benefac-

---

8 Spence qtd. in ibid.

9 Ibid.

10 Ibid., Spence qtd. in ibid.

tor of the Chinese Communist Party (CCP) and its leader, however. Others included those who lived in and worked for the Communists in China: Grigorii Voitinski (born as Grigorii Naumovitch Zarkhin, leading Soviet Comintern emissary, "encouraged a group of [Chinese] intellectuals to establish the CCP, in secret"), Michail Borodin (born Mikhail Markovich Gruzenberg, leading Soviet Comintern emissary), Adolph Abramovich Joffe (Comintern emissary, Soviet ambassador to the official government in Beijing, 1922-1924), Pavel Mif (Comintern emissary, who also worked at the Foreign Languages Institute), Vladimir Abramovich Neumann (born Vladimir Abramovich Nieman, Comintern emissary), Boris Zakharovich Shumiatsky (Comintern emissary), David Crook (worked at the Foreign Languages Institute), Sidney Rittenberg (first American to become a CCP member, discussed below), Israel Epstein (editor-in-chief of *China Reconstructs* and member of the Chinese People's Political Consultative Conference), Sidney Shapiro (worked at the Bureau of Cultural Relations with the Foreign Countries and the Foreign Languages Press), Solomon Adler (co-translator of *Mao's Collected Works* into English), Sam Ginsbourg (worked on the translation of *Quotations from Chairman Mao Tse-tung*), and Michael Shapiro (co-translator of *Mao's Collected Works* into English).[11]

Of special interest for our purposes is Sidney Rittenberg. Rittenberg represents the kind of subversive elite that I referred to in this book's Intro-

---

11   Yitzhak Shichor, "Combining Contradictions: Jewish Contributions to the Chinese Revolution," *International Journal of China Studies* 11, no. 2 (December 2020): 183–212.

duction. In an extensive obituary for *The New York Times* in 2019, Robert McFadden tells how Rittenberg became an intimate of Mao and a legendary figure in the Chinese Communist Party.[12] Born to a prominent South Carolinian family, Rittenberg joined the American Communist Party in 1940, at age 19. Drafted into the military, he was forced to relinquish his party membership, and was trained in foreign languages at Stanford University. In his first (and last) U.S. military assignment, Rittenberg was sent to China to serve as a linguist for the Judge Advocate General.

Upon his discharge in 1946, Rittenberg joined a United Nations relief agency in Shanghai, where he met Communists who convinced him to join their movement. He undertook his own 45-day "long march" to Yan'an, where he met Mao in a mountain military sanctuary and became a member of the CCP, with Mao's explicit endorsement. A translator of news dispatches for the party's propaganda arm and an interpreter of Chinese for communiqués with international leaders, Rittenberg later became the head of China's Broadcast Administration (Radio Beijing). As a leading propagandist, he promoted and glorified the Great Leap Forward and the Cultural Revolution:

> Mr. Rittenberg was an avid propagandist during Mao's Great Leap Forward, a campaign from 1958 to 1961 to transform China from an

---

12 Robert D. McFadden, "Sidney Rittenberg, Idealistic American Aide to Mao Who Evolved to Counsel Capitalists, Dies at 98," *The New York Times*, August 25, 2019, https://www.nytimes.com/2019/08/24/world/sidney-rittenberg-dead.html.

agrarian economy to a collectivized, industrialized society...

He was even more directly involved in the
early stages of Mao's Cultural Revolution, a
decade-long purge of "bourgeois" intellectuals, party officials and others suspected of anti-Maoist thought. Starting in 1966, thousands
of young Red Guards persecuted millions with
imprisonment, torture, public humiliation and
property seizures in struggles to create a Maoist cult of personality. Mr. Rittenberg joined
the Red Guards in denouncing what they called
"establishment" bureaucrats and haranguing
the masses. His speeches and news conferences
were published in the Red Guard newspapers.
One famous picture from the era shows Mao
autographing Mr. Rittenberg's copy of his "Little Red Book" of sayings. Another shows Mr.
Rittenberg on a speaker's platform, holding the
book up and exhorting crowds in Beijing's Tiananmen Square to defend Mao's thoughts.[13]

After serving a second prison sentence in China
on the false charge of being a spy, Rittenberg, who
still believed in the revolution, returned to the U.S.
in 1979. He soon monetized his knowledge of the
Chinese communist culture and the business community and helped Western corporations, especially
Big Tech firms, to cash in on socialism with Chinese
characteristics (or capitalism with Chinese characteristics; see Chapter 4).[14] As such, he contributed

---

13 Ibid.

14 Gary Rivlin, "A Long March from Maoism to Microsoft,"
The New York Times, December 5, 2004, https://www.nytimes.
com/2004/12/05/business/yourmoney/a-long-march-from-maoism-

to China's developing market economy while subverting elements of the U.S. business establishment,
especially the technology sector, which became be-
holden to the ideologically communist country.

But I digress.

Figure 3.1: Mao and Rittenberg, NPR

Mao's Leap into Madness

Khan'kovskiy suggested that Mao's voluntarism[15] soon got the better of him. The 8th National
Congress of the Chinese Communist Party was held
in 1956. The Congress approved the proposals for
the second Five-Year Plan for 1958-1962. "There was
no question of any adventuristic 'leaps' or of 'com-

---

to-microsoft.html.

15 In Marxist thought, voluntarism refers to an overemphasis on
the subjective conditions (will, consciousness) for revolution. It deviates from the orthodox Marxist position, which emphasizes "objective conditions," which are deemed to be determinative.

munes.'"[16] But the Maoists dismissed this original plan, as Mao decided to accelerate development radically. "The Maoists simply threw it overboard, replacing a more or less efficient program with high sounding phrases of 'great leaps' and 'red banners.'"[17]

A second session of the 8th National Congress of the Chinese Communist Party was convened in May 1958. At this convention, Mao introduced his new revolutionary scheme. "The shrieking slogan which all of Mao's stooges soon began learning by rote was: 'By tensing all our forces, by striving forward, let us build socialism on the principle of more, faster, better and more economically!'"[18] Mao aimed "to have China reach the production levels reached by the capitalist countries in the course of 100 to 200 years, in 10-20 or even less years."[19]

The Great Leap Forward was an attempt to increase crop yields dramatically and to industrialize the countryside—to make local communities self-sustaining while increasing agricultural and industrial yields for the state. To accomplish these feats, the peasants were reorganized into massive communes of thousands and even tens of thousands, where all resources were communally shared, including food. Private ownership of land and free trade were abolished, along with the right to leave the collective.[20] To avail women for farming, communal dining halls were established. With women working the commu-

---

16 A. Khan'kovskiy, "The Great Leap Backward," page 2.

17 Ibid.

18 Ibid., page 3.

19 Ibid.

20 That is, the property rights of the peasantry were completely abrogated, the first instance of which is ownership of oneself.

nal farms, many men were likewise made available for small-scale "industrial" production. Communes were instructed to produce steel in homemade, back-yard furnaces. A massive campaign to collect metal tools to transform everything into steel was conducted. Khan'kovskiy mockingly described this effort:

> The Maoists intended to catch up with Brit-ain by creating thousands and thousands of dwarf blast furnaces. It has been described al-ready how everywhere, in cities and villages, on squares, streets and deserts, everywhere ore was to be smelted.[21]

On the agricultural front, to justify the overseed-ing of land, "Mao had proclaimed his belief that 'in company grain grows fast; seeds are happiest when growing together'—attempting to impose class soli-darity on nature."[22] Seeds were sown at five to ten times the normal density, with the predictable result that many young plants were choked off and died. The Chinese adopted farming methods from the Soviet "agrobiologist," Trofim Lysenko, a neo-La-marckian who rejected Mendelian genetics and in-stead held to the Lamarckian inheritance of acquired characteristics. The results were disastrous:

> Wheat and maize never grow well together in the same fields, and the replacement of the tra-ditional barley crop with wheat in the high, cold fields of Tibet was simply catastrophic. Other

21 A. Khan'kovskiy, "The Great Leap Backward," page 4.
22 Stéphane Courtois and Mark Kramer, *The Black Book of Commu-nism: Crimes, Terror, Repression*, Cambridge, MA: Harvard Universi-ty Press, 2004, page 489.

mistakes were made in the nationwide campaign. The extermination of the sparrows that
ate the grain resulted in a massive increase in
the number of parasites. A large amount of hy-
draulic equipment that had been hurriedly and
carelessly built was found to be useless or even
dangerous because of the increased erosion
and the risk of flooding at the first high tide.
Moreover, the cost of its construction in terms
of human life had been enormous: more than
10,000 out of 60,000 workers had died on one
site in Henan.[23]

The peasants exhausted themselves in everything but agriculture, having been drafted into engineering projects and small-scale steel production,
the products of which were virtually worthless. As
Khan'kovskiy put it, Mao had turned "millions of
experienced grain growers into amateur metallur-
gists."[24] The mismatch of competence and assigned
duties represented a devastating loss in productive
output.

The Black Book of Communism, reviled by
Western Marxists, sardonically described the overall
efforts as follows:

> In this happy dream that was to bring real
> Communism within reach, the accumulation of
> capital and a rapid rise in the standard of living
> were to go hand in hand. All that had to be done
> was to achieve the simple objectives set by the
> Party.[25]

23 Ibid.

24 A. Khan'kovskiy, "The Great Leap Backward," page 4.

25 Stéphane Courtois and Mark Kramer, *The Black Book of Commu-*

When the crop yields fell and the death toll rose, the Maoist regime began a campaign of denial, doublespeak, torture, and mass murder. The secretary of the Xinyang district wrote: "The problem is not that food is lacking. There are sufficient quantities of grain, but 90 percent of the inhabitants are suffering from ideological difficulties."[26] Sound familiar?

There is much more to this history. Suffice it to say that the Great Leap Forward precipitated the worst famine in recorded history. Deaths attributable to the famine of 1958-1961 numbered between 20 and 43 million, including those children who were murdered, boiled, and turned into fertilizer.[27]

The Ultimate Great Leap Backward

Before I point to the primary similarity between China's Great Leap Forward and the Great Reset, some notable differences should be conceded. But even these differences do not weigh in favor of the Great Reset. Whereas the Great Leap Forward was a misguided attempt to increase crop yields dramatically and industrialize the countryside, the Great Reset aims deliberately at deindustrialization and will effect a reduction in agricultural output. The Great Leap Forward established the People's Commune and enforced collective "ownership" of land and other resources. Great Reset-initiated policies will lead to the consolidation of farmland in the hands of fewer owners, those with sufficient capital to undertake agriculture under stifling regulations and policies to meet Agenda 2030's sustainable development goals

nism, page 488.
26 Qtd. in ibid., page 492.
27 Ibid., pages 492-493.

(SDGs). Whereas during the early phase of the Great Leap Forward, eating meat was celebrated as a revolutionary act,[28] under the Great Reset, eating meat is deemed reactionary and unsustainable while eating insects and synthetic meats is promoted and celebrated as environmentally conscious.[29] The putative object of the Great Leap Forward was to increase gross domestic product to equal or surpass that of developed nations, particularly Great Britain, and to raise the standard of living of the peasants and the population at large. The Great Reset, on the other hand, represents deliberate de-growth and reduced standards of living of the lower and middle classes in the developed world and the squelching of growth in the developing world. While the Great Leap Forward was implemented to hasten the arrival of full communism, the Great Reset establishes corporate socialism, economic fascism, and neo-feudalism. (See Part I.) Despite the technological innovations of the Fourth Industrial Revolution (discussed in Part IV), the Great Reset is a de-civilizational project.

Yet, the Great Leap Forward and the Great Reset share one essential feature: the arbitrary imposition of a collectivist unscientific ideology on all human activity and nature. During the Great Leap Forward, Lysenkoism was adopted from the Soviet Union for ideological reasons, despite its disastrous effects

28 Ibid., page 488.
29 See for example, Amrou Awaysheh and Christine J. Picard, Ph.D., "5 Reasons Why Eating Insects Can Reduce Climate Change," World Economic Forum, February 9, 2022, https://www.weforum.org/agenda/2022/02/how-insects-positively-impact-climate-change/; Kate Whiting, "How Soon Will We Be Eating Lab-Grown Meat?" World Economic Forum, October 16, 2020, https://www.weforum.org/agenda/2020/10/will-we-eat-lab-grown-meat-world-food-day/.

there. During the Great Reset, climate catastrophism has been adopted on equally ideological, unscientific grounds. "The science" we are told to follow is a sham. Against the facts of science and the benefits of technology, we are told that CO_2 is pollution, that "sustainability" requires imposing an enormous tax on humanity for the respiration of plants, and that farming methods of the original Green Revolution, which have increased yields by many factors, must be eliminated and replaced with a new environmentalist Green Revolution. We are told that industrial production must be carried on using non-fossil-fuel inputs. These demands are as delusional as anything advocated by Chairman Mao.

Carbon neutrality by 2050 is an insanely impossible demand. Our industrial civilization and the population it supports depend on the advances made in fossil fuel extraction and use. Even Vaclav Smil, a believer in climate change, who is an otherwise credible source, agrees:

> For those who ignore the energetic and material imperatives of our world, those who prefer mantras of green solutions to understanding how we have come to this point, the prescription is easy: just decarbonize—switch from burning fossil carbon to converting inexhaustible flows of renewable energies. The real wrench in the works: we are a fossil-fueled civilization whose technical and scientific advances, quality of life, and prosperity rest on the combustion of huge quantities of fossil carbon, and we cannot simply walk away from this critical determinant of our fortunes in a few decades, never mind years.

> Complete decarbonization of the global econo-
> my by 2050 is now conceivable only at the cost
> of unthinkable global economic retreat, or as a
> result of extraordinarily rapid transformations
> relying on near-miraculous technical advanc-
> es.[30]

In short, we risk returning to the pre-industri-
al era of drudgery and intermittent starvation if the
planners of the Great Reset have their way. They
must not have their way.

In the next chapter, I show how, following the
prescriptions of the United Nations and the World
Economic Forum, the Great Reset's environmental
dictates are being implemented in agricultural, industrial, and energy production policies in various
nation-states. The long list of Executive Orders from
the Biden regime tells the story in the United States.

---

30 Vaclav Smil, *How the World Really Works: The Science Behind How We Got Here and Where We're Going*, Viking, 2022,
https://www.amazon.com/How-World-Really-Works-Science/
dp/0593297067, pages 5-6.

CHAPTER FOURTEEN

The Governmental Reset

T HE UNITED STATES government has finally
queued up behind Western Europe and Canada to become one of the leaders among nation-states
administering the environmental policies and prescriptions issuing from the United Nations (UN) and
the World Economic Forum (WEF). The U.S. is the
historic largest emitter of so-called greenhouse gases (GHGs) and the second largest current emitter of
said GHGs after China. The Biden regime's ability to
demonstrate to the world that it is a leader in tackling climate change is paramount to international
climate negotiations and thus Agenda 2030 and the
Great Reset's adoption worldwide.

Likewise, the Supreme Court's ruling in West
Virginia v. the Environmental Protection Agency
(EPA) represents a potential setback for the climate
change catastrophist agenda.[1] While specifically affecting the energy-producing sector, the decision

---

1 Supreme Court of the United States, June 30, 2021, https://www.
supremecourt.gov/opinions/21pdf/20-1530_n758.pdf.

marks a rebuke of the EPA and, by extension, other federal agencies in setting rules for greenhouse gas (GHG) emissions without explicit direction from the U.S. Congress. It has the potential to delay and thus derail the objective of reducing GHG emissions by 50 to 52 percent by 2030, the stated goal of the Biden regime.

The ruling follows on the heels of at least a dozen executive orders (EOs) related to mitigating climate change issued by the Biden regime since Biden's 2021 inauguration.

On January 20, 2021, mere hours after having been sworn into office, Biden signed Executive Order 13990.[2] Among other actions, this EO established the Interagency Working Group on the Social Cost of Greenhouse Gases and charged it with delivering reports on the social cost of carbon (SCC), the social cost of nitrous oxide (SCN), and the social cost of methane (SCM). This Working Group was established to engage all federal, state, and local levels of government, which are now required by law to evaluate each new potential infrastructure or other project on a cost-benefit analysis basis, in which the benefit is supposed to outweigh the cost. An assumed "social cost" of each of these GHGs will be added to the cost of all projects. While the social costs of carbon, nitrous oxide, and methane are yet to be determined, such costs will add millions to every govern-

---

2 "Executive Order on Protecting Public Health and the Environment and Restoring Science to Tackle the Climate Crisis," The White House, The United States Government, January 21, 2021, https://www.whitehouse.gov/briefing-room/presidential-actions/2021/01/20/executive-order-protecting-public-health-and-environment-and-restoring-science-to-tackle-climate-crisis/.

ment project.

The Biden regime has since issued at least 11 additional EOs related to climate change.[3] Together with the first EO, these EOs rescinded all related Trump-era EOs and reinstated related Obama-era EOs. They cancelled the Keystone Pipeline and other projects. They suspended new leases for oil drilling on public lands. They placed a temporary moratorium on drilling in the Arctic National Wildlife Refuge. They recommitted the U.S. to the Paris Accord, whether legally or not. They committed the U.S. to establishing a carbon "pollution-free" electricity sector by no later than 2035. They aimed to ensure that federal funding is not directly "subsidizing" (not charging the assumed social cost is taken to be a subsidy) fossil fuels and required that federal permitting decisions consider the effects of greenhouse gas emissions and climate change. And, they added a welter of bureaucratic administrative actions for a "government-wide approach" to address the "climate crisis." They added several new governmental layers, all of which overlap: the President's Council of Advisors on Science and Technology, a White House Environmental Justice Interagency Council, a National Climate Task Force, an Interagency Working Group on the Social Cost of Greenhouse Gases, and the Special Envoy on Climate (John Kerry). They exhorted "all executive departments and agencies" to tackle the climate change phantom. These EOs—the most ambitious climate change-related U.S. policies

3 Gianna Melillo, "A Look at Biden's Past Executive Orders on Climate Change," *The Hill*, August 17, 2022, https://thehill.com/changing-america/sustainability/climate-change/3603947-a-look-at-bidens-past-executive-orders-on-climate-change/.

to date—were followed by the passage of the Inflation Reduction Act, which will invest $369 billion "in climate solutions and environmental justice" and marked "the largest allotment of federal funds to combat climate change in U.S. history."[4]

While we are yet to feel the full impact of these and other actions taken to mitigate so-called climate change, we already feel the results in increased prices on fossil fuels: gasoline, natural gas, coal-generated electricity, and transportation costs added to the already increased cost of commodities.

Lest one think that these policies and prescriptions have nothing to do with the WEF or the Great Reset, the Biden regime has openly stated that its State Department and climate envoy (John Kerry) are partnering with the First Movers Coalition, of which the WEF is a major organizer:

> The First Movers Coalition (FMC), led by the State Department through The U.S. Special Presidential Envoy for Climate and *the World Economic Forum*, is a platform for building private-sector demand to speed clean energy technology innovation and confront the climate crisis (emphasis mine).[5]

---

4 Melillo, "A Look at Biden's Past Executive Orders on Climate Change."

5 "Fact Sheet: President Biden Tackles Methane Emissions, Spurs Innovations, and Supports Sustainable Agriculture to Build a Clean Energy Economy and Create Jobs," The White House, The United States Government, November 2, 2021, https://www.whitehouse.gov/briefing-room/statements-releases/2021/11/02/fact-sheet-president-biden-tackles-methane-emissions-spurs-innovations-and-supports-sustainable-agriculture-to-build-a-clean-energy-economy-and-create-jobs/.

The WEF notes the partnership on its website and features a photo of John Kerry (with Bill Gates).[6] Once again, the WEF brings its "private-sector" partners to the table. The WEF boasts that "more than 50 companies have joined the First Movers Coalition which aims to decarbonize the heavy industry and long-distance transport sectors responsible for 30% of global emissions." In addition to corporate partners, which include Delta Airlines, FedEx, the Ford Motor Company, United Airlines, and many others, the United States is joined by Denmark, India, Italy, Japan, Norway, Singapore, Sweden, and the United Kingdom. The object is "to create early markets for clean technologies through policy measures and private sector engagement."[7] The First Movers Coalition aims at decarbonizing heavy industry and transportation under the utterly insane notion that heavy industry and even jet transportation can be powered without using fossil fuels in time to avert a supposed climate emergency.

On top of these and other federal policies and prescriptions, states like California and New York have enacted their own laws. California has outlawed the purchase of new gas-powered vehicles beginning in 2035.[8] 17 other states may soon follow suit.[9]

---

6 "First Movers Coalition Is Tackling the Climate Crisis," World Economic Forum, May 2022, https://www.weforum.org/impact/first-movers-coalition-is-tackling-the-climate-crisis/.

7 Ibid.

8 Emma Newburger, "California Bans the Sale of New Gas-Powered Cars by 2035," CNBC, August 26, 2022, https://www.cnbc.com/2022/08/25/california-bans-the-sale-of-new-gas-powered-cars-by-2035.html.

9 Associated Press, "The 17 States That Follow California's Emission Standards and Might Now Ban Gas Cars," *Daily Mail Online*, Asso-

The Agricultural Reset

We already see the results of the Great Reset's agricultural policies throughout the world. In Sri Lanka, where the importation of chemical fertilizers was banned in April 2021 to eliminate the use of nitrates that release nitrous oxide, a so-called greenhouse gas, crop yields fell precipitously, by 30 to 60 percent.[10] Grocery prices increased by as much as 90 percent, in an economy where covid lockdowns had already dealt a huge blow to tourism and business generally. Amid food and fuel shortages, mass revolts left the prime minister's residence aflame,[11] as the president absconded to Singapore, where he tendered his resignation.[12] Shortages of food, fuel, and other necessities continued as the new president, Ranil Wickremesinghe, temporarily took over leadership of the beleaguered country, and Sri Lanka gained provisional approval for a $2.9 billion loan from the International Monetary Fund (IMF).[13] Is this the plan—to further indebt the world's nations

---

ciated Newspapers, September 4, 2022, https://www.dailymail.co.uk/news/article-11176351/17-states-weigh-adopting-Californias-electric-car-mandate.html.

10　Frank Lessiter, "Fertilizer Ban Trims Yields by 30-60%," *No-Till Farmer*, September 1, 2022, https://www.no-tillfarmer.com/blogs/1-covering-no-till/post/11821-fertilizer-ban-trims-yields-by-30-60.

11　NDTV, "Sri Lanka Crisis | Sri Lanka PM's House Set on Fire, Protesters Breach President's Home," YouTube, July 9, 2022, https://www.youtube.com/watch?v=sqNS6mVdjEk.

12　Anbarasan Ethirajan, "Gotabaya Rajapaksa: Sri Lanka's Ousted Former President Returns," *BBC News*, September 2, 2022, https://www.bbc.com/news/world-asia-62765262.

13　Uditha Jayasinghe, "Sri Lanka Gains IMF's Provisional Agreement for $2.9 BLN Loan," Reuters, September 1, 2022, https://www.reuters.com/world/asia-pacific/sri-lanka-imf-reach-preliminary-agreement-29-billion-loan-2022-09-01/.

to the IMF and/or World Bank and thus to dictate the terms of a "green" economic recovery?

WEF-pleasing terms are what led to the crisis in the first place. Sri Lanka fell under the spell of the World Economic Forum (WEF) in 2012, when Asanga Abeyagoonasekera was inducted into the Young Global Leaders (YGL), Sri Lanka's first YGL initiate.[14] Gotabaya Rajapaksa, the now fallen president of Sri Lanka, had embraced the new environmentalist Green Revolution, which targets modern agricultural methods and replaces them with "indigenous," all-organic farming. Rajapaksa halted the importing of chemical fertilizers under the advice of Indian activist Vandana Shiva, who has voiced opposition to the first Green Revolution and has been advocating "indigenous" organic-only farming for decades.[15]

In the Netherlands, colorful tractor, cow, and dung-flinging protests erupted in the spring and summer of 2022, as Dutch farmers resisted Great Reset-initiated policies adopted by Prime Minister Mark Rutte, a WEF member and agenda contributor.[16] The protests featured tractors blocking highways and cattle grazing outside the doorsteps of parliament. Farmers threatened to slaughter cows on site if the coalition government's plans were not

14 "Asanga Abeyagoonasekera - Agenda Contributor," World Economic Forum, accessed September 14, 2022, https://www.weforum.org/agenda/authors/asangaabeyagoonasekera.

15 Michael Shellenberger, "Green Dogma behind Fall of Sri Lanka," July 10, 2022, https://michaelshellenberger.substack.com/p/green-dogma-behind-fall-of-sri-lanka.

16 "Mark Rutte - Agenda Contributor," World Economic Forum, accessed September 14, 2022, https://www.weforum.org/agenda/authors/mark-rutte.

scrapped.[17] The issue at stake: the ruling coalition's plans to cut emissions of GHGs, predominantly nitrogen oxide, by 50 percent nationwide by 2030. The plan would result in an estimated 30 percent reduction in livestock and reduced farming yields, pushing many farmers out of business, according to the coalition government's own admission.[18] The Netherlands is the second largest exporter of food in the world. Thus, the agricultural reductions in the Netherlands will have a world-devastating impact.

The Netherlands is the center of the WEF's Food Action Alliance program[19] and the site of the Global Coordinating Secretariat (GCS) of the WEF's Food Innovation Hubs, launched at the Davos Agenda meeting in 2021.[20] The Invest in Holland website notes that the Food Innovation Hubs have as their goal alignment with the UN Food Systems Summit: "The role of the GCS will be to coordinate the efforts of the regional Hubs as well as align with global processes and initiatives such as the UN Food Sys-

17 Cagan Koc, "Dutch Farmers Bring Cows to Parliament to Protest Nitrogen Cuts," *Bloomberg*, June 28, 2022, https://www.bloomberg.com/news/articles/2022-06-28/dutch-farmers-bring-cows-to-parliament-to-protest-nitrogen-cuts.

18 Mike Corder, "Explainer: Why Are Dutch Farmers Protesting over Emissions," *ABC News*, June 28, 2022, https://abcnews.go.com/Business/wireStory/explainer-dutch-farmers-protesting-emissions-85848026.

19 Sean de Cleene, Lisa Sweet, Wiebe Draijer, and Gilbert Fossoun Houngbo, "Food Action Alliance," World Economic Forum, accessed September 14, 2022, https://www.weforum.org/projects/food-action-alliance.

20 "The Netherlands and the World Economic Forum Launch Food Innovation Hubs Initiative," NFIA, Invest in Holland, March 4, 2021, https://investinholland.com/news/the-netherlands-and-the-world-economic-forum-launch-food-innovation-hubs-initiative/.

tems Summit."[21] And the stated goal of the UN Food Systems Summit is to align agricultural production with Agenda 2030's sustainable development goals (SDGs): "The UN Food Systems Summit, held during the UN General Assembly in New York on September 23 [2021], set the stage for global food systems transformation to achieve the Sustainable Development Goals by 2030."[22]

We have already seen what "sustainability" and "sustainable development" signify. They do not mean, as the words seem to suggest, the ability to withstand shocks of various kinds—economic crises, natural disasters, etc. They mean development constrained by utopian, unscientific environmentalist imperatives, inclusive of reduced production and consumption in the developed world and the thwarting of development in the developing world that would result in the production of additional GHGs. In terms of agriculture, this entails a reduction and eventual elimination of nitrogen-rich fertilizers and the reduction/elimination of methane- and ammonia-producing cattle. Given the long history of enviro-neo-Malthusianism associated with these globalist cadres (see Chapter 9), we cannot rule out the desideratum to reduce the world's population.

Similarly, "the war on fertilizers" has taken root in Canada, where the government is calling for a 30 percent reduction in emissions from chemical fertilizers by 2030. Estimates indicate that if Prime Minister Justin Trudeau's measures to reduce GHGs are fully implemented, reduced crop yields could cost

---

21 Ibid.

22 "Food Systems Summit," United Nations, September 23, 2021, https://www.un.org/en/food-systems-summit.

farmers as much as $48 billion by 2030, dramatically curtailing output and further driving up the cost of food for consumers.[23] The reduced production would come when food security is already a major concern, given the supply-chain issues owing to the pandemic response and the war in Ukraine. Even the *Toronto Sun* opined that the 30 percent reduction in fertilizers is based on a climate zealotry that will send Canada—and those its agriculture supports—into a deadly downward spiral:

> [Climate zealotry] explains why the feds are now bringing in a second carbon tax so soon after fighting the provinces in court over the first carbon tax. It explains why they're now charging ahead with wild abandon to introduce worrisome restrictions on Canadian farming, which industry experts say will cause farms to close and see the price of food only increase more.
>
> That's not all. Everywhere you look, the feds are bringing in climate-related laws and regulations. The feds are also fully aware of the harms these policies will bring about — the big one being increased costs to regular folks, with lower income Canadians most disproportionately harmed. Their own reports acknowledge these looming problems.[24]

23 Jarryd Jaeger, "Trudeau Seeking to Implement Policy Similar to That Protested by Dutch Farmers," *The Post Millennial*, September 1, 2022, https://thepostmillennial.com/trudeau-seeking-to-implement-policy-similar-to-that-protested-by-dutch-farmers.

24 Qtd. in John Hayward, "Canada's Trudeau Declares War on Fertilizer, Following the Footsteps of Sri Lanka," *Breitbart*, July 26, 2022, https://www.breitbart.com/environment/2022/07/26/canadas-

What is behind this drive for the transformation of the agricultural industry—besides, that is, the declared objective of meeting Agenda 2030's SDGs? According to Irish farmer and activist James Conway, the endgame is to make farming in the Netherlands, Canada, Ireland, the U.S., and elsewhere so unprofitable that small farmers will be driven out of business. Banks and other investors can then swoop in and (re)possess farms, either through bank defaults or by buying farms at reduced prices. Conway calls this land grab the greatest transfer of landed wealth in human history.[25]

Such a "scheme"[26] would seem to accord with the WEF's repeated claims that the agricultural supply chain is too "fragmented" for "sustainable" farming. "A resilient, environmentally-friendly food system will require a shift away from our current fragmented supply chains," writes Lindsay Suddon, Chief Strategy Officer of Proagrica, for the WEF's website.[27] In this and many other WEF papers, the "fragmentation" refrain is repeated. Sustainable

---

trudeau-declares-war-on-fertilizer-following-the-footsteps-of-sri-lanka/.

25 Conversations With John Waters, "An Honest Conversation with John Waters and James Conway," *Odysee*, July 24, 2022, https://odysee.com/@johnwaters:7/An-honest-Conversation-full:8.

26 Wiebe Draijer and Gilbert Fossoun Houngbo, "This New Scheme Aims to Make Food Production Fairer for Small Farmers," World Economic Forum, January 22, 2020, https://www.weforum.org/agenda/2020/01/food-action-alliance-smallholders-agriculture-collective-cure/.

27 Lindsay Suddon, How a Smarter Network Could Revolutionise Our Food System," World Economic Forum, November 17, 2020, https://www.weforum.org/agenda/2020/11/field-to-fork-network-could-revolutionize-our-food-system/.

farming cannot be achieved under the "fragmented" agricultural conditions that currently obtain.

One paper, part of the 2020 WEF annual meeting, argues that fragmentation represents the ultimate barrier to sustainability:

> As the heads of leading multilateral and commercial agricultural finance institutions, we are convinced that fragmentation within the current food systems represents the most significant hurdle to feeding a growing population nutritiously and sustainably.[28]

Written by Wiebe Draijer, then chairman of the Managing Board at Rabobank, and Gilbert Fossoun Houngbo, the director general-elect of the International Labor Organization (ILO), this paper is quite telling. It warns that unless fragmentation is addressed, "[w]e will also have no hope of reaching the Sustainable Development Goal of net zero emissions by 2050, given that today's agricultural supply chain, from farm to fork, accounts for around 27% of greenhouse gas (GHG) emissions."[29]

Rabobank is one of the financial sponsors of the WEF's Food Action Alliance.[30] According to its web-

---

28 Wiebe Draijer and Gilbert Fossoun Houngbo, "This New Scheme Aims to Make Food Production Fairer for Small Farmers," World Economic Forum, January 22, 2020, https://www.weforum.org/agenda/2020/01/food-action-alliance-smallholders-agriculture-collective-cure/.

29 Ibid.

30 "Global Leaders Unite under the Food Action Alliance to Deliver a Better Future for the People and the Planet," World Economic Forum, January 22, 2020, https://www.weforum.org/press/2020/01/global-leaders-unite-under-the-food-action-alliance-to-deliver-a-

site, Rabobank operates in the Netherlands, serving retail and corporate clients, and globally, financing the agricultural sector.[31] The ILO is a UN agency that sets labor standards in 187 countries.[32]

What interests could an international bank and a UN international labor agency have in common? According to the joint paper, they have in common a resolve to eliminate fragmentation in agriculture. The banking interest in defragmentation is to gain a controlling interest in fewer and larger farms. The labor union management interest is to have more workers under its supervision and control. The banking and labor interests combined result in large farms worked by organized, non-owning farm laborers, under the controlling interest of the bank. A bonus, or what is more likely, the rationale for this "scheme," is that the SDGs of Agenda 2030 can thereby more easily be implemented across "agricultural value chains and farming practices." The authors conclude: "Most critically, we need to *aggregate opportunities, resources* and complementary expertise into *large-scale projects that can unlock investment* and deliver impact" (emphasis mine).[33] "Collective action" is the "cure."

"Fragmentation" thus means too many discrete

better-future-for-the-people-and-the-planet/.

31 "In Short," Rabobank, accessed September 15, 2022, https://www.rabobank.com/about-us/in-short.

32 "About the ILO," The International Labor Organization, accessed September 15, 2022, https://www.ilo.org/global/about-the-ilo/lang--en/index.htm.

33 Wiebe Draijer and Gilbert Fossoun Houngbo, "This New Scheme Aims to Make Food Production Fairer for Small Farmers," World Economic Forum, op. cit.

and disparate farms. The solution to this problem is consolidation, or the ownership of agricultural assets in fewer and fewer hands. Enter Bill Gates.

The "large-scale projects" will be owned by those who can afford to abide by the European Commission's (EC) Farm to Fork Strategy. "The Farm to Fork Strategy is at the heart of the European Green Deal."[34] The goal of the European Green Deal is "no net emissions of greenhouse gases by 2050."[35]

In a November 2020 report on its study of the EC's Farm to Fork Strategy, the United States Department of Agriculture (USDA) found that the adoption of the plan would result in a decline in agricultural production of between 7 percent to 12 percent for the European Union (EU), depending on whether the adoption is EU-wide only, or global. With EU-only adoption, the decline in EU agricultural production was projected to be 12 percent for the EU, as opposed to 7 percent for the EU, should the adoption become global. In the case of global adoption, worldwide agricultural production would drop by 11 percent. Further, the USDA found:

> The decline in agricultural production would tighten the EU food supply, resulting in price increases that impact consumer budgets. Prices and per capita food costs would increase the most for the EU, across each of the three scenarios [a middle scenario of EU and adoption

34 "Farm to Fork Strategy," Food Safety, accessed September 15, 2022, https://food.ec.europa.eu/horizontal-topics/farm-fork-strategy_en.
35 "A European Green Deal," European Commission, September 15, 2022, https://ec.europa.eu/info/strategy/priorities-2019-2024/european-green-deal_en.

by neighboring nation states is included in the study]. However, price and food cost increases would be significant for most regions if [Farm to Fork] Strategies are adopted globally. For the United States, price and food costs would remain relatively unchanged except in the case of global adoption.

Production declines in the EU and elsewhere would lead to reduced trade, although some regions would benefit depending on changes in import demand. However, if trade is restricted as a result of the imposition of the proposed measures, *the negative impacts are concentrated in regions with the world's most food-insecure populations...*

Food insecurity, measured as the number of people who lack access to a diet of at least 2,100 calories a day, increases significantly in the 76 low- and middle-income countries covered in our analysis due to increases in food commodity prices and declines in income, particularly in Africa. *By 2030, the number of food-insecure people in the case of EU-only adoption would increase by an additional 22 million more than projected without the EC's proposed Strategies. The number would climb to 103 million under the middle scenario and 185 million under global adoption* (emphasis mine).[36]

---

36 "Economic and Food Security Impacts of Agricultural Input Reduction Under the European Union Green Deal's Farm to Fork and Biodiversity Strategies – USDA," USDA, November 2020, https://www.ers.usda.gov/webdocs/publications/99741/eb-30_summary.pdf?v=9641.4. See also, Jayson Beckman, Maros Ivanic, Jeremy Jelliffe, Felix G. Baquedano, and Sara Scott, "Farm to Fork Initiative to Restrict European Union Agricultural Inputs May Increase Food Prices,

So far, the U.S. has not adopted the Farm to Fork Strategy, but its full implementation in the EU alone will result in food shortages and not only in the EU itself. Its global adoption would mean mass famines.

The world over, we see a concerted, coordinated campaign to dismantle the productive capabilities in energy, manufacturing, and farming. This project, driven by elites and accruing to their benefit, is amounting to the largest Great Leap Backward in recorded history. If it is not stopped and reversed, it will lead to economic disaster, including dramatically reduced consumption and living standards. And it will almost certainly result in increased levels of hunger in the developed world and famines in the developing world. WEF Chairman Schwab may outdo Chairman Mao. If we let him.

Further Global Food Insecurity," USDA, March 1, 2021, https://www.ers.usda.gov/amber-waves/2021/march/farm-to-fork-initiative-to-restrict-european-union-agricultural-inputs-may-increase-food-prices-further-global-food-insecurity/.

Part IV

The Fourth Industrial Revolution

Biological inequality is, of course, the bedrock fact
on which all of eugenics is predicated. But it is not
usually realised that the two types of inequality
have quite different and indeed contrary eugenic
implications. The inequality of mere difference is
desirable, and the preservation of human variety
should be one of the two primary aims of eugenics.
But the inequality of level or standard is undesir-
able, and the other primary aim of eugenics should
be the raising of the mean level of all desirable
qualities. While there may be dispute over certain
qualities, there can be none over a number of the
most important, such as a healthy constitution, a
high innate general intelligence, or a special apti-
tude such as that for mathematics or music.

At the moment, it is probable that the indirect effect
of civilisation is dysgenic instead of eugenic; and
in any case it seems likely that the dead weight of
genetic stupidity, physical weakness, mental insta-
bility, and disease-proneness, which already exist
in the human species, will prove too great a burden
for real progress to be achieved. Thus even though
it is quite true that any radical eugenic policy will

*be for many years politically and psychological-
ly impossible, it will be important for Unesco to
see that the eugenic problem is examined with the
greatest care, and that the public mind is informed
of the issues at stake so that much that now is unthinkable may at least become thinkable.*
– Julian Huxley

*Well it seems to me the nature of the Ultimate
Revolution with which we are now faced is precisely this: that we are in process of developing a
whole series of techniques, which will enable the
controlling oligarchy—who have always existed
and will presumably always exist – to get people to
love their servitude. This is the ultimate in
malevolent revolution.*
– Aldous Huxley

CHAPTER FIFTEEN

Digital Big Brother

A T THE 2022 WEF annual meeting, History at a Turning Point: Government Policies, Corporate Strategies, J. Michael Evans, President of Alibaba Group, was asked by the moderator about new innovations that the Chinese multinational e-commerce platform was undertaking to advance "responsible consumption." Evans pointed to a forthcoming technology to reduce carbon emissions by 1.5 gigatons:

> So...we're developing, through technology, an ability for consumers to measure their own carbon footprint. What does that mean? That's where they're travelling, how are they travelling, what are they eating, what are they consuming on the platform. So individual carbon footprint tracker; stay tuned! (28:38-minute mark).[1]

---

1 "Strategic Outlook: Responsible Consumption," World Economic Forum, May 24, 2022, https://www.weforum.org/events/world-economic-forum-annual-meeting-2022/sessions/strategic-outlook-re-

At the mention of the "individual carbon footprint tracker," another participant in the "Responsible Consumption" panel let out an involuntary
"hmmm!" Certainly, this was one of several such
highlights (lowlights) of the annual meeting. Reac-
tions to individual carbon footprint tracking were
soon voiced on Twitter and around the Internet.[2]
Clearly, most people object to the prospect of being
told where they can go, how to get there, what to eat,
and whether they've expended their carbon allowances such that they are forbidden to undertake desired activities.

On the issue of "green travel," Evans continued:

> What we're going to do is allow people to first
> calculate the best route, the most efficient
> route and also the most efficient form of trans-
> portation. And then if they take advantage of
> those recommendations, we'll give them bo-
> nus points that they can redeem elsewhere on
> our platform. So, they're incentivized to do the
> right thing even if they were provided with the
> opportunity to decide to do the wrong thing.[3]

According to Evans, "the right thing" for trav-
elers is to use the routes and means of transporta-

sponsible-consumption.

2   Alec Schemmel, "Critics Slam Personal 'Carbon Footprint
Trackers' Discussed at World Economic Forum," KEYE, May 24,
2022, https://cbsaustin.com/news/nation-world/tech-exec-says-new-
tech-to-help-businesses-track-consumers-carbon-footprint-is-on-
the-way-technology-world-economic-forum-alibaba-group-presi-
dent-michael-evans-privacy-tracking-monitoring.

3   "Strategic Outlook: Responsible Consumption," World Economic
Forum, op. cit.

tion that the Alibaba algorithm recommends. The platform may recommend that you walk, use a bicycle, bus, or carpool. If you don't abide by the recommendation and decide to drive when you've been instructed to walk or take the bus, you will be doing "the wrong thing."

Meanwhile, the development of individual carbon footprint trackers underscores the hypocrisy of the WEF agenda (as if the private jets and limousines of the participants was not enough evidence thereof) and serves as a distraction from disclosures about the worst carbon-emitting culprits, like Alibaba itself, and the fact that the world's richest 10 percent has been responsible for expending one-third of the remaining carbon allotment for 2030, while the world's poorest half was responsible for only 4 percent.[4] The buzz aroused by such controversial statements may have been calculated to distract from the reality that Alibaba, one of the biggest CO_2 emitters in China, will not be carbon neutral until 2030.[5] "It's a big energy user, cloud," Evans admitted, before quickly pivoting to discuss personal carbon footprint trackers. Curiously, Evans never explained how Alibaba is reducing its own operational carbon footprint.

Commentators noted the similarity between the

---

4 Anna Ratcliff, "Carbon Emissions of Richest 1 Percent More than Double the Emissions of the Poorest Half of Humanity," Oxfam International, September 23, 2020, https://www.oxfam.org/en/press-releases/carbon-emissions-richest-1-percent-more-double-emissions-poorest-half-humanity.

5 Luica Mak, Roger Zhang, and Gabbie Fu, "Alibaba Group Announces Carbon Neutrality Goal by 2030," *Business Wire*, December 17, 2021, https://www.businesswire.com/news/home/20211217005249/en/Alibaba-Group-Announces-Carbon-Neutrality-Goal-by-2030.

individual carbon footprint tracker and the Chinese Communist Party's (CCP) social credit scoring system.[6] Under the Chinese social credit scoring system, citizens and other residents are monitored for all on-line and off-line behavior. The Sesame Credit scoring acts as a system of rewards and punishments. The social credit score ranges from 350 to a possible 900, much like the credit score system in the U.S., but it grades a wide array of activities, including spreading "rumors" and other "anti-social" behavior. Private enterprises reward the "right" behavior while data on the "wrong" behavior is stored by the Supreme People's Court of the People's Republic of China, which punishes transgressors. Those who are deemed "untrustworthy" are given low scores that drastically reduce their life options.[7] By 2019, over 30 million people were named by the Chinese government as "untrustworthy." These reprobates were not permitted to leave the country, travel by airplane, travel by highspeed rail, rent a "sharing car," rent a hotel room, dine at luxury restaurants, play golf, buy insurance, or rent a house, among a host of other forbidden activities.

Sesame Credit, which "allow[s] the trustworthy to roam everywhere under heaven, while making it hard for the discredited to take a single step," is run

---

6 Tim Hinchliffe, "'Individual Carbon Footprint Tracker, Stay Tuned': Alibaba Pres at WEF 2022," *The Sociable*, May 25, 2022, https://sociable.co/business/individual-carbon-footprint-tracker-alibaba-wef-2022/.

7 Nicole Kobie, "The Complicated Truth about China's Social Credit System," *WIRED UK*, June 7, 2019, https://www.wired.co.uk/article/china-social-credit-system-explained.

by the Alibaba Group.[8] As of August 23, 2022, Black-Rock, Inc., held over $500 million in Alibaba stock.[9] Sesame Credit represents the kind of corporate-state "cooperation" or "public-private partnerships" lauded and promoted by the WEF, under the Great Reset agenda. Is it any wonder, then, that many fear that carbon footprint tracking represents the early stages of the social credit score in the Western world?

As with Alibaba's innovations, the technologies of what I have called Big Digital—the mega-data services, social media platforms, Artificial Intelligence (AI) agents, apps, and the developing Internet of Things (IoT) and Internet of Bodies (IoB)—are not only managed by monopolies or would-be monopolies but also will continue to be incorporated by the state to become elements of an enhanced corporate-state power. Google Cloud is, in fact, developing an individual carbon footprint tracker, as are many other entities.[10] Like the "privately" produced health passes or vaccine passports, one or more of these technologies could very well be adopted by Western governments as part of an incipient social credit scoring system like the one reputedly implemented in China, with the personal carbon allowance as one of the key components compiled and stored in a digital identity. Likely, ESG metrics will be applied to individuals. What does that mean? It means that in-

---

8 Charlie Campbell, "How China Is Using Big Data to Create a Social Credit Score," *Time*, August 14, 2019, https://time.com/collection/davos-2019/5502592/china-social-credit-score/.

9 "Blackrock Inc. Ownership in Baba / Alibaba Group Holding, Fintel.io," Fintel, August 23, 2022, https://fintel.io/so/us/baba/blackrock.

10 "Carbon Footprint | Google Cloud," Google, accessed August 25, 2022, https://cloud.google.com/carbon-footprint.

dividuals will be rated like corporations for their environmental impact and for their "social" or "social justice" and "governance" compliance. As in China, a governance metric would grade people in terms of whether and how well they abide by state official dictates and "narratives"—like "the Great Narrative" of the WEF.

As nightmarish as personal carbon footprint tracking portends to be, it represents one of the more low-tech, less invasive, and more seemingly benign developments promised as part of the Fourth Industrial Revolution (4-IR). Others include a ubiquitous Internet, smart cities, central bank digital currency (CBDC), digital identities, the Internet of Things (IoT) and the Internet of Bodies (IoB), smart implants, nanorobotic brain-cloud interfaces, algorithms undertaking governmental tasks, augmented reality (AR), virtual reality (VR), mixed reality (MR), the metaverse, and transhumanism. On the one hand, Schwab and company conjure techno-utopian fantasies; on the other, dystopian visions of a totalitarian surveillance society and global domination by the elite.

The 4-IR, we are told, follows the first, second, and third industrial revolutions—the mechanical, electrical, and digital, respectively.[11] The 4-IR builds on the digital revolution, but Schwab and the WEF see the 4-IR as an exponential take-off and convergence of existing and emerging fields, including Big Data; artificial intelligence (AI); machine learning; quantum computing; and genomics, nanotechnology, and robotics (GNR). The consequence is

---

11 Klaus Schwab, *The Fourth Industrial Revolution*, New York: Crown Business, 2016, pages 6-8.

the merging of the physical, digital, and biological worlds. The blurring of these categories ultimately challenges the very ontological categories by which we understand ourselves and the world, including "what it means to be human."[12]

While Schwab and the WEF promote a particular vision for the 4-IR, there is nothing original about their formulations. Transhumanists and Singularitarians (or prophets of the technological singularity), such as Vernor Vinge and Ray Kurzweil, and many others, forecasted these and more revolutionary developments long before Schwab heralded them.[13] The significance of Schwab's and the WEF's take on the new technological revolution is the attempt to harness it to a particular end, presumably "a fairer, greener future."

If existing 4-IR developments are any indication of the future, however, Schwab's language represents euphemism at best and doublespeak at worst. These developments already include Internet algorithms that feed users prescribed news and advertisements and downrank or exclude banned content; algorithms that censor social media content and consign "dangerous" individuals and organizations to digital gulags; keyword and geofence police warrants based on user search engine inputs or untimely whereabouts;[14] facial recognition software

---

12 Ibid., page vii.

13 Ray Kurzweil, *The Singularity Is Near: When Humans Transcend Biology*, London: Duckworth, 2006.

14 Alfred Ng, "Google Is Giving Data to Police Based on Search Keywords, Court Docs Show," *CNET*, October 8, 2020, https://www.cnet.com/news/privacy/google-is-giving-data-to-police-based-on-search-keywords-court-docs-show/.

and other technologies that identify subjects by their gaits, breathing patterns, and irises;[15] apps that track and trace covid or other pandemic-defying suspects, report violators to the police, and shut down their access to banking, transportation, and public life;[16] robot police with QR code scanners to identify and round up the unvaccinated and other dissidents;[17] and smart cities where everyone is a digital entity to be monitored, surveilled, and recorded, while data on their every move is collected, collated, stored, and attached to a digital identity and social credit score[18] —to name a few of the panoptic manifestations of the 4-IR.

4-IR technologies, as forecasted, would subject human beings to a technological management that would make surveillance by the NSA look like child's play. And Schwab lauds developments that would connect brains directly to the cloud to enable the "data mining" of thought and memory, a technological mastery over decision-making that would threaten autonomy and undermine any semblance of free will. The 4-IR accelerates the merging of hu-

---

15 Dake Kang, "Chinese 'Gait Recognition' Tech Ids People by How They Walk," The Associated Press, November 6, 2018, https://apnews.com/article/china-technology-beijing-business-international-news-bf75dd1c26c947b7826d270a16e2658a.

16 Tessa Wong and BBC Chinese, "Henan: China Covid App Restricts Residents after Banking Protests," *BBC News*, June 14, 2022, https://www.bbc.com/news/world-asia-china-61793149.

17 Pei Pei, "Robots Help Enforce Health Safety in Shenzhen," *China Daily*, February 16, 2020, https://www.chinadaily.com.cn/a/202002/16/WS5e492ef6a310128217277de5.html.

18 Michael Rectenwald, *Google Archipelago: The Digital Gulag and the Simulation of Freedom*, Nashville, TN: New English Review Press, 2019, pages 128-147.

mans and machines, resulting in a world in which all information, including genetic information, could be shared, and every action, thought, and unconscious motivation could be known, predicted, and possibly even precluded.

In what follows, I offer an assessment of intersecting, rights-infringing, reality-altering 4-IR technologies and developments, considering their futuristic possibilities, and their implications for liberty and meaning, or the nullification thereof.

The Internet of Things (IoT) and the Internet of Bodies (IoB)

The IoT describes the datafication of physical objects, or the smartification of resources and their connection to networks fed into the Internet. This development represents the vaunted merging of the physical and the digital, such that eventually every known resource will have a data tag, and each and every item will communicate its status to the Internet, allowing the universal coordination of physical resources through remote monitoring. The IoT thus represents a universal inventory of all the world's resources—not only a real-time inventory of their existence but of their statuses and uses as well.

This inventory is accomplished through 5G, which outstrips 4G by many orders of magnitude and allows a vast increase in the volume of connected devices, including natural, manufactured, and cultivated resources. The claim is that by 2025, 5G networks will be distributed around the globe and will make information on resources available to every living person at a negligible cost. However, it is not as if the consumers of resources will have access to all the data that producers and governments will have.

With the connection of human bodies to the IoT, the IoT includes the IoB, with humans registering their whereabouts as well as statuses on various organs and organ systems, which will transmit data to the cloud or other centralized databases. The IoB represents the merging of the digital, physical, and the biological. "Going on the Internet" will become a quaint anachronism, as the Internet becomes ubiquitous and all-encompassing. The IoB represents the universal inventory of human capital. Biometric data on the functioning of human corporal bodies and their organs and organ systems will be registered and translated into machine-readable code to be processed by computer networks fed by numerous inputs of digital information gathering. All humans and other social agents will be bathed in an ambient cyberspace, and for those with access, observing such agents will be as easy as visualizing any other data represented on computer screens. Humans become data points. Cameras, AI bots, electronic door keys, cash registers, RFID tags, wearable devices, implants, vaccination tattoos, brain-cloud interfaces, and numerous other means of data collection, collation, and transmission promise to make possible the timestamping of every human activity. All social human activity may be recorded, digitized, stored, and distributed to the proper agencies as necessary. Every trajectory may be digitized and collected to include almost every action undertaken on the way, possibly even mental operations. All human bodies and minds will be *in* the Internet, as it were, surrounded and even penetrated by cyberspace that will encompass all social space and possibly include access to consciousness as well.

Meanwhile, "the people," or autonomous bodies of the Internet may include not only human agents but also robotic software (softbots); robotic hardware run by AI (hardbots); "robot swarms," or bands of migrating robots undertaking various tasks, including police functions; stationary and migrating apps; virtual assistants; virtual police; virtual teachers; virtual lovers; digital doppelgangers (although this last development involves legal challenges even greater than the release of non-human, "autonomous agents"); and so-called "sentient" AI language systems like Google's LaMDA.[19] These autonomous agents might even be "self-healing" and self-replicating, adding further complexity to the mix of agencies envisioned for the 4-IR. Robots and AI agents may acquire autonomy and rights, just as human beings lose them. Add the metaverse (discussed subsequently), and the moral, psychological, and ontological complexity of the 4-IR world would be unwieldy and confusing at best. Promoted as benefits, the proliferation of connected devices, including wearables, implants, robots, nanorobots, and other elements, will not only be capable of tracking physical behavior and bodily states but also may provide corporations with the ability to assess the movements of consumers, anticipating their consumption, and supplying them with an endless stream of targeted advertising. Predictive algorithms could not only anticipate

---

19 Nitasha Tiku, "The Google Engineer Who Thinks the Company's AI Has Come to Life," *The Washington Post*, June 17, 2022, https://www.washingtonpost.com/technology/2022/06/11/google-ai-lamda-blake-lemoine/.

their consumptive proclivities but also provide the corporate state the augmented means for tracing, tracking, and controlling populations to heretofore unimagined degrees. The IoT, IoB, and digital identities could very well lead to the realization of surveillance regimes more total than those imagined by George Orwell and Aldous Huxley, societies in which the corporate state not only knows every action taken but also those contemplated. Indeed, as we see with the development of a "Chinese-style" social credit scoring system, elements of such surveillance regimes enabled by enhanced Internet connectivity are already operational today.

Digital Identity

As defined by the WEF, digital identity is "the sum total of the growing and evolving mass of information about us, our profiles and the history of our activities online. It relates to *inferences made about us*, based on this mass of information, which become new data points" (emphasis mine).[20] Digital identity is thus not merely a new, more handy, lightweight, digital form of identification. It refers to a collection of data that purportedly defines who we are, including what we do both online and off-line—if "off-line" life can still be said to exist—and not merely to a means by which we can be identified as such.

While it suggests "there will be no 'one-size-fits-all'" digital identity,[21] the WEF promotes the "in-

---

20 "Identity in a Digital World: A New Chapter in the Social Contract," World Economic Forum, September 2018, https://www3.weforum.org/docs/WEF_INSIGHT_REPORT_Digital%20Identity.pdf, page 9.

21 Ibid., page 10.

teroperability"[22] of digital identity so that the same digital identity can function across business and governmental contexts. For businesses, this means expanded markets and business lines and more targeted advertising and marketing, while for governments it means digital governance, which the WEF suggests would result in "better delivery of services, a more engaged citizenry and a tool against corruption and crime." For individuals, digital identity will be sold for the ease of access to financial, political, educational, healthcare, and other services, but could also entail "unwarranted surveillance, discrimination and abuse."[23]

Digital identity is sold by the WEF, the UN, and the World Bank as a means of "inclusion" of the marginalized in the global economy as well as for the "convenience" of those in the developed world. 1.1 billion people, we are told, have no form of identification, and the digital identity would not only supply identification but also incorporate subjects into a system that otherwise excludes them.[24] But digital identity extended to the poor could mean the inability to participate in society without one—*for everyone.* The demand for total "inclusion" means there will be no escape from the digital surveillance afforded by the digital identity. Whenever the word "inclusion"

22 Ibid., passim.

23 Ibid., page 10.

24 "1.1 Billion 'Invisible' People without ID Are Priority for New High Level Advisory Council on Identification for Development," *World Bank Blogs* (blog), October 12, 2017, https://doi.org/10/12/11-billion-invisible-people-without-id-are-prior¬ity-for-new-high-level-advisory-council-on-identification-for-development.

is used, we must consider the totalitarian prospects that it implies. Meanwhile, as New York University Law School's Center for Human Rights and Global Justice argues in "Paving a Digital Road to Hell?," digital identity systems have not only proven to lack inclusivity but the rapid and widescale deployment of digital ID systems to date has proven "dangerous" and has led to "often severe and large-scale, human rights violations...Such systems may exacerbate pre-existing forms of *exclusion* and discrimination in public and private services" (emphasis mine).[25]

Nevertheless, Canada, drawing on a partnership with the WEF's "Known Traveler Digital Identity" (KTDI) program,[26] is developing a new federal "Digital Identity Program" as part of its "Digital Ambition 2022" project.[27] Officials have said that the program is "the electronic equivalent of a recognized proof-of-identity document," such as a driver's license or passport, which "confirms that 'you are who you say you are' in a digital context." However,

25 "Paving a Digital Road to Hell? A Primer on the Role of the World Bank and Global Networks in Promoting Digital ID," Center for Human Rights & Global Justice, NYU School of Law, June 2022, https://covidcalltohumanity.org/wp-content/uploads/2022/07/Report_Paving-a-Digital-Road-to-Hell.pdf, page 6.

26 "The Government of Canada to Test Cutting-Edge Technologies to Support Secure and Seamless Global Travel for Air Passengers," Transport Canada, Canada.ca, Government of Canada, January 25, 2018, https://www.canada.ca/en/transportcanada/news/2018/01/the_government_ofcanadatotestcutting-edgetechnologiestosupportse.html; KTDI, accessed August 22, 2022, https://ktdi.org/.

27 Treasury Board of Canada Secretariat, "Canada's Digital Ambition 2022," Canada.ca, Government of Canada, August 4, 2022, https://www.canada.ca/en/government/system/digital-government/government-canada-digital-operations-strategic-plans/canada-digital-ambition.html.

we have already seen that the digital identity is not a mere digital means of identification but rather is "the sum total of the growing and evolving mass of information about us, our profiles and the history of our activities..." But even if Canada's digital identity system only serves as identification at first, as the Center for Human Rights and Global Justice notes, digital identities are prone to "function creep." That is, "they are intended to be used for multiple purposes that are unforeseen when the system is first designed."[28] Digital identities have the potential to accrete new functions that will be added to those for which the system is developed and implemented. That means that banking and other commercial functions could be added but also potentially political ones, as well as vaccine passports. The digital identity system thus could establish economic, political, and social profiles for all users.

Canada forecasted what it might do with the national digital identity system, when in response to the trucker convoy protest, the government shut down bank accounts[29] and repossessed trucks and other vehicles[30] as punishment for the truckers who

---

28 "Paving a Digital Road to Hell? A Primer on the Role of the World Bank and Global Networks in Promoting Digital ID," Center for Human Rights and Global Justice, NYU School of Law, page 12.

29 Matthew Loh, "Canada Says It Will Freeze the Bank Accounts of 'Freedom Convoy' Truckers Who Continue Their Anti-Vaccine Mandate Blockades," *Business Insider*, February 14, 2022, https://www.businessinsider.com/trudeau-canada-freeze-bank-accounts-freedom-convoy-truckers-2022-2.

30 Erin Marquis, "Ottawa Mayor Suggests Selling Vehicles Seized from Freedom Convoy to Pay Enforcement Costs," *Jalopnik*, February 22, 2022, https://jalopnik.com/ottawa-mayor-suggests-selling-vehicles-seized-from-free-1848575043.

opposed the government's lockdowns and vaccine mandates.

Other major digital ID projects include ID2020, which is collaboration with the United Nations High Commissioner for Refugees (UNHCR) to develop standards for a universal digital identity.[31] ID2020 is not developing digital identity technology systems but works in an alliance with vendors that do.[32] One of the most disturbing elements of ID2020 is its objective of providing "infants with a portable, biometrically-linked digital ID either at the point of birth registration or at the time of routine immunization..."[33] As such, the digital identity could track people from cradle to grave, inclusive of their vaccine statuses. ID2020 has as one of its goals: "Increase the number of fully immunized children."[34] ID2020 is funded by Microsoft, Accenture, Gavi, the Rockefeller Foundation, and IDEO.[35] Gavi is the Vaccine Alliance, which has been "leading global efforts on equitable access to COVID-19 vaccines."[36] Gavi is funded by the Bill

---

31 "Announcing the 2018 ID2020 Summit – Towards 'Good' Digital Identity," UNHCR Blog, September 6, 2018, https://www.unhcr.org/blogs/announcing-the-2018-id2020-summit-towards-good-digital-identity/.

32 "ID2020 | Alliance & Governance," ID2020, accessed September 27, 2022, https://id2020.org/alliance.

33 "ID2020 | Digital Health ID RFP," ID2020, accessed September 27, 2022, https://id2020.org/digital-health-id-rfp.

34 Ibid.

35 Yinka Okeowo, "Meet 5 Founding Partners of ID2020 Alliance," *TechEconomy Nigeria*, March 27, 2021, https://techeconomy.ng/2020/04/meet-5-founding-partners-of-id2020-alliance/.

36 "Responding to Covid-19," Gavi, the Vaccine Alliance, accessed September 27, 2022, https://www.gavi.org/covid19.

& Melinda Gates Foundation.[37] Thus, we see that the digital ID is entwined with the vaccine regime and that the vaccine passport is likely to be a feature of digital identity.

The WEF suggests that digital identity is a fait accompli and that resistance to this development is both futile and undermining of self-interest. After all, digital identities are already in existence, and who wouldn't want the access and convenience that a universal digital identity would provide? As with most 4-IR developments, the WEF promotes digital identity as a boon to society. But of all the other means of identifying and tracking subjects, the digital identity poses perhaps the gravest technological threat to individual liberty yet conceived. It has the potential to trace, track, and surveil subjects and to compile a complete record of all activity. Integrated with a kind of social credit scoring system like the one supposed to be in place in China, as well as a vaccine passport, the digital identity could serve as a definitive means for political profiling, for perfecting the means of political cancellation already a part of Western life.

The digital identity could very well include an ESG score for individuals, thus barring the non-compliant from the civic life and making political deplorables out of millions. Linked with central bank digital currency (CBDC, discussed below), digital identity could bar these undesirables from the economy, forcing them to beg, borrow, and steal in the shadows. Worse yet, it is not beyond governments

37 "The Bill & Melinda Gates Foundation," Gavi, the Vaccine Alliance, July 29, 2020, https://www.gavi.org/operating-model/gavis-partnership-model/bill-melinda-gates-foundation.

to use the digital identity as a pretext for "pre-crime" arrests and political imprisonment.

Augmented Reality (AR)

Augmented reality (AR) involves overlays of digital data on the physical environment. Digital data can include text, sound, graphics, video, global positioning systems (GPS), holograms, and other elements. The data can be accessed using digital cameras, phones, tablets, smart glasses, and other devices as they become available. Apps residing on these devices overlay data on top of physical elements, providing information on what one is seeing and hearing, and could eventually also involve other senses, including taste and smell.

That is, AR represents a hyper-mediated experience of the physical world that interposes information between users and their perceptual fields. Some of the issues involved with AR have to do with the source(s) of overlaid data and the possible agendas of the data suppliers.

Most people have come to trust GPS for its locational and directional data. But AR can and likely will be used to overlay interpretations of elements that accord with official state, corporate, or corporate-state narratives, thus serving as an extension of mass media into the perceptual fields of individuals. In addition to its advertising potential, surreptitious or blatant propagandizing cannot be dismissed as an impossibility, especially given the preponderance of propaganda emanating from mainstream media. Provided that AR becomes a necessity like the smart phone, the propaganda of AR could become nearly inescapable. Of course, companies might produce alternative ARs to counter official AR, but the cost of entry for such systems could be prohibitive. AR, billed as an enhancement of experience, could become an additional means of indoctrination and control. AR represents a technological breakthrough, but the agendas of the producers cannot be trusted.

Central Bank Digital Currency (CBDC)

With central bank digital currency (CBDC), the surveillance possible under the 4-IR is extended to commercial transactions. CDBCs are the digital versions of fiat money, or money backed not by any real marketable assets (like gold) but by the state's promise to pay. CBDC is not a cryptocurrency. Whereas cryptocurrencies represent a decentralized means of storing fungible assets outside of the purview and control of central banks and the state, CBDCs represent state-backed currencies under the complete control of central banks under the purview of the state. While, like cryptocurrencies, CBDCs may use blockchain technology, that is where the similarity ends. Central banks plan to adopt blockchain and other technologies and use them to fulfill their long-held ambition of exercising total centralized surveillance and control over money.

CBDC is the digital equivalent of cash, but it differs from cash in significant ways. Like cash, CBDCs are issued and backed by central banks, but unlike cash, central banks will have complete access to the distribution of CBDCs. Cash can be stored outside of banks, and spending cash cannot easily be tracked. As the Bank for International Settlements (BIS) report on CBDCs makes clear, "[a] key feature of cash is that no centralised records of holdings or transactions exist."[38] With CBDCs, on the other hand, central banks will have access to all accounts stored in their databases. Accounts will be held by central banks directly. This will make every transaction involving digital currency transparent to central banks, which could exercise centralized surveillance and control over spending, debt, and savings. Transaction privacy will be obliterated. As the BIS report states, "Full anonymity is not plausible...For a CBDC and its system, payments data will exist, and a key national policy question will be deciding who can access which parts of it and under what circumstances."[39] The BIS also suggests that CBDCs could be "linked to a national digital identity scheme" and "[a] linked digital identity system would be a necessity to realise real improvement" in making fiscal transfers.[40]

Central banks could also limit holdings and exact real-time taxation on transactions and negative interest rates.[41] They may require spending at a certain rate and make holdings deposited by the state expire if not spent. They may even limit spending to what they deem to be the essentials and freeze the accounts of rebels under the guise of fighting "terrorism."[42] As noted by independent precious metals advisor Claudio Grass, CBDCs give totalitarian regimes another weapon in their vast digital arsenals for

38 "Central Bank Digital Currencies: Foundational Principles and Core Features - Bank for International Settlements," Bank for International Settlements, 2020. https://www.bis.org/publ/othp33.pdf, page 6.

39 Ibid.

40 Ibid., pages 6 and 7.

41 Ibid., page 8, footnote 7.

42 Ibid., page 6.

monitoring and controlling their subjects to hitherto undreamed-of degrees.[43] I should add that CBDCs can make totalitarian regimes out of "democracies."

Under this new banking system, private commercial banks could become obsolete, as banks would no longer offer a legitimate business service for profit. As the BIS notes, "[t]here is a risk of *disintermediating* banks" (emphasis mine)—that is, of obviating and eliminating commercial banks as accounts with central banks become universal. This could cause commercial bank holdings to decline if not disappear entirely, which would devastate the economy as banks "restrict credit supply in the economy with potential impacts on economic growth."[44] This represents a fault line in the Great Reset project. But with CBDCs, banking would take on a police function of rewarding the compliant and punishing nonconformists.

I will not treat the effects of CBDCs on monetary policy, except to say that with digital currency, central banks will be capable of granulated economic planning and interventionism, with an ability to fine-tune tracking of spending on commodities and even to direct spending to particular sectors and commodity types. As the BIS argues:

> [The] Covid-19 pandemic illustrates the benefits of having efficient facilities for the government to quickly transfer funds to the public and businesses in a crisis. A CBDC system with

43 Claudio Grass, "The Dangers Posed by State-Controlled Digital Currency," Mises Institute, July 6, 2020, https://mises.org/wire/dangers-posed-state-controlled-digital-currency.

44 "Central Bank Digital Currencies: Foundational Principles and Core Features - Bank for International Settlements," page 8.

identified users (e.g., *a system linked to a national digital identity scheme*) could be used for these payments (emphasis mine).[45]

The potential for abuse would be even greater than it already is under the state-backed, asset-free, cash-based monetary system in practice today. CBDCs would give central bankers the ability to bail-out favored players in real time and flood markets with currency injections instantaneously. Likely, a requirement for bailouts will be an acceptable ESG score. Price controls could be introduced at will to counteract the inflationary tendencies that such digital currencies would inevitably exacerbate.

Meanwhile, according to International Monetary Fund Chair and Managing Director Kristalina Georgieva, 90 percent of central banks are deliberating the institution of CBDCs.[46] The Bahamas led the way with the first CBDC, the Sand Dollar,[47] while several other countries, including Nigeria and countries in the Eastern Caribbean Union, have launched CBDCs. Pilot projects are underway in many other nations, including Canada, China, France, India, Russia, Saudi Arabia, South Africa, Uruguay, and

---

45 Ibid., page 6.

46 "Central Bank Digital Currencies," World Economic Forum, May 23, 2022, https://www.weforum.org/events/world-economic-forum-annual-meeting-2022/sessions/central-bank-digital-currencies.

47 Vipin Bharathan, "Central Bank Digital Currency: The First Nationwide CBDC in the World Has Been Launched by the Bahamas," *Forbes Magazine*, October 22, 2020, https://www.forbes.com/sites/vipinbharathan/2020/10/21/central-bank-digital-currency-the-first-nationwide-cbdc-in-the-world-has-been-launched-by-the-bahamas/?sh=674ec9cc506e.

Yemen.[48] China is undertaking the largest pilot project, with 140 million participants using the e-CNY.[49] At the 2022 WEF annual meeting, IMF chair Kristalina Georgieva said that China's experimental adoption of the digital yuan prompted her to "embrace" CBDCs.

In Executive Order 14067 of March 9, 2022, the Biden regime stated that it "places the highest urgency on research and development efforts into the potential design and deployment options of a United States CBDC." It further suggested that such a CBDC must ensure that "the global financial system has appropriate *transparency,* connectivity, and platform and architecture interoperability or transferability, as appropriate" (emphasis mine).[50] The Federal Reserve is in the research phase for the introduction of a U.S.-backed CBDC, having published its preliminary exploratory findings in a January 2022 paper.[51] The paper has been opened to comments and most of the comments are decidedly negative regarding the floated introduction of the digital dollar. The

---

48   "Central Bank Digital Currency (CBDC) Tracker," CBDC tracker, accessed July 2, 2022, https://cbdctracker.org/.

49   Arendse Huld, "The Digital Yuan App - All You Need to Know about the New e-CNY Tool," *China Briefing News,* April 14, 2022, https://www.china-briefing.com/news/china-launches-digital-yuan-app-what-you-need-to-know/.

50   "Executive Order on Ensuring Responsible Development of Digital Assets," The White House, The United States Government, March 9, 2022, https://www.whitehouse.gov/briefing-room/presidential-actions/2022/03/09/executive-order-on-ensuring-responsible-development-of-digital-assets/.

51   "Dollar in the Age of Digital Transformation," January 2022, https://www.federalreserve.gov/publications/files/money-and-payments-20220120.pdf.

European Central Bank has signaled its support for a single digital currency, which would cement the centralization sought by European Union leaders. In short, CBDCs are the wave of the future, and the future does not look bright. CBDCs must be resisted at all costs.

Despite all the liberty- and rights-infringing issues that attend the digitalization of everything, the most pernicious development may be the production of digital simulacra to supplement, and to varying degrees, supplant the analog world. This is known as the metaverse, which I treat next.

CHAPTER SIXTEEN

The Metaverse

THE WORLD ECONOMIC Forum (WEF) describes the metaverse as "a unified and persistent virtual environment accessed via extended reality (XR) technologies."[1] On May 25, 2022, during its annual meeting, the WEF announced its metaverse initiative, Defining and Building the Metaverse, which it claims is "the world's foremost multistakeholder initiative to develop and share actionable strategies for creating and governing the metaverse."[2] It's as if the WEF is in a hurry to get the masses hooked up to the metaverse, before the latter eat the elite.

I'll introduce the metaverse with a Facebook post I made about it on October 21, 2021:

> The #Metaverse is where the technocrats want you to dwell as they make the meat world an

---

1 "Who Will Govern the Metaverse?," World Economic Forum, May 25, 2022, https://www.weforum.org/agenda/2022/05/metaverse-governance/.

2 "The Metaverse," World Economic Forum, accessed July 2, 2022, https://www.weforum.org/topics/the-metaverse.

uninhabitable shit hole with the Great Reset. You won't be allowed to move in actual space unless your digital ID is updated for the latest vaccine, administered on a minute-by-minute basis. They'll send their avatars to chase you around with virtual needles in the metaverse too.[3]

While the above post may represent hyperbole, the metaverse certainly may become a means of compensating for and distracting from the real-world impoverishment created by the enactment of Great Reset desiderata, while also serving as an additional enforcement regime for such matters as vaccination. The point is that the metaverse will be used to displace physical-world experience with a simulated reality, and, thanks to the reduced satisfactions of the "real world" because of the Great Reset, the metaverse may become preferable to non-virtual reality. Meanwhile, given its governance by the same elites that govern the physical world, the limitations and threats imposed by authorities in the physical world will be doubled in the metaverse.

The term "metaverse" derives from Neal Stephenson's sci-fi novel, *Snow Crash*. The metaverse is a digitally represented universe that is billed by its very name as something above or beyond the material world, yet also part of it. In the novel's metaverse, humans are represented by their chosen avatars and interact with avatars of others, with everyone occupying cyberspace. Imagine walking along a street that

---

3   Michael Rectenwald, The #Metaverse is where the technocrats... - Michael Rectenwald, Facebook post, Retrieved June 20, 2022, from https://www.facebook.com/michael.rectenwald/posts/10158075161717274.

is either virtual, material, or both, and passing people represented as anthropomorphized cats, dogs,
bears, or other creatures. You are in the metaverse,
where social actors and the physical world have been
reformulated and presented as virtual, augmented,
and mixed realities.

The metaverse is a virtual world replete with
digital assets, including virtual vehicles, homes,
pets, partners, children, and more.[4] One can earn,
spend, and invest virtual money, which intersects
with and to some extent supplements and replaces
"real-world" earnings, spending, and investments.
Given the economic stasis and reduced prospects of
the Great Reset, ownership in the metaverse may be
the only option for many.

The metaverse is the experience of a consensual
fiction in which one is a character among other fictional characters. The fiction, however, impacts the
real world and to some extent supplants it.

The issues attendant upon the metaverse
should be obvious. Identity itself is thrown into
question. Systems for ensuring consistent identity across metaverse platforms are being developed,
but the potential for dissembling is enormous. The
WEF notes that stable identity, trust, and security
represent issues that could plague the users of the
metaverse. Charlie Bell, the executive vice president
of Security, Compliance, Identity, and Management
at Microsoft, has pointed to impersonation, fraud,
phishing, social engineering, nation-state espionage,
and other security threats that could be deal break-

4 The Ontology Team, "Ontology and the Coming Metaverse," *Me-
dium*, Ontology Network, June 22, 2021, https://medium.com/ontol-
ogynetwork/ontology-and-the-coming-metaverse-323596946aa2.

ers.[5] People have even claimed that their avatars have been molested in the metaverse.[6] I would add that the metaverse could become a propaganda box for indoctrinating users while placating them.

The metaverse also poses societal and philosophical problems, as ontological entities become unhinged from their substrata, and identity and the object world are transmuted via avatars and the digital representation of objects. The line between "the real" and the simulacrum is blurred, at best.

The metaverse thus reifies postmodern epistemology. That is, the metaverse instantiates postmodern theory by making its conceptual framework a thing.

In Jacques Derrida's treatment of language in *Of Grammatology* (1967), the link between ontology and language is broken, as language refers only to itself: "There is nothing outside of text."[7] Derrida drew on Ferdinand de Saussure's notion of the sign—the signifier-signified-referent construction—to undermine any relationship between language and the ontological. According to de Saussure's formulation, the signifier is the word (text), the signified is the

5 Charlie Bell, "The Metaverse Is Coming. Here Are the Cornerstones for Securing It," The Official Microsoft Blog, March 29, 2022, https://blogs.microsoft.com/blog/2022/03/28/the-metaverse-is-coming-here-are-the-cornerstones-for-securing-it/.

6 Weilun Soon,"A Researcher's Avatar Was Sexually Assaulted on a Metaverse Platform Owned by Meta, Making Her the Latest Victim of Sexual Abuse on Meta's Platforms, Watchdog Says," *Business Insider*, May 30, 2022, https://www.businessinsider.com/researcher-claims-her-avatar-was-raped-on-metas-metaverse-platform-2022-5.

7 Jacques Derrida, *Of Grammatology*, Translated by Gayatri Chakravorty Spivak, The Johns Hopkins University Press, 1998, page 158.

idea evoked by the word, and the referent is the ontological object or concept to which the signified refers. The signifier has no necessary relationship to its referent (the ontological entity). The signifier points instead to the signified, or an idea, not to the referent, or something ontological. Derrida goes further than Saussure and breaks the connection between the signifier (the word) and the signified (the idea evoked by the word), arguing for the self-referentiality of the signifier. The signifier points only to itself and not even to the signified. Derrida also conflates the signified and the referent, thereby denying any relationship of language to the ontological. Being itself is thus a construction of the signifier: "being is produced...only through the logos, and is nothing outside of it...in the last instance, the difference between signified and signifier is *nothing*."[8]

It should be remembered here that the metaverse transcribes the subject and the object world into data (zeros and ones) or into text itself. In the metaverse, as in Derrida's deconstruction, "there is nothing outside of text." The metaverse reifies this postmodern disjunction from ontology by further breaking the link between representation and the ontological as it displaces the ontological itself and replaces it with data—that is, with a textual simulacrum. Language, thus, not only loses its connection to ontology but also the signifier (data/text) replaces both the idea of the world (the signified) and the ontological world it-

---

8 Ibid., pages 22-23. I refer readers to my lengthier discussion of deconstruction in my course for Libertyclassroom.com: Michael Rectenwald, "Critical Theory, Cultural Studies, and Postmodern Theory," Liberty Classroom, July 7, 2021, https://libertyclassroom.com/course/601ffeddee13c/, lectures 9 and 10.

self (the referent). The metaverse is thus deconstruction made literal.

In his book, *Simulations* (1983), the French postmodern theoretician Jean Baudrillard treated this further disjunction.[9] According to Baudrillard, the postmodern world has become a series of simulacra, a spectacle of simulations without originals. Suburban neighborhoods, amusement parks, jungle dioramas in shopping malls, and even the political Left and Right—these are all simulations without originals, imitations of prototypes that no longer exist. Baudrillard later enraged both the political Left and Right when he remarked that the first Gulf War "wasn't real."[10] He meant that the real had been displaced by images and history by the serial reproduction of imagery. The metaverse represents this further displacement, positing the signified (the idea of world) as the signifier (data/text), which replaces the referent, to which language no longer refers. We are thus lost in a postmodern miasma.

This postmodern miasma is illustrated by Ray Kurzweil in *The Singularity Is Near*. Kurzweil lauds the interchangeability of signifiers (avatars) for identities in what has become known as the metaverse:

> In virtual reality we won't be restricted to a single personality, since we will be able to change our appearance and effectively become other people. Without altering our physical body (in real reality) we will be able to readily transform our projected body in these three-dimensional

---

9 Jean Baudrillard, *Simulations*, New York, NY: Semiotext(e), 1983.
10 Jean Baudrillard, *The Gulf War Did Not Take Place*, Bloomington, IN: Indiana Univ. Press, 2012.

virtual environments. We can select different bodies at the same time for different people. So your parents may see you as one person, while your girlfriend will experience you as another. However, the other person may choose to override your selections, preferring to see you differently than the body you have chosen for yourself. You could pick different body projections for different people: Ben Franklin for a wise uncle, a clown for an annoying coworker. Romantic couples can choose whom they wish to be, even to become each other. These are all easily changeable decisions.[11]

In Kurzweil's example, that is, not only does the signifier (text/data) replace the idea of the world (the signified) and the ontological (the referent), but it also replaces the textual/data representation(s) performed by a given avatar with those of others' avatars. Thus, the signifiers have absolutely no stability. Deconstruction in the metaverse is as utterly confounding as it is in "real" life. Like deconstruction, that is, the metaverse leads to epistemological solipsism and nihilism. Once language no longer has any purchase on ontology, the possibility for knowledge is eradicated.

The philosophical and societal-level problems posed by the metaverse are perhaps best illustrated by referencing the 1999 sci-fi cyber thriller, *eXistenZ*, written and directed by David Cronenberg.[12] Allegra Geller (Jennifer Jason Leigh), the world's leading game designer, and the goddess of what we

---

11 Ray Kurzweil, *The Singularity Is Near*, Penguin Publishing Group, page 314.

12 David Cronenberg, *eXistenZ*, Dimension Films, 1999.

now call the metaverse, is testing her new virtual reality game, eXistenZ, with a focus group.

As the film begins, the project manager of eXistenZ introduces the game: "eXistenZ. Written like this. One word. Small 'e.' Capital 'X.' Capital 'Z.' eXistenZ. It's new. It's from Antenna Research. And it's here. Right now." He writes the name on a chalkboard in an otherwise abandoned church, as he introduces the new game system to an audience of willing players. Allegra moves from a pew to the church altar and begins uploading the game to the players from a fleshy, organic game pod ported directly into her spine via what looks like an umbilical cord. She's immediately attacked by an assassin, a member of the Realist Underground, who shoots her with a bony, cartilaginous gun that we later learn fires human teeth. Allegra survives the assault. She flees with a young marketing trainee, Ted Pikul (Jude Law), who is assigned to be Geller's bodyguard by the project manager of eXistenZ, as the latter lies dying from a tooth wound to the chest. Allegra's pod contains the only copy of eXistenZ. But the organic pod is wounded from the aborted upload. To test the pod and the game, she convinces Ted to have a bio-port installed in his spinal cord, so he can play the game with her.

In eXistenZ, "reality" is as strange and disfigured as the simulated reality of the game space. While the majority apparently dwells in the metaverse, the world's infrastructure is dilapidated and crumbling. Gross biological mutations abound, like the two-headed lizard creeping around Ted's car. There's the maniacal Country Gas Station attendant named Gas (Willem Dafoe), who worships Geller for having given simulated dimension to his otherwise miserable life (he's a gamer), but tries to kill her for the five-million-dollar bounty on her head. And there's the bizarre Scot, Kiri Vinokur (Ian Holm), who operates on Allegra's organic, pulsing, and bleeding pod, and restores it to health, as if this is a routine operation.

When the couple enters eXistenZ, everything about the game experience is entirely "realistic," except for the non-playing characters (NPCs), whose speech is clearly scripted. The active players converse normally, except when their game characters take over so that they can issue the correct cues to the NPCs and move the game forward.

After ordering "the special" in a Chinese restaurant that serves amphibious mutants (the "real" meal will be bugs), the pair plays a game within a game. They insert miniature pods into their gamified bio-ports and begin a new sequence. The double gaming exacerbates Ted's unease. In the middle of a love scene with Geller's game character—which is Allegra herself, but not quite—he jumps up and declares, "eXistenZ is paused!"

Upon awakening in the abandoned ski lodge where their bodies have remained in hiding, Ted is estranged from his surroundings.

"So how does it feel?" Allegra asks.

"What?" Ted responds.

"Your real life. The one you came back for."

"It feels completely *unreal*," Ted intones, bewildered.

Allegra wants to return to the game.

"You wanna go back to the Chinese restaurant? ... because there's nothing happening here. We're safe. It's boring."

316 The Great Reset and the Struggle for Liberty

Ted feels the texture of a chair, as if he's never encountered the "real world" before.

"It's worse than that. I'm not sure...I'm not sure here...where we are...is real at all. This feels like a game to me. And you...you're beginning to feel like a game character," Ted says tremulously.

When they reenter the game space, Ted and Allegra resume their roles at the Chinese restaurant, where Ted's game character is compelled to shoot the waiter with a pistol that he automatically constructs from bones buried in his meal. It's the exact replica of the one fired by the member of the Realist Underground in the "real world," and the bullets are teeth. The Realist Underground has infiltrated the game and eXistenZ has been infiltrated by "reality," and vice versa. When the game-playing appears to be over, we learn that Ted is actually a member of the Realist Underground. That's why he'd never had a bio-port installed. He attempts to shoot Allegra but is killed by her instead.

Having just murdered Kiri Vinokur and Ted, Allegra, believing she's still in the game, asks, "Have I won? Have I won the game?"

We are ported back to a focus group and learn that eXistenZ is just a game within a game. What a relief! All the characters, both "inside" and "outside" of eXistenZ, including Gas, Kiri Vinokur, the Chinese waiter, and Allegra and Ted, are part of a "real" focus group. But if the NPCs were also game players, then Ted and Allegra were also NPCs. Ted and Allegra, it turns out, are a "real-life" couple. The "real" game is transCendenZ, by PilgrImage. The project manager spells it out: "Capital 'C,' capital 'Z,' transCendenZ." The "real" game designer is not Allegra, but Yevgeny

Nourish, "the greatest game artist in the world."

After the focus group finishes a friendly but eerily scripted discussion, Nourish quietly confesses his concerns to the project manager: he did not like the anti-game sentiment expressed in the game-playing that had just transpired. One or more of the gamers must have introduced it into the script. We immediately learn that the culprits are Ted and Allegra and that they are part of the "real" Realist Underground. They approach Nourish angrily. Ted pulls out a rifle from a satchel and shoots the game artist and the project manager, while the other members of the focus group look on dispassionately, like NPCs in a game.

eXistenZ captures the ontological bewilderment, identity transmutation, and reality-disfigurement that the metaverse promises, with its foundering border between "reality" and the simulacrum. One leaks into the other seamlessly, even into the "real" focus group at the end. *eXistenZ* points not only to the emotional detachment from "the real" that the metaverse produces but also the substitutability of the simulation and "the real." The question is, where does the metaverse begin and end? Of course, the film illustrates the technocratic control that the metaverse represents—game players wearing VR headsets, exploring a world produced by alien and distant companies, and sitting or lying dormant for hours on end, while their avatars engage in what, for them, becomes "real life."

Curiously, in its buildup to becoming Meta, Facebook required that its Oculus employees read Ernest Cline's dystopian sci-fi novel, *Ready Player*

One.[13] And Mark Zuckerberg wanted Meta modeled after the novel and Neal Stephenson's *Snow Crash.*[14] As in *eXistenZ,* the "real world" in *Ready Player One* is a dismal place that people play the game to escape. Meta is a partner of the WEF.[15]

The metaverse is a manufactured reality that apparently offers no alternative—other than becoming the member of a neo-Luddite cult bent on its destruction. And that is the brilliance of the metaverse's figuration by its promulgators. All those who oppose the metaverse are considered retrograde anti-technology fanatics, like members of the Realist Underground. Thus, the seduction and compulsion are irresistible, almost. But, like "the special" served in eXistenZ's Chinese restaurant, the meal is a weapon.

13 Jillian D'Onfro, "Facebook Gives Its Oculus Employees a Dystopian Sci-Fi Book to Get Them Excited about Building the Future," *Business Insider,* January 27, 2016, https://www.businessinsider.com/oculus-gives-all-its-employees-ready-player-one-2016-7.

14 Marc Deschamps, "Mark Zuckerberg Wants to Create *Ready Player One*-Inspired Metaverse," *GAMING,* Comicbook.com, August 1, 2021, https://comicbook.com/gaming/news/facebook-mark-zuckerberg-ready-player-one-metaverse/.

15 "Meta," World Economic Forum, accessed September 28, 2022, https://www.weforum.org/organizations/facebook-inc.

CHAPTER SEVENTEEN

Hacking Humanity: Transhumanism

T HE NOTION THAT the world can be replicated and replaced by a simulated reality says a great deal about the beliefs of those who promote the metaverse. The conception is materialist and mechanistic at base, the hallmarks of social engineering. It represents the world as consisting of nothing but manipulable matter, or rather, of digital media mimicking matter. It suggests that human beings can be reduced to a material substratum and can be induced to accept a technological reproduction in lieu of reality. Further, it assumes that those who inhabit this simulacrum can be controlled by technocratic means. Such a materialist, mechanistic, techno-determinist, and reductionist worldview is consistent with the transhumanist belief that humans themselves will soon be succeeded by a new transhuman species, or humanity-plus (h+)—perhaps a genetically- and AI-enhanced cyborg that will outstrip ordinary humans and make the latter virtually obsolete.

The term transhumanism was coined by Julian Huxley, the brother of the novelist Aldous Huxley and the first director-general of the United Nations Educational, Scientific and Cultural Organization (UNESCO). In an essay entitled "Transhumanism," published in the book *New Bottles for New Wine* (1957), Huxley defined transhumanism as the self-transcendence of humanity:

> The human species can, if it wishes, transcend itself—not just sporadically, an individual here in one way, an individual there in another way, but in its entirety, as humanity. We need a name for this new belief. Perhaps transhumanism will serve: man remaining man, but transcending himself, by realizing new possibilities of and for his human nature.[1]

One question for transhumanism is indeed whether this transcendence will apply to the whole human species or rather for only a select part of it. But Huxley gave some indication of how this human self-transcendence might occur: humanity would become "managing director of the biggest business of all, the business of evolution..."[2] As the first epigraph to this Part makes clear, Julian Huxley was a proponent of eugenics. And he was the President of the British Eugenics Society.[3] It was in his intro-

---

1 Julian Huxley, "Transhumanism," *New Bottles for New Wine*, London: Readers Union, Chatto & Windus, 1957, page 17.

2 Ibid., page 13.

3 "Past Presidents," Adelphi Genetics Forum, August 10, 2022, https://adelphigenetics.org/history/past-presidents/. The Adelphi Genetics Forum was originally named the British Eugenics Education Society and was founded in 1911. It changed its name to the

duction of UNESCO, as the director-general that he suggested that eugenics, after the Nazi regime had given it such a bad name, should be rescued from opprobrium, "so that much that now is unthinkable may at least become thinkable."[4] As John Klyczek has noted, "In the wake of vehement public backlash against the atrocities of the Nazi eugenic Holocaust, Huxley's eugenics proper was forced to go underground, repackaging itself in various crypto-eugenic disguises, one of which is 'transhumanism.'" Transhumanism, Klyczek suggests, is "the scientific postulate that human evolution through biological-genetic selection has been largely superseded by a symbiotic evolution that cybernetically merges the human species with its own technological handiwork."[5]

Contemporary transhumanist enthusiasts, such as Simon Young, believe that humanity can take over where evolution has left us to create a new and improved species—either ourselves, or a successor to ourselves:

> We stand at a turning point in human evolution. We have cracked the genetic code; translated the Book of Life. We will soon possess the ability to become designers of our own evolution.[6]

British Eugenics Society in 1926 and changed its name again to the Galton Institute in 1989. In 2021, it changed its name yet again to the Adelphi Genetics Forum.

4 Julian Huxley, "UNESCO: Its Purpose and Its Philosophy," Unesdoc.unesco.org, 1946, https://unesdoc.unesco.org/ark:/48223/pf0000068197, page 21.

5 John Adam Klyczek, *School World Order: The Technocratic Globalization of Corporatized Education*, Trine Day, 2019, page 207.

6 Simon Young, *Designer Evolution: A Transhumanist Manifesto*,

In "A History of Transhumanist Thought," Nick Bostrom details the lineage of transhumanist thought from its prehistory to the present and shows how transhumanism became wedded to the fields of genomics, nanotechnology, and robotics (GNR), where robotics is inclusive of Artificial Intelligence (AI).[7] It is the last of these fields that primarily concerns us here. The transhumanist project has since envisioned the transcendence of humanity via technological means. In the past thirty years, this technological transcendence has been figured as "the singularity."

Vernor Vinge, the mathematician, computer scientist, and science fiction author introduced the notion of the technological singularity in 1993.[8] The singularity, Vinge suggested, is the near-future point at which machine intelligence will presumably supersede human intelligence. Vinge boldly declared: "Within thirty years, we will have the technological means to create superhuman intelligence. Shortly after, the human era will be ended."[9] Vinge predicted that the singularity would be reached no later than, you guessed it, 2030. The question Vinge addressed was whether, and if so, how, the human species might survive the coming singularity.

Prometheus, 2005, Kindle Edition, Location 273.

7 Nick Bostrom, "A History of Transhumanist Thought," in Michael Rectenwald and Lisa Carl, eds., *Academic Writing Across the Disciplines*, New York: Pearson Longman, 2011.

8 Vernor Vinge, "The Coming Technological Singularity: How to Survive in the Post-Human ERA - NASA Technical Reports Server (NTRS)," NASA, March 30, 1993, https://ntrs.nasa.gov/citations/19940022856.

9 Ibid., page 11.

The inventor, futurist, and now Google Engineering Director Raymond Kurzweil has since welcomed the technological singularity as a boon to humanity. Kurzweil, whose books include *The Age of Spiritual Machines* (1999), *The Singularity Is Near* (2005), and *How to Create a Mind* (2012), suggests that by 2029, technologists will have successfully reverse-engineered the brain and replicated human intelligence in (strong) AI while vastly increasing processing speeds of thought. Having mapped the neuronal components of a human brain, or discovered the algorithms for thought, or a combination thereof, technologists will convert the same to a computer program, personality and all, and upload it to a computer host, thus grasping the holy grail of immortality. Finally, as the intelligence explosion expands from the singularity, all matter will be permeated with data, with intelligence; the entire universe will "wake up" and become alive, and "about as close to God as I can imagine," writes Kurzweil.[10]

Thus, in a complete reversal of the Biblical creation narrative, Kurzweil posits a dumb universe that begins with a cosmic singularity (the Big Bang) and becomes God by a technological singularity. This second singularity, Kurzweil suggests, involves the universe becoming self-aware, vis-à-vis the informational, technological agent, humanity. Thus, in the technological singularity, the technological and the cosmic converge, as Kurzweil resembles a techno-cosmic Hegelian. (Hegel figured collective human self-consciousness progressing in self-actualization and self-realization, finally becoming and recogniz-

10   Ray Kurzweil, *The Singularity Is Near*, Penguin Publishing Group, page 375.

ing itself as God, "through the State [as] the march of God in the world."[11]) Incidentally, according to Kurzweil, our post-human successors will bear the marks of their human provenance. Thus, the future intelligence will remain "human" in some sense. Human beings are the carriers of universal intelligence and human technology is the substratum by which intelligence will be infinitely expanded and universalized.

More recently, Yuval Noah Harari—the Israeli historian, WEF-affiliated futurist, and advisor to Klaus Schwab—has also hailed this singularity, although with dire predictions for the vast majority. According to Harari, the 4-IR will have two main consequences: human bodies and minds will be replaced by robots and AI, while human brains become hackable with nanorobotic brain-cloud interfaces (B/CIs), AI, and biometric surveillance technologies. Just as humans are functionally replaced, that is, they will be subject to the total control of powerful corporations or the state (or, what's more likely, a hybrid thereof, a neo-fascist state). Rather than a decentralized, open-access infosphere of exploding intelligence available to all, Singularitarian technologies will become part of the arsenal for domination. The supersession of human intelligence by machine intelligence will involve the use of such data and data processing capabilities to further predict and control social behavioral patterns of the global population. In addition, the biotechnical enhancement of the few will serve to exacerbate an already wide gulf between the elite and the majority, while the "superiority"

11 Georg Wilhelm Friedrich Hegel, *Elements of the Philosophy of Right*, trans. S. W. Dyde, London: George Bell and Sons, 1896, page 247.

of the enhanced functions ideologically to rationalize differences permitted by such a division. That
is, Harari suggests that if developments proceed as
Vinge and Kurzweil predict, this vastly accelerated
information-collecting and processing sphere will
not constitute real knowledge for the enlightenment
of the vast majority. Rather, it will be instrumental-
ist and reductionist in the extreme, facilitating the
domination of human beings on a global scale, while
rendering opposition impossible.

In an article in *Frontiers in Neuroscience*, Nuno
R. B. Martins et al. explain just how such control
could be implemented through B/CIs, which the authors claim will be feasible within the next 20 to 30
years:

> Neuralnanorobotics may also enable a B/CI
> with controlled connectivity between neural ac-
> tivity and external data storage and processing,
> via the direct monitoring of the brain's ~86 x
> 10^9 neurons and ~2 x 10^{14} synapses...
>
> They would then wirelessly transmit up to ~6
> x 10^{16} bits per second of synaptically processed
> and encoded human–brain electrical informa-
> tion via auxiliary nanorobotic fiber optics (30
> cm^3) with the capacity to handle up to 10^{18} bits/
> sec and provide rapid data transfer to a cloud-
> based supercomputer for *real-time brain-state
> monitoring and data extraction.* A neuralna-
> norobotically enabled human B/CI might serve
> as a personalized conduit, allowing persons to
> obtain direct, instantaneous access to virtually
> any facet of cumulative human knowledge (em-

phasis mine).[12]

Such interfaces have already reached the commercialization stage with Elon Musk's Neuralink,[13] Kernel,[14] and through DARPA,[15] among others.

When neuralnanorobotic technologies that conduct information and algorithms that make decisions interface with the brain, the possibilities for eliminating particular kinds of experiences, behaviors, and thoughts becomes possible. Such control of the mind through implants was already prototyped by Jose Delgado as early as 1969.[16] Now, two-way transmission of data between the brain and the cloud effectively means the possibility of reading the thoughts of subjects, interrupting such thoughts, and replacing them with other, machine-cloud-originating information. The desideratum to record, label, "informationalize," rather than to understand, let alone critically engage or theorize experience will take exclusive priority for subjects, given the possi-

12 Nuno R. B. Martins, Amara Angelica, Krishnan Chakravarthy, Yuriy Svidinenko, Frank J. Boehm, Ioan Opris, Mikhail A. Lebedev, et al., "Human Brain/Cloud Interface," *Frontiers in Neuroscience* 13 (March 29, 2019), https://doi.org/10.3389/fnins.2019.00112, no page numbers.

13 "Home," Neuralink, accessed September 26, 2022, https://neuralink.com/.

14 "Home," Kernel, accessed September 26, 2022, https://www.kernel.com/.

15 Staff, E&T editorial, "DARPA Funds Brain-Machine Interface Project for Controlling Weapons via Thoughts," RSS, May 23, 2019, https://eandt.theiet.org/content/articles/2019/05/darpa-funds-brain-machine-interface-project-for-controlling-weapons-via-thoughts/.

16 Jose M. R. Delgado, *Physical Control of The Mind: Toward a Psychocivilized Society*, New York, NY: Harper and Row, 1969.

bilities for controlling neuronal switching patterns. Given the instrumentalism of the Singularitarians— or, as Yuval Harari has called them, the "Dataists"— decisive, action-oriented algorithms will dominate these brain-cloud interfaces, precluding faculties for the critical evaluation of activity, and obliterating free will.[17] Given enough data, algorithms will be better able to make decisions for us. Nevertheless, they will have been based on intelligence defined in a particular way and put to particular ends, placing considerable emphasis on the speed and volume of data processing and decision-making based on data construed as "knowledge." Naturally, Aldous Huxley's *Brave New World* comes to mind. Yet, unlike Huxley's mind-numbing soma, brain-cloud interfaces will have an ideological appeal to the masses; they are touted as enhancements, as vast improvements over standard human intelligence.

Harari peels back the curtain masking transhumanism's Wizard of Oz promises, suggesting that even before the singularity, robotics and machine intelligence will make the masses into a new "useless class."[18] Given the exorbitant cost of entry, only the elite will be able to afford actual enhancements, making them a new, superior species—notwithstanding the claim that Moore's Law closes the technological breach by exponentially increasing the price-performance of computing and thus halving its

17 Yuval Noah Harari, "Yuval Noah Harari on Big Data, Google and the End of Free Will," *Financial Times*, August 26, 2016, https://www.ft.com/content/50bb4830-6a4c-11e6-ae5b-a7cc5dd5a28c.

18 Yuval Noah Harari, "The Rise of the Useless Class," ideas.ted.com, February 24, 2017, https://ideas.ted.com/the-rise-of-the-useless-class/.

cost per unit of measurement every two years or less. How the elite will maintain exclusive control over enhancements and yet subject the masses to control technologies is never addressed. But perhaps a kill switch could be implemented such that the elite will not be subjected to brain-data mining—unless one runs afoul of the agenda, in which case brain-data mining could be (re)enabled.

In a 2018 WEF statement, Harari spoke as the self-proclaimed prophet of a new transhumanist age, saying:

> We are probably among the last generations of homo sapiens. Within a century or two, Earth will be *dominated* by entities that are more different from us, than we are different from Neanderthals or from chimpanzees. Because in the coming generations, we will learn how to engineer bodies and brains and minds. These will be the main products of the 21st century economy (emphasis mine).[19]

No longer capable of mounting a challenge to the elite as in the nineteenth and twentieth centuries, and having no function, the feckless masses will have no recourse or purpose. Exploitation is one thing; irrelevance is quite another, says Harari. And thus, as Harari sees it, the remaining majority will be condemned to spend their time in the metaverse, or worse. If they are lucky, they will collect universal basic income (UBI) and will best occupy themselves by taking drugs and playing video games. Of course,

19 World Economic Forum, "Will the Future Be Human? - Yuval Noah Harari," YouTube, World Economic Forum, January 25, 2018, https://www.youtube.com/watch?v=hL9uk4hKyg4.

Harari exempts himself from this fate.

As for the elite, according to Harari, their supposed superiority to the masses will soon become a matter of biotechnological fact, rather than merely an ideological pretension, as in the past. The elite will not only continue to control the lion's share of the world's material resources; they will also become godlike and enjoy effective remote control over their subordinates. Further, via biotechnological means, they will acquire eternal life on Earth, while the majority, formerly consoled by the fact that at least everybody dies, will now lose the great equalizer. As the supernatural is outmoded, or sacrificed on the altar of transhumanism, the majority will inevitably forfeit their belief in a spiritual afterlife. The theistic religions that originated in the Middle East will disappear, to be replaced by new cyber-based religions originating in Silicon Valley. Spirituality, that is, will be nothing but the expression of reverence for newly created silicon gods, whether they be game characters, game designers, or the elites themselves.

Harari's pronouncements may amount to intentional hyperbole to make a point, but his statements are remarkable for the cynicism and disdain for humanity they betray. They are revelatory of the unmitigated gall of believers in the transhuman future. Coupled with the neo-Malthusian impulses of the elite, centered around the UN and the WEF, a picture emerges of an elite whose objective is to reduce the population of "useless eaters," while keeping the remainder in their thrall.

Part V

The Question of Conspiracy Theory

It is also important for the State to inculcate in its subjects an aversion to any "conspiracy theory of history;" for a search for "conspiracies" means a search for motives and an attribution of responsibility for historical misdeeds. If, however, any tyranny imposed by the State, or venality, or aggressive war, was caused not by the State rulers but by mysterious and arcane "social forces," or by the imperfect state of the world or, if in some way, everyone was responsible ("We Are All Murderers," proclaims one slogan), then there is no point to the people becoming indignant or rising up against such misdeeds. Furthermore, an attack on "conspiracy theories" means that the subjects will become more gullible in believing the "general welfare" reasons that are always put forth by the State for engaging in any of its despotic actions. A "conspiracy theory" can unsettle the system by causing the public to doubt the State's ideological propaganda.
—Murray N. Rothbard, *Anatomy of the State*

CHAPTER EIGHTEEN

The Question of Conspiracy Theory

S O, IS DISCOURSE critical of the Great Reset nothing but a conspiracy theory after all? Most of the legacy media and reputable cultural institutions still seem to suggest as much.[1] According to the *New York Times*, the Great Reset is "a baseless conspiracy theory about the coronavirus."[2] The Anti-Defamation League claims that adherents to the Great Reset conspiracy theory believe "elites want to use the coronavirus as a tool to reorganize global societies and economies to their benefit at the expense of ordinary people, with the ultimate goal of [establishing] a global totalitarian regime." Such

---

1 *Time* is an exception, devoting an entire issue to the Great Reset and hailing it as the solution to our problems post-covid. "The Great Reset: How to Build a Better World Post-Covid-19," *Time*, October 21, 2020, https://time.com/collection/great-reset/.

2 Davey Alba, "The Baseless 'Great Reset' Conspiracy Theory Rises Again," *New York Times*, Nov. 17, 2020, https://www.nytimes.com/live/2020/11/17/world/covid-19-coronavirus#the-baseless-great-reset-conspiracy-theory-rises-again.

beliefs, the organization suggests, represent regurgitated conspiracies about the New World Order and reek of an underlying, age-old antisemitism.[3] *BBC News* suggests that the Great Reset proposal and the World Economic Forum (WEF) "face legitimate criticism from a variety of sources...but the real energy online is not about legitimate political questions—discussions about fossil fuels and income equality—but [comes] in the shape of wild and unsubstantiated claims."[4]

Part of the problem with these characterizations is that the Great Reset is not, *on its face*, a conspiracy. It's not strictly "a secret plan on the part of a group to influence events partly by covert action."[5] It's not a conspiracy, as such, because, as we have seen, there's nothing particularly clandestine about the Great Reset project. When "What is the Great Reset?" is entered into a search engine, for example, the query yields, among other items, an essay of mine, and numerous items from the WEF announcing and describing the project. As we know, Klaus Schwab and Thierry Malleret even wrote a book entitled *Covid-19: The Great Reset*. The WEF held a summit called *The Great Reset*. More recently, Schwab and

3 "'The Great Reset' Conspiracy Flourishes Amid Continued Pandemic," Anti-Defamation League, December 29, 2020, https://www.adl.org/blog/the-great-reset-conspiracy-flourishes-amid-continued-pandemic.

4 BBC Monitoring and BBC Reality Check, "What Is the Great Reset - and How Did It Get Hijacked by Conspiracy Theories?," *BBC News*, June 23, 2021, https://www.bbc.co.uk/news/blogs-trending-57532368.

5 Charles Pigden, "Popper Revisited, Or What Is Wrong with Conspiracy Theories?," in David Coady, ed., *Conspiracy Theories: The Philosophical Debate*, Routledge, 2018, page 20.

Malleret published a second book on the Great Reset, entitled *The Great Narrative* (The Great Reset Book 2). It repeats and amplifies many of the arguments made in book 1. It's not as if the Great Reset is some hidden plot. It's an "open conspiracy"—that is, it's not a conspiracy at all.

But the charge of conspiracy theory is usually levied at Great Reset discourse not because the Great Reset doesn't exist. Few, if any, claim that conspiracy theorists are just making it up. The problem, according to establishment sources, is that the Great Reset has been blown up into a nefarious plot of a technocratic global elite to establish a socialist, communist, or fascist New World Order, with themselves in charge. The Great Reset, so the "conspiracy theory" goes, will abolish the property rights of the majority as well as obliterate individual and national sovereignty and autonomy, while wiping out the last vestiges of personal freedom. The Great Reset propagators use Covid-19 and climate change as pretexts to enslave what will remain of humanity using lockdowns, experimental vaccines, and pervasive, inescapable surveillance.

Let's suppose that this characterization accurately represents most of the moral panic surrounding the Great Reset. Let's further allow, just for the moment, that this construal is demonstrably mistaken, or hyperbolic at best. Would that mean that the Great Reset agenda is nothing to worry about?

I think not. The Great Reset project might lead to other results, results that are not quite so dramatic, yet still decidedly negative. Maybe the general population becomes poorer but not entirely propertyless. Maybe only some rights are abrogated—although, arguably, all rights are property rights. Perhaps national sovereignty is weakened rather than entirely abolished. Or maybe the Great Reset leads to entirely different prospects, as bad or even worse than those suggested by critics. And yet another possibility is that the Great Reset leads to outcomes that the propagators openly avow and intend, but which their critics deem to be deleterious. It is worth adding again that virtually all "great" plans have unintended consequences, most of them disastrous. There are many illustrations of this, including plans enacted with genuinely good intentions. So, one more reason to worry about the Great Reset is simply the fact that a world-shaping plan is in progress and may have unintended consequences. None of these possibilities should be ruled out in advance.

To ward off the usual dismissals of "conspiracy theory," in this final chapter, I treat the epistemological status of conspiracy theory itself. Are all conspiracy theories necessarily to be disqualified a priori? What kinds of conspiracy theories, if any, can be eliminated? What kinds, if any, should be entertained? And finally, what about theories regarding the Great Reset?

The Epistemological Status of Conspiracy Theory

The term conspiracy theory is one of the most potent epithets that can be hurled at a writer or speaker. Originally, the phrase simply meant a theory...of a conspiracy—theories ranging from the speculative, plausible, likely, to the absurd. Today, the phrase is almost always used to delegitimize and dismiss its target. The phrase represents a condensed, shorthand means of labeling a claim negatively and humiliating the claimant, disqualifying the claimant and the claim a priori.

In the United States, the term "conspiracy theory" is often credited to a disinformation or deflection campaign of the CIA, in connection with the assassination of President John F. Kennedy—to discredit and dismiss all but the official narrative concerning that event.

But the *Oxford English Dictionary* finds the first known usage of the term in a 1909 review of a doctoral dissertation in *The American Historical Review*.[6] The reviewer, Allen Johnson, used the phrase to describe a theory that P. Orman Ray, the author of the dissertation, revived to explain the repeal of the Missouri Compromise in 1854. The repeal of the Missouri Compromise is unimportant here, but I decided to track down this text to check its use of the term conspiracy theory. I found that nothing in Johnson's review of Ray's dissertation suggested that the claim made by Ray should be dismissed because it was a conspiracy theory. In fact, Johnson suggested that Ray made good use of the existing materials in support of his theory: "No new manuscript material has been found to support the theory, but the available bits of evidence have been collated carefully in this volume."[7] Allen took Ray to task for not providing sufficient evidence to back his claim, but he did not reject it for being a "conspiracy theory." As we can see, the term has not always served to discredit those

---

6   Allen Johnson, "The Repeal of the Missouri Compromise: Its Origin and Authorship by P. Orman Ray," *The American Historical Review*, July 1909, Vol. 14, No 4, pages 835-836.

7   Ibid., page 836.

who proposed such theories.

More recently, the conspiracy theory question has become a subject of a growing scholarly debate including historians, psychologists, sociologists, anthropologists, political scientists, and, within the last twenty years, philosophers. It is curious that philosophers are latecomers to this debate because discussions of the conspiracy theory question began with a philosopher. While most, if not all, of the psychological research on conspiracy theorists and conspiracist thinking is worthless,[8] a review of the philosophical literature should prove rewarding.

Karl Popper was arguably the first major thinker to treat conspiracy theory. In *The Open Society and Its Enemies* (1945), the philosopher introduced the conspiracy theory as a type of explanation that should be excluded from the social sciences.[9] In volume 2 of *The Open Society*, Popper defined the conspiracy theory of society as follows:

> It is the view that an explanation of a social phenomenon consists in the discovery of the men or groups who are interested in the occurrence of this phenomenon (sometimes it is a hidden interest which has first to be revealed), and who have planned and conspired to bring it about.[10]

Popper called the conspiracy theory of society

---

8 Iain Davis, "The BBC's Psychology behind Conspiracy Theories," *UKColumn*, August 4, 2022, https://www.ukcolumn.org/article/the-bbcs-psychology-behind-conspiracy-theories.

9 Karl R. Popper, *The Open Society and Its Enemies*, Princeton: Princeton University Press, 2020, https://doi-org.proxy.library.nyu.edu/10.1515/9780691212067.

10 Ibid., page 306.

"a typical result of the secularization of a religious superstition," an explanation of historical causality that replaces the causal agency of the gods or God with that of "sinister pressure groups whose wickedness is responsible for all the evils we suffer from—such as the Learned Elders of Zion, or the monopolists, or the capitalists, or the imperialists."[11]

Popper's problem with the conspiracy theory of society was not that conspiracies do not happen but rather that they seldom succeed. Conspiracy theory, he suggested, grants too much credence to the power of the human actors involved. Instead of drawing on conspiracy theory, Popper argued that the main task of the social sciences should be to explain why intentional human actions (including conspiracies) often result in unintended outcomes, or why conspiracies fail:

> Why is this so? Why do achievements differ so widely from aspirations? Because this is usually the case in social life, conspiracy or no conspiracy. Social life is not only a trial of strength between opposing groups: it is action within a resilient or brittle framework of institutions and traditions, and it creates—apart from any conscious counter-action—many unforeseen reactions in this framework, some of them perhaps even unforeseeable.[12]

Actions have unintended as well as intended consequences because they take place in a social context that cannot be fully predicted or controlled

---

11 Ibid.
12 Ibid., page 307.

by social actors. The conspiracy theory of society is wrong, Popper claimed, because it holds that the results of actions are necessarily those intended by the actors interested in such results. For this reason, as Popper would see it, we should reject "conspiracy theories" about the Great Reset.

Popper defined the conspiracy theory of society as a thoroughgoing explanation of all outcomes:

> The conspiracy theory of society cannot be true because it amounts to the assertion that *all results*, even those which at first sight do not seem to be intended by anybody, are the intended results of the actions of people who are interested in these results (emphasis mine).[13]

It's clear from this statement that Popper's charge does not apply to all conspiracy theories. It only includes conspiracy theories that purport to explain everything. Popper admitted that conspiracies "are typical social phenomena."[14] He claimed that most conspiracies fail, but that implies that some conspiracies succeed.

Conspiracy theories, or better, conspiracy hypotheses, it would seem, merely explain some outcomes in terms of attempted conspiracies. Theories that don't aim at explaining every outcome in terms of a singular, overarching conspiracy are based on an acknowledgement that conspiracies do transpire and that some outcomes are the results of conspiracies. An attempted bank robbery involving more than one person is technically a conspiracy. An explanation

---

13   Ibid.
14   Ibid.

of the plot, without first-hand knowledge of the details, is technically a conspiracy theory. It seems that nothing in Popper's definition of the conspiracy theory of society suggests that conspiracy hypotheses should be dismissed in advance. Likewise, it appears to be reasonable to conclude that conspiracy theory should be retained as one of the explanatory modes for understanding social outcomes.

This accords with the assertions of the leftist philosopher Charles Pigden. In his essay, "Popper Revisited, Or What Is Wrong With Conspiracy Theories?,"[15] Pigden—apparently the first philosopher to engage the question of conspiracy theory after Popper—takes exception to Popper's refutation of the conspiracy theory of society. Or, I should say, he shows that Popper left plenty of room for exceptions. According to Pigden, Popper's refutation is a refutation of a theory—the conspiracy theory of society—that no one believes anyway. Popper was attacking a straw man.

To summarize Pigden's argument: first, Popper's conspiracy theory of society always involves the discovery of the men or groups interested in an event and who planned and conspired to effect it. Therefore, every social phenomenon would have to be the product of a conspiracy for the theory to be true. Second, Popper seems to suggest that for the conspiracy theory of society to be true, all social outcomes must be explicable solely in terms of a plot by conspirators. That would mean that the conspiracy would have to be entirely successful. Third, Pop-

---

15 Charles Pigden, "Popper Revisited, Or What Is Wrong with Conspiracy Theories?," in David Coady, ed., *Conspiracy Theories: The Philosophical Debate*, pages 17-43.

per's refutation suggests that conspiracy theories by themselves can explain social events. That would eliminate other causal factors.

But the conspiracy theory of society describes practically no conspiracy theories. Few conspiracy theories hold that every social phenomenon can be explained with reference to a conspiracy; few conspiracy theories claim that all conspiracies are successful; and few, if any, conspiracy theories rule out other causal factors of social events. Likewise, Popper's refutation does not exclude the possibility that conspiracies happen, that they may succeed, or that conspiracy theories may explain some outcomes, including outcomes that result from failed conspiracies. Popper claimed that believing in the conspiracy theory of society is superstitious. But there is nothing in Popper's refutation of the conspiracy theory of society that is incompatible with conspiracy theories per se. Believing that conspiracies never happen and that conspiracy theories are therefore necessarily invalid is at odds with reality.

Is this all that can or should be said about the epistemological status of conspiracy theories? I'm afraid not. Several other philosophical objections have been raised against conspiracy theories since Popper's refutation of the conspiracy theory of society and Pigden's rebuttal. Philosopher Lee Basham objects to conspiracy theories based on pragmatism: *"There is nothing you can do."*[16] Since most events that are alleged to involve conspiracies cannot be prevented, he says, we waste our precious time and personal resources in attempting to uncover and ex-

16 Lee Basham, "Living with the Conspiracy," in David Coady, ed., *Conspiracy Theories: The Philosophical Debate*, page 74.

plain them. Instead, we should pursue "what is good and valuable in life."[17]

Basham's dismissal of conspiracy theories is based on practical rather than evidentiary considerations: what's the use? But conspiracy theories might indeed be useful, especially since, if correct, they could help us to stop ongoing conspiracies in their tracks and prevent at least some of their negative consequences. Likewise, it may be anything but pragmatic to dismiss conspiracy theories without due consideration.

In "Of Conspiracy Theories," the philosopher Brian L. Keely argues against what he calls "unwarranted conspiracy theories," or UCTs. I'll consider this argument in some detail because it can help us to determine whether theories about the Great Reset are unwarranted.

Keely suggests that UCTs share five features. The fifth feature is most important for Keely's discussion. "The chief tool of the conspiracy theorist is what I shall call errant data," he writes.[18] Data is errant when it is unaccounted for by the received theory, or else contradicts that theory. This is not Keely's example, but an example of errant data is the collapse of Building 7 of the World Trade Center on 9/11/2001.

However, conspiracy theories are not unique in accounting for errant data. In fact, errant data has been significant in the history of science. Errant data is the precondition for Thomas Kuhn's "paradigm

---

17 Ibid.
18 Brian L. Keely, "Of Conspiracy Theories," in David Coady, ed., *Conspiracy Theories: The Philosophical Debate*, Routledge, 2018, pages 51-52.

shift." In *The Structure of Scientific Revolutions* (1962), Kuhn argued that the overwhelming accumulation of "anomalies," or errant data, eventually becomes the basis for the introduction of new, rival theories. This is how science advances.[19]

The importance of errant data in conspiracy theories is not simply that conspiracy theorists explain data left unaccounted for by official theories. The significance of errant data for conspiracy theories is that the propagators of official theories allegedly squelch errant data: "the conspiracy theorist is struggling to explain phenomena that other, presumably powerful, agents are actively seeking to keep secret."[20] Therefore, the epistemological situation of the conspiracy theorist differs from that of the natural scientist. Presumably, nature does not actively seek to hide evidence of its own activity: "Imagine if neutrinos were not simply hard to detect, but actively sought to avoid detection! This is exactly the case with which conspiracy theorists contend we are confronted in the cases they seek to explain."[21]

Because conspiracy theories portray the conspirators as actively suppressing errant data and piling on evidence that contradicts their theories, Keely suggests that the main problem with UCTs is not that they fail to meet the criteria of falsifiability for scientific statements. Falsifiability, according to Karl Popper's *The Logic of Scientific Discovery* (1934), is the requirement that any statement alleging scientific status must meet. It must be testable and falsifi-

---

19 Thomas S. Kuhn, *The Structure of Scientific Revolutions*, Chicago, IL: The University of Chicago Press, 2015.

20 Keely, "Of Conspiracy Theories," page 55.

21 Ibid.

able, at least theoretically.[22] UCTs gain support from errant data, and from the contradicting data of official accounts, because conspiracy theorists contend that the suppression of errant data is part of the conspiracy itself. Likewise, the argument that conspiracy theories are unfalsifiable cannot be reasonably levied against them. The requirement of falsifiability does not obtain when powerful forces are impeding the discovery of facts and insisting on a particular explanation while subverting the inquiry: "My claim here is that unfalsifiability [sic, he means falsifiability] is only a reasonable criterion in cases where we do not have reason to believe that there are powerful agents seeking to steer our investigation away from the truth of the matter."[23] That is, the criterion of falsifiability cannot be reasonably demanded from conspiracy theories.

But this point leads Keely to his main reason for rejecting UCTs. It's not that UCTs are unfalsifiable—although they are—but rather that they require an excessive degree of skepticism to maintain, skepticism that implies disbelief in almost all official sources of information.

Keely argues that most of what we accept regarding nature and society does not depend on direct evidence gleaned by us individually. Most people do not believe claims about nature or society because they themselves have conducted the experiments or observations that support such claims. Our beliefs are not necessarily warranted by direct observation or investigation. They are warranted by trust in

---

22 Karl Raimund Popper, *The Logic of Scientific Discovery*, Mansfield Centre: Martino Publishing, 2014.

23 Keely, "Of Conspiracy Theories," page 55.

those who have conducted the observations or investigations in our stead. That is, we (supposedly) trust the institutions and the methods that have delivered such knowledge to us. In science, the institutions and methods include the mechanisms of scientific publication, the elaborate peer-review process, professional reputations, university accreditation, and so forth. The analogous mechanisms in the public sphere, where conspiracy theorists operate, include the free press, government agencies, and free agents. We don't necessarily trust individuals per se. We trust the long-established institutional methods and processes within which they operate. Or do we?

Keely's problem with UCTs is that they require an increasingly expanding skepticism. In addition to the original conspirators, new elements—the media, government agencies, institutions, individual experts—must be drawn into the circle of the conspirators. For example (and again, this is not an example that Keely gives), to maintain the belief that the moon landings were an elaborate hoax, one would have to believe that thousands of NASA employees were part of the conspiracy to deceive the public, or that they were otherwise duped by a small circle of conspirators, and that no one has blown the whistle for over fifty years.

Keely rejects UCTs—which he admits cannot be theoretically distinguished from credible conspiracy theories in advance—because without trust in those in positions of authority, we'd be left in a world where we'd have no reason to believe anything anyone says. But ultimately, he objects to UCTs because they depend on an outmoded worldview:

Conspiracy theorists are, I submit, some of the last believers in an ordered universe. By supposing that current events are under the control of nefarious agents, conspiracy theories entail that (sic) such events are capable of being controlled...

Such beliefs are out of step with what we have generally come to believe in the late twentieth century. The rejection of conspiratorial thinking is not simply based on the belief that conspiracy theories are false as a matter of fact. The source of the problem goes much deeper. The world as we understand it today is made up of an extremely large number of interacting agents, each with its own imperfect view of the world and its own set of goals. Such a system cannot be controlled because there are simply too many agents to be handled by any small controlling group. There are too many independent degrees of freedom. This is true of the economy, of the political electorate, and of the very social, fact-gathering institutions upon which conspiracy theorists cast doubt...

The rejection of the conspiratorial worldview, however, is not something about which I am particularly thrilled. If conspiracy theories are genuinely misguided, then I fear we are left with an apparently absurdist image of the world. A lone gunman can change the course of history when the US President just happens to drive past the window of his place of work during the gunman's lunch hour. The conspiratorial world view offers us the comfort of knowing that while tragic events occur, they at least occur for a reason, and that the greater the event, the greater and more significant the reason.[24]

Keely rejects the conspiratorial worldview because it assumes an ordered universe, where major events happen for a reason. Under this worldview, the ultimate reason for events had hitherto been God, while penultimate reasons, presumably, could be assigned to the devil. In the case of conspiracy theories, the reason for major events is the nefarious intentionality of the conspirators themselves. (The evil demiurges?) But only believers in a universe organized by a grand intentionality believe that major events necessarily happen for a reason. The "sophisticated" among us, supposedly having imbibed a materialist worldview under which there is no God, no longer ascribe events to such a grand intentionality: "Our contemporary world view," Keely writes, "which the conspiracy theorist refuses to accept, is one in which nobody—not God, not us, not even some of us—is in control."[25]

It's clear that, like Popper, Keely thinks that conspiratorial thinking is secularized superstition. But the rejection of this worldview, Keely admits, leads to an acceptance of absurdity, and absurdity is precisely what the conspiracy theorist has been trying to avoid. In the end, we are left with either the nihilism of hyper-skepticism or the nihilism of absurdism. The first represents the conspiratorial worldview, while the second is the "sophisticated" one. Take your pick.

Yet, Keely suggests that conspiracy theories are not, by definition, unwarranted. Not all conspiracy

---

24 Keely, "Of Conspiracy Theories," pages 57-59.
25 Ibid., page 58.

theories are UCTs. "We seem to be confronted with a spectrum of cases, ranging from the believable, to the highly improbable."[26] Some conspiracy theories turn out to be correct, and thus we are mistaken to dismiss all conspiracy theories in advance. Instead, we should evaluate conspiracy theories for the degree of skepticism that they require and dismiss those that involve more debunking of official explanations than explanation itself. When they require "more skepticism than we can stomach," we should relinquish them.[27]

Who is the "we" that Keely refers to? There are those who can stomach endless skepticism and those who can stomach total absurdity. And there are those who can toggle between the two. Rather than considering the question in terms of what "we can stomach," I suggest that we consider the range of possibilities in terms of the degree of chance that obtains for any social event. At one pole, we have absolute social accidentalism, where no causal agency can be located. (Things just happen, and no one intends anything.) At the other pole, we have the conspiracy theory of society, where everything can be explained in terms of conspiracy. I submit that neither of these antipodes describes the caused (or un-caused) nature of social events. Rather, every social event involves some degree of intentionality, and some events can only be explained in terms of collective social agency. Some (but not all) events involving collective social agency, moreover, entail conspiracy. Thus, the range of events might be plotted as follows, where only the bolded elements represent actual possibilities:

---

26 Ibid., page 60.

27 Ibid.

social accidentalism | **individual agency —>collective agency —>conspiracies** |conspiracy theory of society

To round out the philosophical debate regarding conspiracy theories, I'll consider an important intervention by philosopher Steve Clarke entitled "Conspiracy Theories and Conspiracy Theorizing."[28] Clarke suggests that conspiracy theories have suffered from guilt by association with anti-elitist, anti-intellectual populism, which intellectuals generally abhor. Clarke finds the dismissal of conspiracy theories on this basis by intellectuals to be unjustified, and his essay reflects his intention to justify "an entitlement to an attitude of prima facie skepticism towards the theories propounded by conspiracy theorists."[29] As I read him, Clarke intends to partially exonerate the bias of intellectuals, while rescuing conspiratorial thinking from automatic dismissal.

Clarke interprets Keely's argument as more negative toward conspiracy theories than I read him and he proposes a competing understanding of conspiracy theories. Conspiracy theories, Clarke argues, can best be evaluated in terms of what Imre Lakatos called "degenerating research programmes." Lakatos built on Thomas Kuhn's notion of the scientific paradigm—research traditions developed around a core theory that researchers work to elaborate and defend against disconfirming evidence. Lakatos distinguished between "degenerating research pro-

28 Steve Clarke, "Conspiracy Theories and Conspiracy Theorizing," in *Conspiracy Theories: The Philosophical Debate*, Routledge, 2018, pages 77–92.

29 Ibid., page 79.

grammes" and "progressive research programmes," as follows:

> A progressive research programme is one in which novel predictions and retrodictions are made that are generally successful. In a degenerating research programme successful novel predictions and retrodictions are not made. Instead auxiliary hypotheses and initial conditions are successively modified in light of new evidence, to protect the original theory from apparent disconfirmation.[30]

Conspiracy theorists, Clarke argues, are particularly prone to cling to their theories even after it has become clear that they have become "degenerating research programmes"—after they have been forced to introduce auxiliary hypotheses and to modify initial conditions in light of disconfirming evidence.[31] Why is this so? Why do conspiracy theorists cling to their theories even after they have clearly become "degenerating research programmes?"

Clarke offers a reason for this recalcitrance: conspiracy theorists commit what social psychologists call "the fundamental attribution error." The fundamental attribution error is endemic to human cognition and entails a tendency on the part of ob-

---

30 Qtd. in Clarke, "Conspiracy Theories and Conspiracy Theorizing," page 81.

31 One might argue that Charles Darwin's theory of natural selection had already begun to degenerate during Darwin's lifetime and in his own work. In later editions of *On the Origin of Species*, Darwin reintroduced the formerly rejected Lamarckian inheritance of acquired characteristics to account for modifications in organisms that he couldn't square with natural selection.

servers to explain the behavior of others in terms of their dispositions, that is, in terms of intent, rather than in terms of the situations in which they find themselves. Conspiracy theorists are less likely to relinquish their theories because they are particularly prone to the fundamental attribution error. In explaining behavior in terms of the dispositions of social actors, conspiracy theorists provide unifying accounts of events, but at some (indefinite) point, this epistemic virtue undermines credibility.

Clarke suggests that despite their often erroneous conclusions, conspiracy theorists serve three valuable social functions. First, they help us to hone our non-conspiratorial explanations of social events. Second, they may be right, and their theories may be essential for understanding some occurrences. Third, by casting suspicion on institutions, governments, and well-placed individuals, they promote openness in society. Ironically, that is, conspiracy theorists help to foster the open society that Popper extolled. (This last point is my evaluation, not Clarke's.) Given their skepticism of authority figures, conspiracy theorists may, in fact, perform the fourth-estate function when the media lacks this skepticism. And they may keep drawing our attention to errant data, forcing even the disbelievers in conspiracy theories to amend their own explanations until they are complete.

Finally, the philosopher of education, David Coady, has written extensively on the problem of conspiracy theories.[32] He argues that there is no

32 David P. Coady, *What to Believe Now: Applying Epistemology to Contemporary Issues,* Chichester, West Sussex, etc., Wiley-Blackwell, 2012; David Coady, "Psychology and Conspiracy Theories," in D.

problem with conspiracy theories themselves. The problem is with the use of the term "conspiracy theory," as well as with the use of such cognate terms as "'conspiracy theorist', 'conspiracism', and 'conspiracist ideation.'"[33] Coady points out that this problem is relatively new, dating from the 1950s (or soon after the publication of Popper's *The Open Society*). Conspiracies happen, and explaining some events involves a choice between rival conspiracy theories and not between a conspiracy theory and a non-conspiratorial explanation. 9/11 is just one such case. No one doubts that a conspiracy took place, not even the government. The question is a matter of who the conspirators were. Thus, conspiracy theories are not wrong because they are conspiracy theories but because they may simply identify the wrong conspirators.

Rather than demonstrating the irrationality of the conspiracy theorist, the use of these terms (conspiracy theory, conspiracy theorist, etc.) demonstrates the irrational charge given to these phrases:

> When someone asserts that a conspiracy has occurred (especially when powerful people or institutions are involved) that person's word is inevitably given less credence than it should because of an irrational prejudice produced by the pejorative connotations of these terms.[34]

Coady & J. Chase, eds., *The Routledge Handbook of Applied Epistemology*, Routledge, 2019, pages 166-175; David Coady, "Conspiracy Theory as Heresy," *Educational Philosophy and Theory*, 2021, pages 1–5, https://doi.org/10.1080/00131857.2021.1917364.

33 Coady, "Conspiracy Theory as Heresy," page 1.

34 Ibid., page 2.

Conspiracy theories are not wrong or irrational for being conspiracy theories. They are wrong or irrational for other reasons:

> There are of course many conspiracy theories that are untrue or irrational. However, it does not follow, and it is not true, that they are untrue or irrational because they are conspiracy theories. To dismiss them as conspiracy theories is to dismiss them for the wrong reason and it leads to a variety of harms both to the individuals who are dismissed in this way and to society as a whole.[35]

The use of the terms "conspiracy theory" and "conspiracy theories," etc., Coady suggests, is analogous to the use of the term "heresy" during the Middle Ages. Coady advocates retiring the conspiracy theory language altogether.

I do not wish to go further down the philosophical rabbit hole. From this discussion, it should have become clear that there is no clear-cut philosophical basis for rejecting conspiracy theories wholesale. Pigden is right that few people hold to a conspiracy theory of society. However, its refutation by Popper does not eliminate the viability of all conspiracy theories. Conspiracy theories are not necessarily superstitious. In fact, it may be superstitious to discount all conspiracy theories in advance.

Against Basham, I don't believe that dismissing conspiracy theories is pragmatic. In fact, we may dismiss some conspiracy theories, especially those that explain putatively ongoing conspiracies, at our peril.

---

35 Ibid., page 3.

I agree with Keely that Popper's criterion of falsifiability for a scientific statement does not apply where conspiracy theories are concerned. The social field into which conspiracy theories intervene makes falsifiability an impossible standard because the accumulation of counter evidence against conspiracy theories may be part of the conspiracy itself. But I will add that even if we accept falsifiability as a criterion for the natural sciences, which is up for debate,[36] the social sciences simply cannot conduct experiments designed to falsify a conspiracy theory. Finally, I agree with Keely that conspiracy theories fall along a spectrum, from the plausible to the incredible. However, I suggest that we should be more disposed to reject conspiracy theories the closer they approach the conspiracy theory of society, not because they require too much skepticism.

Clarke's contribution to the debate effectively exonerates (most) conspiracy theorists and, at least theoretically, rescues conspiracy theories from the knee-jerk derision of intellectuals (and pseudo-intellectuals). Without saying so, he also suggests a better way of thinking about conspiracy theorists. We should avoid the fundamental attribution error. We should consider evaluating conspiracy theorists in terms of their situations, as opposed to their dispositions. Instead of looking at conspiracy theorists as irrational, we might look to the situations in which they find themselves for explaining their conspiratorial thinking. We should grant them the benefit of the doubt—ascribing their behavior to situation-

---

36 See, for example, Robin Craig, "Science, Doubt, and Certainty," *The Savvy Street*, October 29, 2014, https://www.thesavvystreet.com/science-doubt-certainty/.

al conditions rather than to their dispositions. This is especially the case when confidence in elites and elite institutions has been eroded by a series of confirmed or partially confirmed conspiracies. When obscurity and mendacity prevail at the highest levels of society, as has been the case with the covid crisis, for example, we should expect a greater frequency of conspiracy theories. As I have suggested, given its immediate connection to the covid crisis and other questionable circumstances, and given the language of the authors of this project, the Great Reset lends itself to conspiratorial thinking.

Finally, given that the uses of the terms "conspiracy theory" and "conspiracy theorist" are epistemologically unsound and irrational, it would be best to retire the terms entirely. However, this is unlikely to happen. As Murray N. Rothbard suggested (see the epigraph to this Part), the campaign against conspiracy theories and conspiracy theorists may be part of a conspiracy to protect conspiracists themselves.[37] All those who conduct conspiracies, including state actors, have every reason to divert and deflect attention from their activities; only well-placed conspirators have the power to do so. Apparently, such well-placed actors have adopted the taboo against conspiracy theories from Popper and propagated it. Their vassals in academia, the media, and society at large obediently enforce the taboo and routinely denigrate offenders. This is one way of keeping conspiracies hidden and conspirators off the hook. It should be clear by now how this circumstance relates to the perpetrators of the Great Reset.

---

37 Murray N. Rothbard, *Anatomy of the State*, Ludwig von Mises Institute, 2009, pages 26-27.

Before I close out this discussion of conspiracy theory, I will relate a curiosity regarding Karl Popper. Popper wrote *The Open Society and Its Enemies* at the tail end of World War II, partly to distinguish the open society from the kind of closed society that had produced Nazi Germany. Nazi antisemitism was likely the basis for Popper's refutation of the conspiracy theory of society. But I believe that Popper's refutation of the conspiracy theory of society later became useful to the CIA, when the assassination of President John F. Kennedy led to alternative theories about that event and perhaps also in the context of the Cold War. I began to wonder whether the CIA had used Popper's writing, or Popper himself, as a means to discredit alternative theories.

Wouldn't it be ironic, I thought, if Karl Popper's campaign against conspiracy theory—which begat all the abuse behind the use of that term—was itself part of a conspiracy, a conspiracy to pooh-pooh conspiracy theories? Call me a conspiracy theorist. Likewise, I searched the Internet for "Karl Popper CIA." What I found is inconclusive but nevertheless intriguing. It turns out that one J. Ader of the *MuckRock* news organization had wondered about Popper's CIA connections as well. On August 9, 2020, Ader filed a Freedom of Information Act (FOIA) request to the CIA for "All records mentioning Karl Raimund Popper (28 July 1902 – 17 September 1994), Austrian-born British philosopher and social critic..."[38] On November 30, 2020, the CIA replied with what is

38 J. Ader, "FOIA - CIA - Karl Popper," *MuckRock*, August 9, 2020, https://www.muckrock.com/foi/united-states-of-america-10/foia-cia-karl-popper-100101/.

known as a Glomar Response:[39]

> We completed a thorough review of your re-
> quest and determined that in accordance with
> Section 3.6(a) of Executive Order 13526, the
> CIA can neither confirm nor deny the existence
> or nonexistence of records responsive to your
> request. *The fact of the existence or nonex-*
> *istence of such records is itself currently and*
> *properly classified* and is intelligence sources
> and methods information protected from dis-
> closure by Section 6 of the CIA Act of 1949, as
> amended, and Section 102A(i)(l) of the Nation-
> al Security Act of 1947, as amended. Therefore,
> your request is denied pursuant to FOIA ex-
> emptions (b)(l) and (b)(3).[40]

According to UNREDACTED, the independent
non-governmental research institute and library located at The George Washington University, a Glomar Response is different than a regular FOIA denial: "When an agency replies with a Glomar Response,
it refuses even to admit that documents exist; this
makes research (and the appeals process) much
more difficult." Further, requests are "Glomar'ed"
either because they are requests about national security intelligence or because they may violate an individual's privacy.[41]

39 "Where Did the Phrase 'I Can Neither Confirm nor Deny' Come
from?," *The Flag*, May 8, 2021, https://theflag.org/trivia/where-did-
the-phrase-i-can-neither-confirm-nor-deny-come-from/.
40 "FOIA - CIA - Karl Popper," MuckRock, November 30, 2020,
https://www.muckrock.com/foi/united-states-of-america-10/foia-
cia-karl-popper-100101/#file-923894 (emphasis added).
41 "Foia Tip No. 7-the Glomar Response," UNREDACTED, January
7, 2010, https://unredacted.com/2010/01/07/foia-tip-7-glomar-re-

Since Popper died in 1994, it is unlikely that his privacy would be violated by the release of whatever information the CIA has (or doesn't have) on file. Likewise, the denial is more likely related to national security intelligence.

"Are They That Stupid, or Are They Doing It on Purpose?"[42]

Because the Great Reset is not, on its face, a conspiracy but rather an open and avowed plan, no one can say that all discourse concerning it is conspiracy theory. If one were to deem all such discourse conspiracy theory, one would have to include the discourse generated by the WEF itself, including the open pronouncements on the WEF website and the books by Schwab and Malleret. But that would be ridiculous. Conspirators, by definition, do not publicly announce their plans.

No, if the Great Reset is a conspiracy, it must be that the project is not what the conspirators say it is. Likewise, all the talk about "equity," "fairness," "sustainability," "shared destiny," and so on, must mean something other than what Schwab and company suggest. These must be euphemistic stand-ins for what they really intend. "You'll own nothing, and you'll be happy" must mean that only the majority will be without property. The elite will continue their ownership and, in fact, will make ownership exclusive to themselves. You will own nothing means they will own everything.

Reading the Great Reset in this way means pre-

---

sponse/.

42 Thanks to Lori Price for this expression offered in the context of brainstorming for this book's title.

suming access to knowledge about the intentionality of its proponents. It means explaining their behavior in terms of their dispositions. This is one way of interpreting much of the discourse surrounding the Great Reset. The "conspiracy theorists" allege nefarious intent on the part of the WEF and their collaborators.

Another interpretation is that expressions—such as "they will make us propertyless while they own everything and treat us like cattle"—amount to shorthand for underscoring the probable outcomes should the Great Reset prove successful. It's not as if such expressions necessarily impute nefarious intentions to the propagators. They are merely placeholders to make crystal clear what the results would be if the Great Resetters have their way. It's just that their plans would amount to such an outcome, however they phrase it, and whatever they believe about their efforts. They may believe that they are doing good works, that they are indeed saving "the planet," and so on, while we realize that their "good works" would lead to our enslavement.

I admit that this book has vacillated between these two modes—between apparently ascribing evil intentionality on the one hand ("the attribution error") and on the other, implying that the propagators of the Great Reset are unintentionally doing evil. But in my defense, I will say that it is difficult to avoid ascribing evil intentions to other social actors when we deem the probable outcomes of what they attempt to be evil. Call it the fundamental attribution error. At the same time, my adoption of such rhetoric may be understood as expressing the difference between what is alleged and what would occur. The reader may have found such vacillation in this book. I make no apologies for it.

Conclusion:
The Grand Refusal

A S WE HAVE SEEN, the Great Reset is a multi-tentacled, many-headed hydra of mythical proportions. This monstrosity is entangling itself with every conceivable area of life. The Great Reset project has already reached into and altered the behavior of nearly every industry, multinational corporation, local and national government, and our personal lives. It harnesses the information technology and biotechnology sectors to establish a stranglehold on the entire world. The minute we cut off one head, another seems to grow in its place.

Thus, it might seem that the Great Reset is a fait accompli. But this is not the case. We can still stop this juggernaut in its tracks—if we act now. Although much water is already under the bridge, the project is still very much underway. The momentum is against us, but we still have time to avert the total disaster that is unfolding and to elude the manifold shackles of this global hegemon.

What can we do? I offer a nine-point plan of specific actions we can take.

Nine-Point Plan for Stopping the Great Reset

1. Refuse CBDC (Central Bank Digital currency).

2. Reject Internet of Bodies (IoB) technologies, the installation of devices in your body, the Metaverse, and transhumanism.
   a. Refuse wearables reputedly meant for health concerns.
   b. Reject personal carbon footprint tracking technologies, including those embedded in credit cards.
   c. Reject mRNA "vaccines."
   d. Reject "enhancements."
   e. Reject the Metaverse.
   f. Reject brain-cloud interfaces.

3. Refuse digital identity.
   a. "Inclusion" means totalitarianism.

4. Practice the free market.
   a. Reduce/eliminate dependence on the state.
   b. Disengage, as much as possible, from establishment institutions, including most educational institutions.
   c. Become or remain as entrepreneurial as possible.
   d. Buy locally, from farmers' markets, etc.
   e. Establish parallel economies and parallel social networks.[1]

---

1 Michael Rectenwald, "Human Action in the Context of Covid

f. Consider joining independent communities, such as freedom cells.[2]

5. Divest from ESG stocks and electronically traded funds (ETFs) that include ESG-indexed stocks.

 a. Transfer your investments into non-ESG-reporting stocks and EFTs.[3]

 b. Assist in bringing antitrust legislation against ESG investing by coordinating a class. If you are an attorney-at-law specializing in antitrust, consider organizing a class action or filing a motion.

6. Remove money from ESG-reporting banks and avoid buying insurance from ESG-reporting insurance companies.[4]

Totalitarianism," Michael Rectenwald.com, October 19, 2021, https://www.michaelrectenwald.com/essays/human-action-in-the-context-of-covid-totalitarianism.

2 "Home," Freedom Cells, accessed September 21, 2022, https://www.freedomcells.com/.

3 This effort is being made easier by the emergence of new ETFs that explicitly avoid ESG-oriented investing. The charge is being led by Vivek Ramaswamy, whose Strive Asset Management has introduced at least four new ETFs focused "exclusively on excellence over social agendas imposed by ESG-linked asset managers." See "Strive of DRLL Anti-ESG Fame to Launch Four New Etfs – Dailyalts," *DailyAlts*, August 25, 2022, https://dailyalts.com/strive-which-scooped-250m-on-the-drll-anti-esg-etf-to-launch-four-new-etfs/.

4 Most national banks are onboard the ESG train but so too are many credit unions and local and regional banks. For a list of the latter, see Amy Bergen, "15 Banks Putting Social Responsibility First: MONEYUNDER30," *Money Under 30*, June 1, 2022, https://www.moneyunder30.com/socially-responsible-banks-and-credit-unions.

7. Put extreme pressure on government representatives to do the following:
    a.   protect national sovereignty and individual rights;
    b.   divest and disassociate from the World Economic Forum and all its tentacles;[5]
    c.   withdraw from the UN and the World Health Organization;
    d.   withdraw state and other pensions from ESG-indexed stocks, withdrawing from ESG-investing asset managers such as BlackRock, Inc., State Street, and The Vanguard Group, among many others;[6]

Check your bank by searching for the bank name and "ESG."

5 A bill has been introduced in by U.S. House Republicans to do just that. The "Defund Davos Act," H.R. 8748 reads: "No funds available to the Department of State, the United States Agency for International Development [USAID], or any other department or agency may be used to provide funding for the World Economic Forum." See Scott Perry, Tom Tiffany, and Lauren Boebert, "H. R. 8748: To Prohibit Funding for the World Economic Forum," Congress.gov, August 26, 2022, https://www.congress.gov/117/bills/hr8748/BILLS-117hr8748ih.pdf. See also Natalie Winters, "New: 'Defund Davos' Bill Would Deny World Economic Forum Taxpayer Cash," *The National Pulse*, August 29, 2022, https://thenationalpulse.com/2022/08/29/bill-introduced-to-block-wef-funding/.

6 As noted in Chapter 6, this effort is already underway. See "To: Laurence D. Fink, CEO BlackRock Inc., from 19 U.S. Attorneys General," Texas Attorney General, August 4, 2022, https://www.texasattorneygeneral.gov/sites/default/files/images/executive-man¬agement/BlackRock%20Letter.pdf. Florida Governor Ron DeSantis has already eliminated ESG considerations from state pension investments. See "Governor Ron DeSantis Eliminates ESG Considerations from State Pension Investments," Florida Governor Ron DeSantis, August 23, 2022, https://www.flgov.com/2022/08/23/governor-ron-desantis-eliminates-esg-considerations-from-state-pen-

e.   bring antitrust legislation against ESG investing.[7]

8. Encourage the defection of elites from the globalist agenda.
   a.   Identify elites who might oppose the agenda for moral, ethical, or economic reasons and appeal to them by writing emails, letters, and by putting this book into their hands.

9. Network with like-minded individuals and spread this plan digitally and analogically.

All in all, these steps are part of what I am calling the Grand Refusal. We can take as our inspiration for this Grand Refusal the iconic character of Howard Beale, from the classic Paddy Chayefsky movie, *Network*. Although he delivered his message through television, this newscaster gone rogue encouraged his viewers to turn off their televisions, to thrust open their windows, and to scream, "I'm mad as hell, and I'm not going to take this anymore!" Although his viewers were framed by the rectangular

---

sion-investments/.

7 ESG-indexing may very well constitute an antitrust violation. See Mark Brnovich, "Opinion | ESG May Be an Antitrust Violation," *The Wall Street Journal*, March 6, 2022, https://www.wsj.com/articles/esg-may-be-an-antitrust-violation-climate-activism-energy-prices-401k-retirement-investment-political-agenda-coordinated-influence-11646594807. Even industry experts acknowledge the "risk." See "The Intersection between ESG Efforts and Antitrust Law: Insights: Vinson & Elkins LLP," Vinson & Elkins, July 14, 2022, https://www.velaw.com/insights/the-intersection-between-esg-efforts-and-antitrust-law/.

boxes of their windows, which resembled TVs, and thus replicated Beale himself, Beale's individual and collective viewers nevertheless issued a clarion call— to each other, and to the elites.

Like Beale's, our Grand Refusal is both individual and collective, although it is not a call for revolution. It is a call to counter-revolution against the revolutionary schemes of the subversive elites, who mean to condemn us to total helplessness. These elites have subverted all systems of government, including democracy, and have instituted a worldwide prison for captives subjected to their machinations and the onslaught of perpetual gaslighting in the media.

This is not a drill. We really can't take it anymore. If we do, we surrender our liberty and that of our descendants. Our Grand Refusal may not be issued in grandiose jeremiads like Beale's, but nevertheless, we must declare and enact our insubordination. We seek to turn a tragedy-in-making into a comedy— that is, in Shakespearean terms, to restore order to the world through a cleansing of extreme wickedness in high places. This is not a utopian scheme to counter another "utopian" one. We do not seek perfection but rather sanity—although, like Beale, we will surely be called insane. But we must not allow the elites and their minions to deter us with such epithets. We have a world to save.

Index

Numbers

369

371

First Movers Coalition 268, 269
first worldism 120
First World Population Conference 176, 177
fishing rights 246
Five-Year Plan 257
Jon Fleetwood 194, 212
Melissa Fleming 44
Sam Fleming 47
Richard Florida 37
Food Action Alliance 272, 276
Food Innovation Hubs 272
food production 172
food security 239, 242, 274
Forbes 53, 56, 90, 91, 210, 211, 304
Ford Motor Company 269
Foreign Countries 254
Foreign Languages Institute 254
Foreign Languages Press 254
Forum of Young Global Leaders 196, 197 (see also: Young Global Leaders (YGL) program)
fossil fuels xvii, 97, 218, 220, 244, 245, 267-269, 334
Foundation Board (WEF) 155, 156, 172, 187, 191
Fourth Industrial Revolution xix, 22-27, 30, 112, 132, 195, 249, 262, 281, 288
fracking 243
fragmentation 275-277
Framework Convention on Climate Change (UNFCCC) 228, 229, 245
France 125, 138, 198, 200, 304
Frankfurt school 33
Freedom of Information Act (FOIA) 357

Chrystia Freeland 100, 138, 139, 198
free market 34, 56, 59, 75, 110, 206, 236, 363
Milton Friedman 58, 63, 96
Frontiers in Neuroscience 325, 326
Fruits of Philosophy, or the Private Companion of Young Married People 165
Francis Fukuyama 31
the fundamental attribution error 351, 352, 355, 360

G

G-20 144
G-20 Growth Framework and Mutual Assessment Process 144
Galileo 225
Francis Galton 177
Christina Garsten 130, 147, 191
gasoline 244, 268
Bill Gates 200, 269, 278
Gavi 298, 299
gender equality 163, 182, 206, 240, 243
General Agreement on Tariffs and Trade (GATT) 155
General Motors (GM) 87
genomics, nanotechnology, and robotics (GNR) 288, 322
Geological Survey of Denmark and Greenland 223
The George Washington University 358
Kristalina Georgieva 199, 304, 305
David Gergen 137
Germany 200, 225, 357

377

S

Salzburg 156
Sand Dollar 304
San Francisco 169, 191
Margaret Sanger 164, 177, 240
Nicolas Sarkozy 200
SARS-CoV-2 21, 197
Saudi Arabia 304
Eric Schmidt 155
Guido Schmidt-Traub 143
Klaus Schwab x-xii, 21, 22, 24,
    26, 27, 34, 35, 37, 38, 41-
    43, 51, 52, 54-57, 66, 75,
    77, 78, 95, 100, 110-113,
    130, 137, 138, 146, 154-
    156, 188, 191, 193, 197,
    198, 200, 201, 206, 210,
    211, 248, 249, 280, 288-
    290, 324, 334, 359
Roger Scruton 85
Sesame Credit 286, 287
Shanghai 253, 255
Michael Shapiro 254
Sidney Shapiro 254
shared destiny 30, 82, 359
shareholder(s) 55, 58, 62-64,
    75-78, 94
Vandana Shiva 271
Boris Zakharovich Shumiatsky
    254
Tasneem A. Siddiqui 146
Silicon Valley 329
Simulations 312
Singapore 136, 200, 269, 270
S. Fred Singer 219, 223, 230
Singularitarian(s) 324
Singularitarian technologies 324
singularity 289, 322, 323, 324,
    327

The Singularity Is Near 289, 312,
    313, 323
W. Cleon Skousen 32
Eliot Slater xvi, 167
smart cities 245, 288, 290
Vaclav Smil 263, 264
Snow Crash 308, 318
social accidentalism 349, 350
social distancing 196, 204
socialism x-xii, xix, 24, 25, 30,
    31, 34, 55, 60-75, 79, 80,
    82-85, 109, 110, 116, 118,
    121, 122, 225, 234, 235,
    256, 258, 262
socialism-communism x, 31, 69,
    70-72, 118, 121, 122, 225
socialist-communist ideology
    83, 117, 118, 121
socialists 60, 65, 83, 118, 153,
    154, 232, 233
social media 40, 44, 210, 287,
    289
Adrienne Sörbom 130, 147, 191
George Soros 211, 233
South Africa 107, 304
Southern Poverty Law Center
    228
Soviet(s) xx, 32, 33, 69, 72, 73,
    82, 154, 156, 157, 225,
    250-254, 259, 262
Soviet Comintern 254
The Soviet System in China 253
Soviet Union (USSR) xx, 32, 69,
    72, 73, 82, 251, 252, 262
Special Envoy on Climate 98,
    267
speciesism/anthropocentrism
    120
The Spectator 199
Jonathan Spence 252
Sri Lanka 270, 271, 274

383

UN Secretary-General 44, 143, 144, 145, 199, 206
UN Sustainable Development Solutions Network 143
unvaccinated 141, 142, 290
unwarranted conspiracy theories (UCTs) 343-346, 349
UN-WEF memorandum of understanding 208
Uruguay 211, 304
U.S. Congress 251, 266
U.S. peace movement 225
USSR 154
U.S. State Department 157
utopia 35, 54, 122
utopian 35, 273, 288, 367

V

vaccination(s) 41, 196, 204, 210, 242, 292, 308
vaccination tattoos 292
vaccine passports 27, 287, 297
Vancouver Declaration on Human Settlements 234
Peter Vanham 75
Versailles Peace Conference 149
Vernor Vinge 289, 322
virtual assistants 293
virtual police 293
virtual reality 288, 308, 312, 314
virus 21, 39, 43, 44
Grigorii Voitinski 254

W

Wall Street 32, 84, 92, 102, 212, 251, 366
war on fertilizers 273
The Washington Post 155, 157, 293
wealth liquidation 59

wealth transfer(s) 226, 248
wearables 293, 363
Ivan Wecke 112, 208, 209
World Economic Forum (WEF) 10-xiii, xv, xvi, xix, 21-26, 30, 33-35, 37-45, 47, 51-54, 56, 57, 66, 74, 75, 78, 79, 85, 95, 98, 100-102, 105, 111, 112, 127-133, 136-147, 150-159, 166, 170-176, 179, 187, 188, 190-213, 226, 229, 233, 239, 241, 245, 247, 248, 249, 262, 264, 265, 268, 269, 271, 272, 275, 276, 280, 283, 284-289, 294-296, 299, 304, 305, 307, 309, 318, 324, 328, 329, 334, 359, 360, 365
WEF Board of Trustees 138
WEF Food Systems Stewardship Board 144
WEF Foundation Board 156
Wei Zhao 73, 74
Leana Wen 141, 142
West Virginia v. the Environmental Protection Agency (EPA) 265
White House 169, 266-268, 305
Gail Whiteman 158
whiteness 33, 120
Ranil Wickremesinghe 270
woke x, xii-xv, 25, 30, 82-85, 87-91, 93-96, 102, 105, 108-111, 113, 119, 121, 122, 204
woke capitalism 25, 83, 87-89
wokeness xiii, xv, 88, 89, 109-111, 118-122
World Bank-IMF Global Monitoring Report 144

CPSIA information can be obtained
at www.ICGtesting.com
Printed in the USA
BVHW031144060123
655719BV00018B/863/J